DATE DUE

AUG 1 7 1998			
FEB 0 3 03			

DEMCO 38-297

Families of Value

GAY AND LESBIAN PARENTS AND THEIR CHILDREN SPEAK OUT

Advance Praise for *Families of Value!*

"An important book whose time has come! We are delighted to see that gay and lesbian families are finally being recognized and look forward to the day when lesbian and gay people are welcomed completely as full members of the human family."

——**Adele Starr,** First President of PFLAG (Parents and Friends of Lesbians and Gays) National; and **Larry Starr,** Co-Founder of PFLAG, Los Angeles, California

"For too long, our families have been obscured and marginalized by silence, shame, and secrecy. *Families of Value* puts an end to this silence, allowing the diverse voices of lesbian and gay parents, and their wonderful children, to ring true, celebrating the joys and challenges of family life."

——**Tim Fisher,** Executive Director, Gay and Lesbian Parents Coalition International, Washington, D.C.

"*Families of Value* is an important resource for both the lesbian and gay community and for anyone who wants to understand the changing nature of the American family. Dr. Drucker enables lesbian and gay parents and their children to give testament with their own voices to the richness of their family life and the normalcy of their lives."

——**Rabbi Denise L. Eger,** Congregation Kol Ami, West Hollywood, California

Families of Value

GAY AND LESBIAN PARENTS AND THEIR CHILDREN SPEAK OUT

JANE DRUCKER, Ph.D.

INSIGHT BOOKS

Plenum Press • New York and London

Library of Congress Cataloging-in-Publication Data

Drucker, Jane.
    Families of value : gay and lesbian parents and their children
  speak out / Jane Drucker.
        p.   cm.
    Includes bibliographical references and index.
    ISBN 0-306-45863-2
    1. Gay parents--United States.   2. Lesbian mothers--United States.
  3. Gay fathers--United States.   4. Children of gay parents--United
  States.   I. Title.
  HQ76.3.U5D78   1998
  306.85--dc21   98-12619
                                                                      CIP

ISBN 0-306-45863-2

© 1998 Jane Drucker
Insight Books is a Division of Plenum Publishing Corporation
233 Spring Street, New York, N.Y. 10013-1578

http://www.plenum.com

An Insight Book

Printed in the United States of America

To the millions of children of gay and lesbian parents whose lives
are unwittingly setting an example for the rest of us

Contents

Foreword

Families of Value: Gay and Lesbian Parents and Their Children Speak Out, authored by Dr. Jane Drucker, is an important book that has much to teach us about families, values, and relationships. Regretfully, one of the major obstacles to a compassionate understanding of the varieties of sexual orientation and the raising of children is "religion" and "the Bible." Men and women of faith are frequently misled by those who turn a living, revealed word into a stone cast down from above. Yet, to leave a text bare, uninterpreted by history and/or conscience forms a letter into an idolatrous icon.

No text is impervious to moral criticism, and a mature faith encourages such criticism as the highest form of faith. We have much to learn from our interactive tradition. Where there is conscience against the Law, the Law must bend. The bending of that Law is not blasphemy but a refinement of the Law and a tribute to God's morality. On many occasions, the rabbis have abrogated Biblical laws, because they ran counter to moral sensibility.

Many years ago, the issue of homosexuality was for me a matter of theoretical interest. Intellectually I knew there were homosexuals, but personally I knew none. Whoever they were, they were well closeted, out of sight, out of mind. But in the intervening years, blood and flesh persons have come into my study, visible and audible with faces, eyes, lips. They have come to see me. Out of desperation, they have left their cloistered lives to reveal themselves.

Why have they come to me? I am not their parents. But parents are the last ones they would speak to. They are too ashamed and too frightened. They have come because I am a rabbi and because I represent Jewish ethics and Jewish law. They have come because they have heard me speak about God, love, compassion, and justice in class and from the pulpit. They have heard me teach that a root principle in Judaism is our belief that God has created each of us in His divine image.

They do not feel that they were created in God's image. Quite the contrary, they feel that no one regards them as human, normal, or recognizes their personhood. They come carrying a terrible and fateful knowledge. As they grew up, they heard whispers grown into roars, stories about gays who are unnatural, perverse, pathological, sinful. Those who come to me know that they are hated, rejected, mocked, scorned, reviled. They are frightened.

What greater humiliation is there than to discover that in the eyes of your society you are really not human? What makes a human being human more than his or her ability to love and to be loved? But they are told they are not lovable and are not allowed to love. They live in silent shame, fearful of the revelation that will shake the foundations of their being. Theirs is a monstrous burden to carry.

Scholars have long puzzled as to the meaning of the sentence, "Thou shalt not lie with mankind as with womankind; it is an abomination." Over the centuries, scholars have recognized that there were sexual practices that were abominable because they were part of a system of "sacred prostitution." It is not at all clear as to what the abomination was all about in ancient times. It is abundantly clear that one cannot visit the iniquities of the past upon the present.

There is within our tradition an evolving moral sensitivity, and we are part of our moral growth. Looking into the eyes of gay and lesbian parents and hearing their testimony requires that we look a second and a third time into the literal text and ask ourselves whether or not their application is compatible with the spirit and the purpose of Biblical law. For the Bible's words are of pleasantness, for peace and understanding and love.

As a rabbi, I am faced not only with a text of a few verses, but also with human beings I know and whose families I know. I look from the Law into the eyes of those before me. Without them, it might be an easier matter to judge, but the Talmud says, "You have to judge according to that which you see with your own eyes." (Baba Bathra 43a)

What do I see with my own eyes? I see honest, decent, God-fearing, loving men and women. And I hear the words of Micah the prophet who tells me that God wants me "to do justice to love mercy . . ."

What is just and merciful here? The persons who have come to me carry their own testimony. "It has been a living hell. I no more chose my attachments to another of my own gender than you, Rabbi, chose the love of a woman. It was not something taught or modeled or revered in my home or in my circle. I sensed it in early childhood. I denied it, fought it, but it would not be denied."

I read that psychologists maintain that sexual orientation is determined by the time the child is five years old. I am told by the wisdom of Jewish law and tradition to listen to the heart of the one who stands before me.

Scholars agree that the authors of the Bible and the Talmud took their position on the issue of homosexuality on the assumption that homosexual behavior was an act of freedom of choice, that the homosexual acted either to defy God, or to oppose the law, or as a holy prostitute using his or her body to serve a pagan cult. The assumption of the ancients about the motivation of the homosexual was based on factual error. One cannot blame the rabbis of the first centuries for not knowing the etiology of homosexuality. They judged acts with the knowledge of their time. But this does not exonerate rabbis living on the edge of the twenty-first century.

For homosexuals, the interpretation of the ancients offers no option except denial of their sexual life. Following it means for me to deny them the deepest expression of love. That counsel is contrary to the affirmation of life and of sexuality that is so basic in Judaism, which lauds the joys of sexuality as manifestations of God's beneficent creation.

Others argue that the purpose of union is procreation and that homosexuality is prohibited because it denies history, denies the future, and defies the purpose of marriage. Are we not mandated to multiply and fructify and fill the earth? *Families of Value* . . . clearly demonstrates the intense drive that so many gay and lesbian parents feel to fulfill just this purpose in their lives. They are creating, out of their love, families to fill the future.

The Law reminds us that we are to love the stranger and to know his heart. If we don't know the heart, if we do not know the humanity of the pariah, we do not know our own humanity. As long as we have not discovered the stranger in our midst as "human being," we will not discover our own humanity. We are all required to protect the persecuted, the humiliated, the ostracized, the pariahs created by humankind. We are commanded to accept the dignity of each individual, to know the heart of the strangers, to make them feel at home with us and to encourage them to live out their own lives with dignity and within a compassionate community.

Rabbi Harold M. Schulweis

Preface

I stood in a quiet gallery of the Los Angeles County Museum of Art moving forward and back, forward and back, forward and back, mesmerized by the transformation of a mass of dots into the glistening waters of the River Seine in Paul Signac's clear and beautiful rendering of *The Seine at Herblay*. As the Pointillists discovered, a painter may well be able to reconstruct reality from flecks and dots of information, but it is in standing back from the details and allowing the points to merge into a glistening or flowing or striking overview that we can best feel and understand the world in which we live. As I have come to deeper levels of understanding my own nature, I have also sought to step back and to find a way to make who I am feel more connected to the larger world around me.

As the daughter and granddaughter of survivors of the Nazi Holocaust, the *Shoah,* I have always felt a deep connection to family and have held as my most precious desire the dream of continuing the family that was so nearly extinguished over fifty years ago. I grew up assuming that I would marry a nice Jewish man, have babies, and create a good home. I learned from family, from friends, and from the culture around me that being a wife and mother was the ultimate achievement to which I should aspire. Even when it became politically incorrect to admit so, I was always drawn to becoming a mother. Unlike so many of my contemporaries, my interest in establishing a career as the focal point to my life was never very strong. As the years went on, however, and I slowly came to terms with my own lesbianism, I was faced with the unfathomable possibility of not being able to turn my dream of raising a family into a reality.

From the time of my own childhood, I have been very connected to the idea of bearing and raising children. In my mid-thirties, I came to accept that if I were ever to raise a child, I would do so in a lesbian household. My acceptance of my own sexual orientation and of its implications for how I would create a family has led me to a great deal of soul searching and questioning of the efficacy and ethics of creating an "alternative" family. *Families of Value: Gay and Lesbian Parents and Their Children Speak Out* was conceived from my personal desire to assure myself that the life I want to live is ethical. In my heart, I have always believed so, but the controversy that I have witnessed and experienced since coming out as a lesbian who wishes to raise children has often made me question my heart. I became interested in exploring the panoply of lesbian and gay family structures in order to satisfy my own need for reassurance that my personal interest in raising a family is healthy, and that it can be implemented in an environment that would be healthy to a child.

I approached the creation of *Families of Value: Gay and Lesbian Parents and Their Children Speak Out* with a strong belief that families headed by lesbian or gay parents are healthy, vibrant, and numerous. My intent has been to shed a brighter light on the reality that these families do already exist and that the children in them are growing up as well adjusted or as poorly adjusted as the children of heterosexual parents. I hope that through my writing I also provide the foundation for a network of support for those lesbian and gay parents and their children who might not yet be connected to a community of other such families. In addition, I offer to the extended families, friends, professionals, and general skeptics who encounter gay and lesbian parents and their children a vehicle by which to see and to understand their lives.

I wanted *Families of Value: Gay and Lesbian Parents and Their Children Speak Out* to come from the hearts and pens of real families, because I believe that opening a window into the lives of real people is the most powerful means by which to touch readers. Through word of mouth and through advertisements in gay- and lesbian-family-oriented publications, I found dozens of individuals and families who wished to participate in the project. I sent out questionnaires and awaited their return. Most, not all, came back with responses of varying detail. I was fortunate enough to be able to speak directly, either in person or over the telephone, with members of about a third of the families who returned completed surveys to me.

Compiling the documents for this project became at once a more joyful and a more arduous task than I had anticipated. I relished reading each questionnaire as it arrived. I felt truly honored to be the recipient of so many touching contributions, and I often found myself smiling, laughing, or crying as I read each story. A pattern of human experience began to emerge as I traveled through the pile of papers that grew before me. It revealed a tapestry of love, sacrifice, joy, and the kind of growth that is experienced by strong people who find ways to master the challenges that life puts in their paths.

Once the reading was done, though, there were many technical and editorial decisions to be made. Some of the responses seemed to fit into different categories than I had imagined when I first wrote the questions. How should I organize them? How much should I include in the final work? I wondered about the actual format of the book, and I asked myself at times if the material would be too repetitive. I considered using only some of the contributions to illustrate particular points of information gathered from my own research. Then I thought about presenting each family's contribution intact, essentially as it appeared from top to bottom on each questionnaire. I began to see that there were more questions I now wished I had thought to ask and became concerned that perhaps there would be too *little* information. Would it be useful to contact any of the respondents for clarification of their answers? Should I attempt to edit responses into a common style, or should I leave each story in the voice of its author? I wrestled with various foci for each chapter. As I worked, I often despaired at how slowly I was able to transcribe the material into my computer! Would I *ever* get through it all?!

I eventually chose the final format as it appears here. Every family's responses to questions within a topic area appear at the end of each chapter. This is the format that most engages my interest as a reader and most loyally implements my original idea of presenting families' stories as they have experienced them. All of the material from the questionnaires is included essentially *verbatim*. The only alterations I made were a few spelling corrections and some minor grammatical changes. Because of the nature of the material and the sometimes cruel realities of the world, the names of all contributing family members have been changed in order to protect their privacy and to ensure their safety.

In my own search for the means and community support for the responsible creation of a family by a homosexual person in a homophobic culture, I have peered into the family lives of many gay men and lesbians. They are certainly no more perfect than any other group of families. There are struggles and challenges, times of disharmony and times of confusion as well as times of coming together and being happy, but I find with great joy that the families of gay men and lesbians are primarily filled with love, courage, and purpose.

Acknowledgments

The creation of *Families of Value: Gay and Lesbian Parents and Their Children Speak Out* was at once a solitary and a communal project. It would not exist if it were not for the loving support, ongoing encouragement, and honest contributions of many people. I wish to thank Dr. Bobbi Liberton, whose professional guidance and personal involvement have been fundamental to my being able to complete this project. I am blessed by the close friendship that developed between us. I also wish to thank the following: my dear friend, Alicia Magal, who has been my touchstone, my confidante, my critic, and my pep team through more crises than any friend should be asked to endure; Alicia's husband, Itzhak, also a dear friend, who put up with his wife's being busy much more often than he liked; Dr. Sharon Siegel, who started me on the path that ultimately led to the writing of this book by being the right person in the right place at the right time; Dean Shapiro and Dr. Phil Starr, who read through the many poorly printed pages of my rough drafts and provided invaluable insights; Steve Porus, whose zest and unconditional support taught us both many lessons about relationships and resulted in a manuscript becoming a book; Frank Darmstadt, my editor, whose enthusiasm and belief in my work has brought this book to life; the members of "Response," who showed me there was community interest in my work; the parents of "Maybe Baby," who unknowingly helped me formulate questions for myself and for my questionnaires; my own parents, who did not always know what I was working on, but continued to trust that it was important anyway; and most importantly, the twenty-two families of value who shared so much of themselves by contributing the material that makes this book worth reading. And lastly, love and thanks to Wendy.

DISCLAIMER

Although all the families represented in *Families of Value: Gay and Lesbian Parents and Their Children Speak Out* are real, the names and identifiable characteristics of all contributing family members have been changed. The author has been granted specific permission from all contributors to publish the information contained herein.

Introduction

Minds are like parachutes . . . they only function when open.

   Seen on a bumper sticker

Opening a window into the lives of real people.

*A*n unholy roar fun-neled its way through the house, and I was cata-pulted from a deep sleep. I grasped the sides of my bed so tightly that my hands ached as I listened to the wrenching creaks of my bedroom walls. The room lurched from side to side and then for-ward and back. A final upward jolt ended the mayhem. The bedside clock flashed 4:31 a.m. Los Angeles had just experienced an earthquake.

   I was not pleased to be awakened so violently and unex-pectedly. I was disoriented and had difficulty recalling where I could find such basic necessities as shoes and a flashlight. In the hours and days to come, my neighbors and I would realize increasing layers of confusion on both a personal and community level.

There was work to do. In a matter of minutes I had arrived with a carload of injured neighbors at our local emergency room. Three hundred strangers and a filled neonatal intensive care unit were waiting ahead of us. It would take the hospital staff nearly eight hours just to triage the wounded and begin to treat the more severe injuries. Much of the community was in the dark, both literally, as even emergency generators failed, and figuratively, as we furtively sought the as-yet-nonexistent news reports that we hoped would tell us what had just happened.

Time passed. The injured were treated and released. The death toll was mercifully low. Repairs to structures and psyches were begun, and ever so slowly life returned to its normal routine. With the passing of a few years, "the big one" of '94 is seldom mentioned any longer in conversation.

America is in many ways in the midst of the early hours of a social earthquake.

Recent events in American politics and American jurisprudence have focused the nation's attention on the "Lifestyles of the Gay and Lesbian." The 1992 passage of Colorado's Amendment Two sought to restrict the civil rights of gays and lesbians. It was ultimately overturned by the U.S. Supreme Court in 1996. That same year, President Clinton signed the "Defense of Marriage Act," which essentially defines marriage exclusively as a contract between one man and one woman. Also in 1996, Judge Kevin Chang issued a decision in the case of *Baehr v. Miike,* the well-publicized legal battle regarding marriage between same-gender partners in Hawaii. All of these actions have undeniably raised eyebrows, questions, and expectations regarding the etiology and social/ethical implications of homosexuality in America.

The shaking up is reaching into our homes and schools as well. Children are read books such as *Heather Has Two Mommies,* schools are using the videos *Both of My Moms' Names are*

Judy[1] and *It's Elementary*,[2] and a fair share of homes have in recent TV seasons tuned into "My Two Dads" and "Ellen" as part of their TV fare. A spotlight has begun to illuminate many formerly hidden lives of individuals, couples, and families. I offer *Families of Value: Gay and Lesbian Parents and Their Children Speak Out* into that light.

Families of Value: Gay and Lesbian Parents and Their Children Speak Out is comprised of two interwoven aspects. The first is its theoretical conception. The second element is the actual compilation of the material that emanates from my questions into a physical body of information to be made available for others to use for their own learning and growth.

I have gathered background information wherever I could find it. Facts, figures, and ideas arrived via journals, newspaper and magazine articles, books, and television and radio programs, and in conversations with gay and straight friends and their children. I had other conversations with the director of a gay-friendly sperm bank, adoption facilitators, lawyers, psychotherapists, and members of the clergy. Other ideas and information came from my own musings, feelings, and self-exploration, and from meetings I attended with several support groups for gay and lesbian parents in my own corner of the community.

My primary desire, however, was to hear from the children who are growing up with gay fathers and lesbian mothers, because, after all, it is their lives that have come to intrigue me. Simply reading and talking *about* them was not sufficient to answer my questions or to do justice to their unique experiences. I needed to work directly with the people who were the subjects of my interest.

I personally know a growing number of gay and lesbian families, but I never wanted this to be a project about my friends. My vision was always to create a larger, more representative picture of the gay and lesbian parenting community. I also ardently believed that privacy for my participants would be a critical factor in gathering the information that would make my work most compelling, so I found myself contemplating means by which to collect candid input from anonymous contributors.

At first, I wanted to hear only from the children of gay fathers and lesbian mothers, because I had the idea that the young people's words would be most powerful if they could stand on their own and not be contrasted to their parents' experiences. It soon became clear, however, that parents felt that their children's safety might be compromised by participation in the study. Their concern was too deep to trust that their children's identities could be adequately protected. Many of the parents, however, expressed an enthusiastic interest in the concept of the project and were clearly willing to participate themselves.

Once I opened my mind to collecting input about whole families, my efforts became more productive. I talked to parents about various formats for gathering the responses that I would need. I considered a wide range of possibilities, including video- or audiotaped interviews with individual families, an open-ended call for family anecdotes, creation of a local support group that would also evolve into an opportunity for data collection, and visiting existing support groups for children and/or parents.

Ultimately logistics prevailed. I am a writer, not a video producer, so I chose to go with my strength and focus on a written project. My desire to include families from around the country clearly negated the idea of creating or attending support groups just in my own city. I still liked the idea of collecting family anecdotes, but I came to think that leaving the requests too unstructured would be likely to result in material that was less focused than I wanted for this particular work. I question now whether or not that was a wise conclusion to draw, for I may have missed some wonderful material, but it is the assumption from which I worked.

My final response to the data-gathering challenge was to formulate a set of questions that would become a vehicle through which families could give a narrative about their experiences. I developed three separate surveys. Parents, young children, and teenage/adult children were each provided with a lengthy questionnaire of open-ended inquiries that fell into six major categories of information. Each category was to become a separate chapter in the book.

Families of Value: Gay and Lesbian Parents and Their Children Speak Out became a psychological and sociological examination of the phenomenon of parenting by homosexuals and the effects on their children of growing up in nontraditional families. Each of its six chapters consists of two parts. The first segment in each is a conceptual discussion based on a review of relevant literature and other appropriate media and community resources in a specific topic area. The second section in each chapter is a series of vignettes contributed by each of twenty-two gay- or lesbian-headed families.

In Chapter 1, "What Is a Family? Defining Ourselves," the word "family" is defined and discussed. Among the questions addressed are the following: Who comprises a family? How are families, specifically gay and lesbian families, formed? How are family rights protected or denied? Case law and common social trends are cited, and pros and cons of alternative insemination, adoption, foster parenting, and surrogate parenting are discussed.

Chapter 2, "It's All 'Relatives': Creating Family Ties," addresses issues related to family relationships. Gay- and lesbian-headed families are viewed as minority families, and their structures as well as the nature of interactions among family members are examined. Questions and common concerns that are addressed include: "Won't a child raised by gay parents grow up to be gay him/herself? "How can a child succeed if there is no father/mother in the home?" "Will my child be teased for being different because I am gay?" And "Are gays and lesbians emotionally capable of nurturing a child?" These issues are addressed from the perspective of decades of psychological research on child development, homosexuality, and parenting. The primary focus is on the emotional and physical well-being of the children.

In the third chapter, "Parents and Children Together: A Unique Bond," the focus sharpens to a discussion of this special relationship. What are the roles, rights, responsibilities, and sacrifices of parenthood, and how does a parent's sexual orientation affect his or her children? Several myths are introduced and refuted based on prior psychological research and the contributions of the families who participated in the creation of *Families of Value: Gay and Lesbian Parents and Their Children Speak Out*. The myths include: "Gay men and lesbians don't like or want children." "The children of lesbians and gay men will be sexually abused." "Lesbians and gay men are inherently unfit to be parents." "The children of gays and lesbians will be encouraged to become homosexual." "Lesbians cannot provide proper homes for boys." "Gay men cannot provide proper homes for girls." "Children should not grow up in a single-parent home." And "Children are confused by having two same-gender parents." Additional issues that are discussed include whether or not children should know that their parents are homosexual, what to have children call their multiple moms and multiple dads, and possible effects of legalized civil same-gender marriage on these families.

Community relations is the core topic of Chapter 4, "Out and About in the Community: When and How Do We Reveal Ourselves?" Here is an examination of the pros, cons, and intricacies of 'coming out' to the larger community of neighbors, friends, extended family, schools, doctors, religious institutions, work associates, and strangers. How do parents' interests and children's interests differ? When and where should families come out, and when and where should they keep information about parental sexual orientation private? How might coming out help or hinder a child and a family? What are the best ways and the healthiest times to come out?

Chapter 5, "To Be or Not to Be? Sexual Orientation Is Not a Choice," examines sexual orientation and psychological identity. Four aspects of human sexuality (sexual orientation, biological sex, gender identity, and social gender roles) are defined and discussed. Further discussion is offered from the perspectives of historical and cultural influences, the effects of parenting styles, and the role of psychosocial development in determining an individual's sexual orientation.

In Chapter 6, "God and Goddess: Religion and Spirituality in Gay and Lesbian Families," the focus turns to spirituality and the interplay of deity, religion, and sexual orientation in the spiritual lives of gay- and lesbian-headed families. Historical background is presented and recent developments in various religious denominations and their institutions are explored. This chapter offers a look at the challenges that face gay and lesbian parents in providing a religious or spiritual foundation for their children.

The concluding chapter poses questions for further research, and the appendices that follow offer community and media resources that relate to the needs and interests of gay fathers, lesbian mothers, their children, extended family, and friends.

Although I originally entered into this study with the bias that I would find typical families that happen to be headed by lesbian or gay parents, I often wondered what the *real* story would be. It turned out to be even more intriguing than I had imagined. The twenty-two families who have contributed their stories to *Families of Value: Gay and Lesbian Parents and Their Children Speak Out* are to be highly commended for their openness and their generosity in sharing so many personal experiences and insights with complete strangers.

More lesbians than gay men responded to my request for participants. I believe that this is due to the reality that more women are currently parenting than men,[3] although it has long been known that the proportion of gay men has been increasing in the gay and lesbian parenting community.[4]

I have chosen not to dissect, analyze, or interpret the stories of my contributing families, but I present them as a collection of anecdotes that have been shared with me by the courageous men, women, and children who are living ordinary lives in an extraordinary way. My hope is that individual voices telling their own life experiences should blend together into a shimmering rendition of gay and lesbian family life.

I see in the lesbian and gay parenting community a need for contact, mutual support, and information. If *Families of*

Value: Gay and Lesbian Parents and Their Children Speak Out can fill some piece of the vacuum that appears to exist, I will feel that I have created something worthwhile. I wish for this book to become an avenue by which our families can be seen as vibrant and healthy by themselves, by their extended family and friends, and by strangers who may or may not even realize that they know people who are living in gay- or lesbian-headed families.

Meet the Families of Value

FAMILY 1

Jeremy is the 27-year-old single gay father of an adopted son, Micah, who is two and a half. Jeremy is white and Jewish. Micah is African American. They live in a single-family suburban home with Jeremy's mother.

FAMILY 2

Alan and his wife, Margaret, live together with their 15-year-old daughter, Brett, and their 7-1/2-year-old-son, Joey. Two years ago, at age forty-four, Alan realized he was gay and came out to his family.

FAMILY 3

Rob is the gay 53-year-old biological father of three children. His daughters are ages nine and and twenty-two, and his son is nineteen. He is currently divorced from their mother, but is sharing parenting with her. Rob is becoming more active in the gay and lesbian community.

FAMILY 4

Samantha and her lesbian partner adopted their now 19-month-old son together. After her partner left the family, Samantha became a single parent with shared custody.

FAMILY 5

Linda and Donna are lesbian mothers in their forties. They are full-time coparents to their 9-month-old son. Donna also has three teen-aged children from a heterosexual marriage. Linda works as a psychologist.

FAMILY 6

Leah and Ali are raising their 2-year-old adopted son, Jacob, in a suburban Jewish home. Both moms are in their early forties and hold professional jobs as an occupational therapist and an associate professor, respectively.

FAMILY 7

Lydia and Sari are an interracial lesbian couple who are raising their 5-year-old birth son, Nathan, and their 1-year-old adopted daughter, Starr. They remain very close to the friend who donated sperm to become Nathan's biological father. The family lives in a large metropolitan area.

FAMILY 8

Carol and Rose are a lesbian couple raising their 16-month-old daughter, Drew. Both moms work in the mental health field. They live in the Midwest.

FAMILY 9

Jenny and Ann are in their thirties and have been a couple for 12 years. They are loving parents to Jenny's 13-year-old daughter, Jo, and their 4-year-old daughter, Cait.

FAMILY 10

Dee and Sherry are raising Sherry's two teen-aged sons, and Dee is trying to conceive a third child for their family. They live in a small town on the West Coast.

FAMILY 11

Liz and Kathy are two lesbian moms with a 2-year-old daughter and a new baby on the way. Both moms are in their early thirties and love their daughter dearly. They chose to use the same sperm donor for both of their children.

FAMILY 12

Joyce is the single 52-year-old mother of a 20-year-old son, Keola. They are native Hawaiian and very proud of their heritage.

FAMILY 13

Roz and Stacy, both lesbians in their early twenties, are the moms of a 2-year-old daughter, Skye. Skye knows who her dad is, but doesn't see much of him.

FAMILY 14

Carole and Andrea are a lesbian couple who work professionally in the health care field. They are raising Andrea's 13-year-old daughter and Carole's 7-year-old son.

FAMILY 15

Christine is a 60-year-old lesbian mother of seven grown children from her former heterosexual marriage. She is currently a minister at a Metropolitan Community Church in a large city on the West Coast. Four of her daughters, who are all happily straight, share their stories in this book.

FAMILY 16

Dale and Kat are a lesbian couple who have been coparenting Kat's 8-year-old son and the 8-year-old daughter of close relatives for the past year. Both women identify themselves as disabled. Dale is a human rights activist, and Kat is an artist.

FAMILY 17

Jim is the biological father of two daughters, ages seventeen and thirteen. He shares legal custody with his ex-wife, but the girls do not live with their dad. Jim lives with his male partner of 3 years.

FAMILY 18

Becka is now a single lesbian mom of her alternatively conceived 7-year-old son, Tommy. Her ex-partner lives separately, but both women are actively involved in Tommy's life.

FAMILY 19

Sandra has a teen-aged daughter and son from a previous heterosexual marriage. She is now in a lesbian relationship and raising her children with her partner of four years. 17-year-old Miranda is very supportive of her moms' relationship.

FAMILY 20

Melissa and Trish are in their late thirties and are the co-parents of Melissa's 14-year-old biological daughter, Dawn.

FAMILY 21

Denise and Alisha, who have been a couple for 8-1/2 years, are the lesbian moms of 5-month-old Zoe, who is Denise's biological child.

FAMILY 22

Werner is the widowed father of 3-1/2-year-old Anna. He came out as a gay man after the death of Anna's mother, Katrina. Werner and Anna live in Austria.

What Is a Family?
Defining Ourselves

1

I thank all who have loved me in their hearts, with thanks and love from mine . . .

Elizabeth Barrett Browning, *Sonnets from the Portuguese,* #41

*O*ne of my colleagues recently came into our staff meeting with a new brochure for the family counseling center where I work. On the cover was an attractive graphic of a smiling man and woman holding each other's hands, and each had their free arm around a child. It showed that we promoted healthy, happy familyhood. Or did it?

"Family" . . . conjures up images of a lifetime.

After much discussion about the focus of the group and the nature of our clientele, we mutually decided that the graphic would not be a welcoming sign to many of our clients whose lives and significant relationships were not included in its message. There is no one grouping of people that can adequately embrace all that we mean when we refer to family.

FAMILY . . . The word conjures up images of a lifetime: Thanksgiving dinners, summer vacations, schedules to organize early-morning bathroom occupancy. Who among us can say that we are not who we are because of the family with whom we grew up? And who among us does not, at some core level of our souls, identify *our* family experience as the norm against which all other families will forever be measured?

The previous generation of pop culture, which is currently enjoying a resurrection, suggested that the Nelsons, the Andersons, and the Cleavers are the models toward which all families should strive. Perhaps this revival represents a group longing for a return to simpler times, times in which we knew our roles and were less burdened with the need to make choices from an overwhelming number of options. In their respective and consummately respectable milieus, each of these TV-land families projected an image of social perfection. To be like them would suggest familial normality. We have been given, and have long accepted, the archetype of one breadwinning father, one home-making mother, and two or three happy and well-behaved offspring all living comfortably in a well-appointed suburban home as the ideal, perhaps only real, American family constellation.

But wait a moment. What do we see going on in the homes around the bend in the road? How do we justify our near worship of Ozzie Nelson, Jim Anderson, and the Beav with our concurrent affection for Opie and Andy Taylor and Aunt Bea; Eddie and Mr. Eddie's Father; the rambunctious three sons, single father, and elderly uncle of the Douglas clan; single mother Alice and her teenage son Tommy; and the mix-n-match Bradys? Something is not quite consistent in the collective American memory of healthy family values.

A new recognition of nontraditional families is, indeed, arising. With the re-airing of such shows as "Alice" (from *Alice Doesn't Live Here Anymore*), "The Brady Bunch," "The Andy Griffith Show," and more recently the addition of shows such as "Ellen," there is a depiction of single-parent households, blended families, and other alternative family arrangements. There are groupings of friends who relate to each other as only family members would have a generation ago, and there is a diversity of individual identities. In short, the media are exposing a fuller palette of the true-life variety of families.

Real families mix-n-match. Despite everyone's best efforts, real families sometimes fall apart. Real families recreate themselves by reconstituting with other, formerly separate real families. Real families often bring in seemingly unlikely members when circumstances create a need, a space, a bond of affection that falls beyond the 'norm' of our white picket fence fantasy of America. Real families are created in a myriad of different manners and configurations, and a smaller and smaller percentage of them conform to traditional nuclear family structure.

The formal dictionary definitions of "family" are changing, as we see below, and attempting to broaden the collection of relationships that are contained within this single, deceptively simple word.

> **family**\ ´fam-(ə)lē\ . . . [ME⁺(*familie*, fr. L*familia* household
> . . .] . . . **1** . . . : FELLOWSHIP . . . **3:** a group of individuals living under one roof and usu. under one head . . . **5:** the basic unit in society having as its nucleus two or more adults living together and cooperating in the care and rearing of their own or adopted children . . .[1]
>
> **fam-i-ly** (\fam´e lē, fam´lē\ **1.** parents and their children, considered as a group, whether dwelling together or not. **2.** the children of one person or one couple collectively . . . **3.** the spouse and children of one person . . . **4.** any group of persons closely related by blood, as parents, children, uncles, aunts, and cousins . . . **7.** a group of persons who form a household . . . **10.** a group of people who are generally not blood relations but who share common attitudes, interest, or goals and, frequently, live together . . .[2]

The dictionaries strive hard to reflect the reality of our collective experience of "family" by including groupings of people that run the gamut from traditional nuclear families to single-parent homes and even to the more informal relationships established by friends sharing common interests or goals. The country singers Naomi, Ashley, and Wynona Judd; Mark Twain's unforgettable Huckleberry Finn, Tom Sawyer, and Aunt Polly; and teenage sleuth Nancy Drew and her father, Professor Drew, are as much family as are the mom and pop arrangements. Clearly, though, "family" is more than a dictionary definition, and its truths travel well beyond our time-worn electronic and literary illusion. Family is more than a social structure; it is also a base for social functioning. Families are for teaching morals and ethics, for sharing the world, for leaving or creating a human legacy, for increasing joy and satisfaction with life, for shoring us up when life throws a curve, for creating intimate relationships, for "cementing" marriages, for providing support among the generations, and for many of us they are the ultimate fulfillment of the "American Dream."

A new awareness is arising in America. With the opening of the closet door, gay and lesbian adults are revealing a truth that has long existed but has only recently begun to be acknowledged. We have families. Many of us do, indeed, come from relatively stereotypical nuclear families. According to *Gay and Lesbian STATS*, a collection of lists of statistics and facts about gay and lesbian issues,[3] ninety-eight percent of gay and lesbian children come from homes where they were raised by heterosexual parents along with our gay, lesbian, bisexual, and straight siblings. These are the families of our own childhoods.

As we grow up, move out, and come out, we do what most adults do—we form new families. In many cases, the new families formed by gay men and lesbians are loosely connected associations of friends. A significant number of gay men and lesbians buck the traditional values of the surrounding community, however, and establish stable romantic relationships with members of their own gender. More and more gay and lesbian couples are maintaining their monogamous relationships for years, even decades, thus creating a measure of familial stability that is only beginning to be recognized within the gay community and in the larger straight community. *Gay and Lesbian STATS* also states that, between 1977 and 1983, studies revealed that 40 to 60 percent of gay men were in steady relationships, and 75 percent of lesbians made the same claim, and over 80 percent of these couples had been together for over 1 year, with the average duration of their relationships being 6 years.[4] The average heterosexual marriage now lasts 7 years.[5] Considering the social pressure for same-gender couples to separate and for opposite-gender couples to remain together, this parity of longevity seems noteworthy.

An integral part of many gay- and lesbian-headed families is the raising of children. As of 1993, there were known to be between one and five million lesbian mothers and between one and three million gay fathers. From six to fourteen million children in the United States were recognized as having at least one gay or lesbian parent, and ten thousand children were being raised by lesbian mothers who had become pregnant through alternative insemination.[6]

Between 1979 and 1983, a series of court cases in New York State[7] established a case law trail that shuttled the legal definition of family between strict recognition on one hand, based solely upon the contractual agreements of marriage or adoption or upon genetic relationship, and a more behavioral definition on the other hand, that was based upon the reality of people's lives together. These cases dealt with opposite-gender couples who sought renters' rights and protections as well as with gay and lesbian couples. In 1989, a New York court ruled that

> The term family should not be rigidly restricted to those people who have formalized their relationship by obtaining, for instance, a marriage certificate or an adoption order. The intended protection against sudden eviction should not rest on fictitious legal distinctions or genetic history, but instead should find its foundation in the reality of family life[8]

Despite controversy, corporations such as The Disney Company, the ultimate icon of American family values, and municipalities such as West Hollywood, California, and San Francisco are granting family-like status to domestic partners regardless of marital status or gender.

For those who say that family values apply only to domestic arrangements that involve the raising of children by married, heterosexual couples, allow me to point out the exploding increase over the past decade of households in which children are indeed being raised by their gay and/or lesbian parents. The "gayby boom," the sudden spurt of births and adoptions within gay- and lesbian-headed families, is real. Gay and lesbian parenthood is achieved via many routes. Until fairly recently, the majority of gay men and lesbians who were parents produced their children the old-fashioned way. They were married to or in a relationship with a member of the opposite sex. For a variety of reasons, and in a multitude of ways, these individuals came to understand and accept their homosexuality, and they chose to come out of their closets. Many lost custody and even visitation rights to their children upon revealing their sexual orientation, even though they had been considered to be fine parents prior to their revelation. Many retained custody and/or visitation, either by continuing to deny their homosexuality publicly or despite having come out.

There is also a substantial number of gay and lesbian parents who are adoptive or foster parents. Whether or not these parents are part of a couple, the lack of legal recognition of gay and lesbian relationships dictates that they must adopt their children as single parents. Not all states will allow gays or lesbians to adopt or foster children. At the present time, Florida, for example, does not grant adoptions to gays or lesbians.

If you are considering adopting a child, there are questions you may wish to consider. How much personal information do you reveal to the adoption agency, to the adoption facilitator, or even to the birth parents? Are domestic adoptions or foreign adoptions more feasible or appropriate for you? Are you willing to adopt an older or disabled child?

Adoption can be time-consuming and expensive, but it is a major vehicle by which adults who cannot procreate can become parents. Often, the possibility of adoption grows out of foster parenting. Are gays and lesbians eligible to serve as foster parents where you live? Are you willing to open your heart and your home to a needy child who may or may not stay with you for the long haul?

If you choose adoption, inform yourself about the birth mother's and birth father's rights to consent and change of heart in your area. Most adoptions are permanent once the case is finalized. In a small number of cases, this has not been so. Are you more comfortable with an open or a closed adoption? In other words, how do you feel about your child and the biological parents knowing or knowing about each other either now or in the future? Would you adopt a relative's child?

In a number of states, including Alaska, California, Minnesota, New York, Oregon, Vermont, Virginia, and Washington, aas well as in the District of Columbia, second- or coparent adoptions are possible[9] so that the life partner of the first adoptive parent can also be granted legal custody of the child or children he or she is raising. These arrangements are currently under legislative consideration across the country.[10]

In some states where second-parent adoption is not possible, or in personal situations in which potential parents choose not to formalize their relationship through adoption, such legal contracts as formal or informal "Guardianship," "Power of Attorney," or "Appointment of Agent" can be signed in order to effect at least minimal parental rights and responsibilities. There is, however, no uniform legal vehicle by which the relationship between the child and the second parent can be recognized.[11,12]

An increasing number of lesbian couples are making alternative insemination their first choice for adding the pitter-patter of little feet to their families. Difficulties abound in this and all other methods of family creation for gays and lesbians. Some localities or institutions may prohibit or discourage offering insemination services to unmarried women.[13] Insurance companies rarely cover the costs of insemination or semen purchase. Direct transfer of semen from the donor to the recipient woman may be illegal if the two are not married. Even where the transfer is legal, doing it without a physician as an intermediary may confer parental rights and responsibilities upon the donor.[14]

Nonlegal considerations regarding the choice of alternative insemination are numerous. Again, there are many questions for potential parents to consider. Do you want a known donor (sometimes called a yes donor) or an unknown donor for your child? After all, your decision to use an unknown donor now may well affect your child's knowledge about his or her second biological parent for the rest of that child's life.

If you choose a known donor, how well do you wish to know him? Should he be a relative? a friend? the acquaintance of a friend? Should he live near you or far away? You may be opening up a potential Pandora's box regarding future decisions about child support or custody should either you or a known donor have a change of heart in the future. In some parts of the country, knowing who the sperm donor is confers parental rights on him whether or not you or he desire such an arrangement. How safe are the screening procedures for genetic anomalies or sexually transmitted diseases? Do you feel confident that you and your child are safe from HIV infection, and are you comfortable with any possible risk of genetic abnormalities based solely upon the word of someone you don't know? How do you fill in the birth certificate? Will leaving the space for the father's name blank leave your child with an emotional void? What effect will writing "father unknown" have on your child? It is currently illegal in all fifty states to include the name of your female partner as a second parent on the birth certificate.[15] What roles do the mother(s) and the donor each see themselves and the others playing in the resulting child's life? Signed agreements and contracts offer a fair amount of protection for your current wishes, but no contract is an absolute guarantee of safety should one or more of the parties choose to make a concerted effort to have it nullified.

For gay men who wish to have a biological link to their offspring, being a known sperm donor may offer a means by which to parent. Gay men and lesbians do sometimes choose to share parenting responsibilities either by living together with or without romantic partners, or by sharing custody of their children in more than one home.

The use of surrogate motherhood programs is becoming increasingly available in addition to adoption or shared parenting. Although single men and gay male couples are not high on the eligibility lists of surrogacy organizations, this is a possible avenue for gays to have a direct biological connection to their child. Further information is available in Appendix A under "Growing Generations." Men do need to be aware, however, that surrogacy contracts are not necessarily legally binding.

These are some of the facts and statistics. They reveal a great deal about the hidden corners of our neighborhoods, but they also obfuscate the humanity of our lives. Only the voices of those walking the walk are truly able to tell the real stories of their real lives. Who are the players beyond the cold facts and the statistics? How are these families creating themselves? What are their day-to-day experiences, concerns, and dreams? The answers to these questions are diverse.

The stories below come from the mouths and pens of gay and lesbian doctors, lawyers, carpenters, social workers, clergy, politicians, nurses, teachers, artists, waiters, songwriters, accountants, Christians, Jews, pagans, atheists, Generation Xers, Baby Boomers, and the children they are raising.

Family 1—Jeremy ▲▼▲ Gay Father—27—New York

"Okay, so these are the players: Didi, my mom who lives with me; Hank, my dad who is deceased; Al, my paternal grandpa who lives in the same town as I do; Brenda, my sister; Andy, her husband; Jay, my brother; Davida, his wife; Emma (age seven) and Eli (age three), their children; me; and Micah, my 2-1/2-year-old adopted son. We spend time with each other, of course, but we also help compensate for needs that others have.

"To get Micah, I lied. I did not say I was gay, which was a lie of omission, I filled out my medical report rather than giving it to my doctor, and I colored the race demographics of the area I lived in so that there wouldn't be any reason standing in my way to adopt. I always feel awkward admitting this. I just felt none of those tidbits of information has anything to do with my ability to parent. I went to a private agency after being told by a State adoption counselor that single male parents were essentially at the end of the line for available infant adoptions. I also ruled out international adoption because I wanted to bond with an infant."

Family 2—Alan ▲▼▲ Gay Father—46—Massachusetts

"I was married to Margaret for many years before I came out as gay. We are what I consider a normal Christian family: husband, wife, daughter, and son. We have only two children to replace ourselves—no overpopulation. Our only problems in forming our family came when trying to live up to others' expectations of what a family should be. I feel we are unique as well as a '90s family. Only the children's biological parents live in the home, but the kids also have contact with their mother's 'significant other.' The children's mother and I are co-parents, housemates, and have joint custody. We are also still very best friends."

Margaret (Straight Mother . . . Married to Alan—44—Massachusetts): "We are 'normal looking' in appearance. The children's father and I share in co-parenting our children. My 'significant other' (male) is very supportive of our family system. We're very open and truthful with each other."

Brett (Alan and Margaret's 15-year-old daughter—Massachusetts): "Alrighty then. I have a biological straight mom, a biological gay dad, and a 7-year-old brother. My mom is a day care provider with green eyes, and she dyes her hair strawberry blonde. My dad is an X-ray technician with brown hair, mustache and brown eyes. He's weird but funny. My parents are separated but living together. They are best friends."

Family 3—Rob ▲▼▲ Gay Father—53—California

"I am separated from my wife after 24 years of marriage. I have 3 biological children. My daughters are 22 and 9, and my son is 19. The two older children are in college. My younger daughter lives with her mother, and she is with me every other weekend. The kids all have regular contact with both parents, although my son has distanced himself from me since I have separated from his mother and 'come out.' He expressed feeling betrayed by finding out about my sexual orientation from a source other than myself. Despite our difficulties, there is mutual love among all members of the family."

Family 4—Samantha ▲▼▲ Lesbian Mother—33—Vermont

"I am now a single parent, 2 months following a 'divorce.' My woman partner of 7 years left me for a man who is considerably older than she is. She and I have a 19 month old son whom we adopted when he was 6 weeks of age from a third world country. We're currently pursuing co-guardianship documentation and sharing custody 50/50."

Family 5—Linda ▲▼▲ Lesbian Mother—40—Utah

"Our family consists of my partner, our 9-month-old son, and myself. My partner also has 3 children, ages 17, 15, and 11, from a prior marriage. We had the baby through artificial insemination, and he lives with my partner and me. She and her ex-husband have joint custody of the older children who live with their father. The two younger children go back and forth, but the oldest does not acknowledge us as a couple or a family, and he never visits."

Family 6—Leah and Ali ▲▼▲ Lesbian Mothers—
40 and 42—Texas

"Our family consists of Mommy (Leah), Mama (Ali), Jacob, our 2-1/2-year-old son, and our dog Cagney. We have been a couple for almost 18 years. We discussed raising a child often, but we didn't get serious until 1992. Ali began artificial insemination, working with an infertility specialist for 1-1/2 years. After much time and expense, we decided on adoption. This was investigated, and ultimately Leah did a single-parent adoption. We have been a family since Jacob was 6 days old, although Leah was at the hospital 15 hours after he was born. Ali now has equal legal, medical, financial rights for our son through Managing Conservatorship. This was completed once our adoption was finalized."

Family 7—Lydia and Sari ▲▼▲ Lesbian Mothers—
43 and 42—California

"In our family, there are two adults, two children, our son Nathan age 5 and our daughter Starr age 1 year. We also have two dogs, Doogie and Rampage, and three cats, Hoover, Naylor, and Whizdom. Our immediate-extended family includes Nathan's biological father, and Starr's two godfathers. Our family is also populated with grandparents, uncles, aunts, and cousins.

"Our family was formed in 1985 when Sari and Lydia joined our lives, hopes, and dreams. One of the first things we discussed was the importance of family, including children, to both of us. Beginning in October of that year, we began laying the foundation for our family. We bought a house, we raised a puppy together, we cemented our relationship with time and love.

"Nathan is Lydia's biological son. He was conceived via alternative insemination, using a friend as our donor. Sari inseminated Lydia and was with her in the delivery room for the C-section. Nathan was lifted out of Lydia and literally placed in Sari's waiting arms. Nathan loves this story, especially the part when he is placed in Sari's arms and she says 'It's my boy.' Nathan's father also is an active participant in his life.

"The first 'problem' we encountered in forming our family was finding a donor when we decided we were ready to have a child. We agreed that Lydia would have the first child and then, when we were ready, Sari would have the second. After several considerations and dead ends, Lydia was speaking with a friend at a party when he asked who our child's father would be. I told him we had our eye on his lover. He became very excited, and said, 'Ask him. He'd love to do it.' Before we could call, he called us and said he had always wanted a child. We arranged a meeting to discuss our definitions of what our family would be. We wanted someone who would be present in our child's life but not a roommate. We agreed to release him from all financial responsibility in exchange for his agreement to give up all parental claims to the child.

"Once that blank was filled in, Lydia went to a woman obgyn to whom we were referred by a friend. When she understood that we were a couple, she stated 'I knew I would have to deal with this sooner or later in my practice, but I did not think it would be so soon.' When she examined Lydia, she found that she had fibroid tumors and suggested a hysterectomy, 'because it was easier.' She then offered that 'Maybe Sari could have the baby, if it did not interfere with your roles.' We never saw that doctor again. Then, through another referral, we found our current doctor who performed the necessary surgery. Four months later, Nathan was conceived.

"When we decided it was time for our next child, we again went through the 'donor' lookout. We were approached by the friend of a friend, and after a lot of discussions and planning, with the same arrangements as we had with Nathan's donor, Sari and our second donor began the process of conception via alternative insemination. Sari became pregnant with identical twin girls. It was a very difficult pregnancy and ended with the unspeakable happening. Three days before our girls were due to be born by a scheduled C-section, there was a cord accident, and our babies died. Sari became pregnant five months later and miscarried. Although we really wanted more children, the pain was too great to risk Sari's becoming pregnant again. We opted for adoption.

"Starr is adopted. Sari was chosen by her birth parents as her adoptive mother. Sari was in the delivery room when Starr was born, again via C-section, and Starr was placed in her arms at that time. Sari was responsible for her care in the hospital and brought her home to her big brother and other Mama when she was 14 hours old."

Family 8—Carol ▲▼▲ Lesbian Mother—41—Kansas

"My partner Rose and I met 4-1/2 years ago at work. We began living together 6 months after and decided we wanted a baby. We started alternative insemination at a local medical center with sperm from an anonymous donor. As a result, our daughter Drew was born almost a year and a half ago. Now there are three of us in the family, and Rose is pregnant with our second child. I have 'Appointment of Agent' papers which supposedly give me authority to make decisions about Drew equal to the authority her biological mother has. No formal arrangements have been made should we ever split."

Family 9—Jenny and Ann ▲▼▲ Lesbian Mothers—
33 and 38—Illinois

"Our family is complete, perfect, and quite loving. Although not traditional, we are certainly solid, nurturing, and supportive of one another. We are the portrait of the 'perfect' family of our generation. We are two middle class working parents, two beautiful children, two cars, a new home, two dogs, and more credit cards than we need. Our family fits together so simply, so perfectly, so naturally.

"We became a family by fate, and I'll forever believe that. I met Ann when I was 15 years old. She was so free-spirited and unlike anyone I had ever been attracted to before. In fact, the thought of being with a woman had never entered my mind . . . but then there was Ann. I struggled with my fascination about her, and I finally came to the conclusion that I should at least investigate my feelings. Ann was quite accommodating to all of my curiosities. Although I loved her, I began struggling with my own issues of being accepted by those closest to my heart. I soon dismissed the attraction as just a phase, and by age 18 I was married to the man that made my family proud. I gave birth to my first child, Jo, 10 months later. The following Christmas, Ann came to my grandparents' home for the holidays. I kept my distance, but my heart was racing as if I were meeting her again for the very first time. I watched her as she rocked Jo, and I began to wonder what my life would be like if I lived with Ann. We kept in touch via phone and letters for the next 15 months. I had decided that I was going to leave my husband and move back to my home town. Ann met me at home when I returned. I knew that moment I saw her that it was just something 'meant to be.' Jo acted as if she had known Ann all of her life. She bonded with 'Boo' immediately. The three of us were meant to be a family . . . I no longer had any doubts.

"For the next several years, we lived in bliss. Ann had stepped into the parental shoes as if they had always belonged to her. Jo had no contact with her father, as he made himself scarce to avoid paying child support. Actually, Ann and I felt this was a blessing and just provided Jo with all she needed to flourish in life. Jo was very accepting of her family . . . I mean, doesn't everyone have a mommy and a Boo-Boo? At age seven, Jo came home from school explaining that she wanted to talk to her dad because her friends at school had dads and she didn't. Ann wanted to explain to Jo at that very moment what the terms gay, lesbian, queer, and faggot meant. I thought this might be too much for Jo to take in, but Ann insisted that if we made our relationship a secret, it would become something hidden and dirty. Jo was told that our family was special, and that others might say things about her parents that would hurt her feelings. After an evening of family discussions, Jo concluded that we had wasted our time explaining our love for each other, because it was something she was fully aware of. She then stated she would never understand why someone outside of our family might think it was a bad thing.

"In the Fall of 1990, I approached Ann with the idea of having another baby. We were comfortable financially, and I had always intended to have more than one child. Ann agreed that a baby would really complete the family. The talk began to excite me, then Ann asked if I would want an anonymous donor, or should we approach someone we knew? I made it clear that I wanted to know the donor, as this was going to be a labor of love. A few weeks later, we approached my cousin and her husband. They were flattered by our request and said that they would think about it. In January 1992, Cait came into our lives. In the delivery room were Ann at my left, and my cousin on my right. My mother, Jo, and a handful of our closest friends were in the waiting room to welcome Cait into the world. It was awesome!

"Our children live with the two of us. Jo's father has not seen her since she was 8 years old, although she has a good relationship with her paternal grandmother. We are in the process of terminating all parental rights with Jo's father. This will enable us to give Ann guardianship, while I retain legal custody. This is the current legal status for Cait as well.

"As for Cait, her biological father sees her on a regular basis. Cait knows him as the man who helped make her, and she has a wonderful relationship with him and with my cousin.

Cait does not have a father's name on her birth certificate. We attempted to put Ann's name as co-parent on the birth certificate, but our efforts to date have been futile."

Jo (Jenny and Ann's 13-year-old daughter): "My family is cool. I have two moms (Mom and Boo) and a little sister. We are a happy family. My parents don't fight. We spend a lot of time together. I know my mom, but I only have pictures of my dad. It makes me mad that I don't know him. If I did know my dad, it would be a normal family in people's eyes, but I don't know if it would be a good family. Right now I have two loving parents that are cool. I can't think of any disadvantages. My mom is very caring. She worries a lot about us. Boo-Boo is very cool. She taught me to ride a bike when I was little and always likes to do fun stuff."

Family 10—Dee and Sherry ▲▼▲ Lesbian Mothers— 31 and 46—California

Dee: "There are four of us in our family right now. Sherry, her two biological sons from a previous heterosexual marriage, and me. The boys are 17 and 15 years old. We are also hoping to have a baby, so I have been trying for 8 months to conceive. Sherry and I started dating in August of 1992, and within a week we became engaged. I moved into the house where Sherry and her two sons lived. A year later, on our anniversary, we got married in the Metropolitan Community Church in San Francisco, which we were attending at the time. The boys attended the wedding and helped out at the reception. Our 17 year old has been with us most of the time we have been together, except for 6 months when he was 15 and ran away from home. Our 15 year old has been with us also for all but 6 months. In his case, we sent him to stay with his Dad when he was 12 because we were afraid he was getting involved with a gang. Now we realize this was not the case. It didn't work out for him to stay with his father and Dad's newer family, so he came home. We have not faced any major problems in forming our family. I used to fear that the boys would say, 'You're not my mother,' but they never did. After we'd been a family for a year and a half, we moved from the city to the suburbs, and this was harder on the boys than we expected. Until recently, the boys' father lived only an hour or two away, and they went to see him one to three times a year. Now Dad has moved to Kansas, so contact will probably be less. They talk by phone every month or two."

Sherry:"Dee's already described the basics of our family. I have primary physical custody of the boys, and I share joint legal custody with their father. When we were first forming our family, my parents and ex-husband were hostile and combative. I had to get a new set of friends, too. Now the boys and their father have a good relationship. They enjoy seeing him. My parents have come to accept Dee as part of the family, and I am now on good terms with them. In the home, it was hard for Dee to feel connected to the boys when they did stuff we experienced as negative, because she didn't have the good nurturing, bonding years when they were young. The boys also probably took a few years to develop a bond to her for the same reason."

Family 11—Liz and Kathy ▲▼▲ Lesbian Mothers— both 32—Pennsylvania

"We are a two-mom family with a 2-year-old daughter conceived via known donor self-insemination. We are expecting a new baby in a couple of months via the same known donor. It was our preference to select a donor who is biologically related to the non-biological mom. We also have three large dogs who are an integral part of the household. We had a successful co-parent adoption prior to our daughter's first birthday and plan to repeat the process after the birth of the second child. We also had a 'parenting agreement,' a 'partnership agreement,' and a 'donor agreement' prior to the adoption. We encountered no problems forming our family beyond the logistics of planning for and succeeding with donor insemination and co-parent adoption. We were, in fact, fortunate, as Liz cannot have children, and we had another "mom" option, which heterosexual couples don't have. Our intention is for our children to have the opportunity to establish a comfortable relationship with their donor. As our daughter is only two, we have not yet had any major discussions. We do, however, communicate regularly with the donor, who lives 2500 miles away, and she spends time with him several times during the year. As she grows older, we will provide her and the new child with age-appropriate information, and they will be able to decide what they would like to call him and how close a relationship he and they feel is comfortable. We intend to raise our children with two moms as the primary caregivers and parents. It was an important part of our decision to have a known donor who did not want to take a parenting role and who is biologically as close to Liz as possible. We were very fortunate to have this option available to us. We are more than happy with the results from all sides. Both of our daughter's grandfathers have passed away, but both grandmothers visit or are visited regularly. One lives very close by, and we spend time weekly together and talk by phone almost daily. We encourage close relationships with both and are sad that our fathers were unable to be a part of our children's lives."

Family 12—Joyce ▲▼▲ Lesbian Mother—52—Hawaii

"When my son was born, I had a 7-1/2-year-old daughter from a prior heterosexual marriage. I was out as a lesbian at that time when Keola's dad and I had a brief affair (my bi phase!). When my son was two, his dad married a woman with two children, then they had another child together. When my son was four, my daughter died. Now our family includes several close lesbian friends, and also included a gay man who recently died. There are two sets of grandparents and assorted aunts and uncles. At first there was pressure from Keola's father and all our parents for me to marry his father. That subsided during the first year. His father and I shared custody (no court order), and my son lived with me through high school. Currently, at age 20, he lives with his father and his father's current girlfriend. When my son's dad was married, his wife targeted our son and was mean to him. This was something my son kept from me until later, so we had difficulties I didn't understand at the time. Now we have a friendly and loving relationship with my son's dad. Our relationship with my parents is one of close long-distance contact. His relationship with his dad's parents is cordial but infrequent. The relationship with my daughter's dad is cordial and respectful, and we have occasional, friendly contact with her grandparents. My son was and is close to his step- and half-siblings, and he deeply loved his sister. My daughter lived with me and spent weekends with her dad."

Family 13—Roz and Stacy ▲▼▲ Lesbian Mothers— 22 and 23—Arizona

Roz: "We have a 2-1/2-year-old daughter, Skye, and we feel that anyone who loves all of us is part of our family. Skye is Roz's natural daughter, and we have arranged a Power of Attorney for Stacy. Basically, Stacy has all the legal and moral responsibility for Skye that any biological parent would have, without taking away the parental rights of Roz as biological mother or of Roz's ex-husband, Skye's biological father. We are also planning to have Stacy's last name added to Skye's name, as I have done with mine. We have emotional support from Stacy's family but resistance from Roz's family. Dave is and always will be Skye's Daddy. Even though we can't get along all the time, we are still friends, and we are civil to each other. I would only take her away from him if he were abusive to her, and he has not been. We do still love each other, and we always will, but that is not what we want for us or for Skye. Skye lives only in one home, ours. Her father is in the Navy and based in California, while we live in Arizona. Even if he were not in the military, she would still be with us. We feel that even though he helped to create her, she is more of me and mine than she could ever be of his. I know that sounds spiteful, but it's fact. Our daughter's father's extended family may not even be aware of our situation.

"Our story actually begins in 1988. We met in high school and became best friends. One night, while playing an acting game, we kissed, and something was sparked. I was confused about the way I felt. I had been with guys before and had considered myself 'straight.' The thought of being with a woman never really occurred to me. Stacy had boyfriends before but had never been with anyone sexually until me. We started dating and kept it hidden for a while. Her mother would say things like, 'If I didn't know better, I'd think that you guys were more than just friends.' We figured she was kind of figuring it out. We told my parents before hers. They thought it was just a phase, and that it was okay because I'd grow out of it. Stacy was really scared to tell her parents because her mother had made a comment once that nothing she or her brother could do would shock her unless one of them were gay. In that case she said that she would disown them.

"Stacy and I decided to run away so that we could be together. All in all, we ended up running away three times. Her mother refused to accept anything, and after about a year, my parents began to accept it better.

"The whole time, we were together. I was really confused. I wanted the sex from a man but the love from a woman. If we got married, our union would be stronger, and I wouldn't want a man anymore (pretty dumb, huh?). We got married. My mother made me gloves for the wedding, and she told her friends at work. They all sent gifts. Stacy's parents didn't even know until much later. Soon after, we broke up.

"I fell in love with Dave, a man that I worked with and moved in with him. Stacy fell in love with an older woman who had a 17-year-old son. Dave went into the Navy, and I bounced between Texas, where my parents live, and Virginia, where Dave was stationed. Dave and I married, and I got pregnant. When I told him, he said, 'Oh.' Things went downhill from there. Stacy moved to Oklahoma with her girlfriend, until her girlfriend left her for another woman.

"Dave and I fought all the time. I started talking to Stacy again and realized that I was still in love with her. She wanted me to try and work it out with Dave, but I had gotten to the stage that I no longer wanted to be with him. Dave and I separated, and I moved back in with Stacy. The understanding was that we would only be roommates and see where my marriage was going.

"At one point, the three of us tried to make a relationship work. I loved them both and didn't know what to do. After a year of trying that, I realized that I loved Dave, but that I'm not happy when I'm with him. I can't see Dave and me living together and raising our daughter together for the rest of our lives, but I can see that with Stacy. Once again, we are separated. Stacy, Skye, and I are very happy as a family now. I am happier than I ever was when I was with Dave, and I know that this is the right path for me now. I still love Dave, but I am no longer in love with him."

Family 14—Carole and Andrea ▲▼▲ Lesbian Mothers— 47 and 44—California

Carole: "We are two moms, a 13-1/2-year-old daughter, and a 7-year-old son. Our daughter is my partner's biological daughter from a prior marriage. Her marriage ended, and we got together 12 years ago. Integrating two households was difficult. It was difficult in some ways to develop a relationship with a child already in the picture. Our son was conceived by artificial insemination. We know his donor's age, religion, education, health history, likes and dislikes, and a little about his personality. As his birth mother, I have sole custody of Jonathan. Alix's father is around but does not maintain regular or consistent contact with her. When he is around, our relationship is cordial/friendly, but he's not around much and is not very responsible. Alix's biological parents share legal custody, but Andrea (her birth mother) has physical custody."

Andrea: "As Carole said, there are two moms, a daughter, and a son in our family, and we all live together. We have been a family since Alix was one and a half. Jonathan has been with us since birth. Our daughter has regular, daily contact with both moms but seldom sees her father. Our son doesn't know his biological father, who is an anonymous donor. I have physical custody of our daughter and share legal custody with her father. Only Carole has custody of our son."

Alix (Carole and Andrea's 13-1/2-year-old daughter—California): "Andrea and Lou are my parents. I know both of my parents, but they're divorced, and I never see my dad. I kind of think of Carole as another one of my parents. What I like best about my family is that we have fun together. I have never really thought about advantages or disadvantages of having two same-sex parents, except one disadvantage is when I have a boyfriend, then there isn't a dad to be overprotective of me. My mom will probably take care of that. Plus I can't go to any father–daughter events. I'd like to be able to say that I have two moms."

Jonathan (Carole and Andrea's 7-year-old son—California): "My family is different from other families that I know because I have two moms. Carole is my biological parent. I don't know who else. In my family I also have a sister, no brothers, a dog, and a rat. My parents are Carole and Andrea, but I call them Mommy and Mimi."

Family 15—Christine ▲▼▲ Lesbian Mother—60—California

"I am the mother of seven children. Currently, they are all grown with ages ranging from my oldest girl, who is 38, to my 29-year-old twin girls. I also have 14 grandchildren ranging from 6 months to 19 years. We started out with one father, one mother using the usual techniques. After 17 years of marriage, I divorced my husband. At that time, the children ranged from 6 to 15 years of age. Only after the divorce was in the planning stage, did I learn there was an alternative to being a miserable heterosexual! I wound up filing for divorce, changing religious affiliation, and coming out within 6 months. Nineteen seventy-two was quite a year!

"I was always the steady parent during the years of raising my children. I had custody. Their father had visitation every other weekend plus up to two weeks one time a year. In reality, since 1972, the children have seen him only six or seven times for brief visits of a few hours. He now lives overseas.

"My first partner was Agnes, a 'dry' alcoholic. We met at a church function. She brought a son into the relationship. He was 1 month younger than my only son, so they were a lot of company for each other. Agnes had been a lousy mother—she identified herself as this—so raising the children was pretty much my scene. If necessary, she would discipline, but usually she was not much good at it. She expected perfection from the children and found any form of compromise difficult. Her rigidity in all aspects of daily life finally caused us to go separate ways. She did remain friendly to the children and me for quite a few years, but I do not know where she is any more. Our relationship lasted 3-1/2 years.

"Another partner was Bo, who was with us about 1 year. It was not actually a relationship, since she had fallen, broken both wrists, and needed help. She was older and retired, so we moved her in with us, as we provided the care she needed. About the time she healed, I needed some very serious spinal surgery, so she stayed to help care for the family and me until

I was able to return to work. She left the area after that, and we did not hear from her again.

"Janet was a partner for about 2 years, 2 very rocky years. She was a heavy drinker and when drinking, she was not very nice. When I tired of her bad example, I asked her to leave. Only then did I learn that she had given both drugs and alcohol to my son and to one of the girls. Needless to say, they had really liked her. Janet was a lot of fun when not drinking, and we used to do quite a bit of camping as a family. Once she was 'invited' to leave, all connections were severed. I understand she left the state.

"After 2 years or so of being alone with my children, I re-met an old friend of about 11 years. We'd lost contact during the period I was with Janet. Rosemarie and I remained together for about 4 years, but we were lovers for only the first three. We loved each other enough to be honest. I was in seminary by that time, and Rosemarie realized she would not be a good pastor's spouse. She did not wish to relocate as my position would require. Even after we broke up, we lived as a family until I was ready to leave the area for my first church."

Marybeth (Christine's 35-year-old daughter—California): "I am on my second marriage of 8 years. My husband adopted my daughter, who is now 16 years. We have one or two foster kids, depending on when they go home and when we have new ones.

"What I like best about our family is that no matter what happens, at least some of us get together. Even as adults, we still have family time, although it is challenging trying to get seven kids, their families, Mom, and her friend together."

Jean (Christine's 29-year-old daughter, Tara's twin—California): "I am married for a little over a year. I have a 4-year-old son and a 9 year old that was put up for adoption. My biological parents are my mom and dad, but I don't know my dad except for a letter twice a year and a check. What I do know, I don't care much about. I do like my stepmother more than my dad. If it weren't for her, I would have nothing to do with him. Mom's partner Rosemarie has been more important in my life than my dad. She is more a parent to me than my dad. I grew up with her being very important. I think that the advantage was I grew up with an open mind. I saw first hand what discrimination was like. I hope that I am less likely to put people down until I know them. When I was 9 years old, I found out my mom was gay, but it wasn't until I was 13 or 14 that I realized that no one else was like our family. I just thought I was extra special to have two moms!"

Tara (Christine's 29-year-old daughter, Jean's twin—California): "I have five sisters and one brother. I am close to two of my sisters. My parents are divorced, which is great! My dad I don't know. He and I are not close. He tried to drown my twin sister and me when we were three. My mom is a lesbian. She is also my best friend, my minister, and the world's best mom! I've always talked to my mom about everything. She's a very important person to a lot of people. There are fourteen grandchildren in the family, three adopted out and one who died. I worry about what people think about me but not my family. I really don't care what they think. My family is different, but that's okay with me. I've always known it was. I like that we are all different, but we all do love each other in our own ways."

Barbara (Christine's 38-year-old daughter—California): "My mom is probably the strongest person I know and has had a great deal of influence in my life. I love her dearly. My dad is just who helped give me life. He doesn't really matter anymore. He was never around when I needed him. As a teenager, I was the oldest of seven kids living with Mom and her friend(s). As an adult, I am the wife of a very good man, the mother of three teenage boys and a teenage daughter. It's a good family. The family I grew up in was never the norm. Dad wasn't around much, then not at all. Then Mom had a friend move in. I think it was more in the norm after she moved in. At least we had a happier family."

Family 16—Dale and Kat ▲▼▲ Lesbian Mothers—
38 and 37—Florida

Dale: "Kat is an artist. I am a human rights civic activist. We are both physically challenged. Kat has the most gentle, loving spirit of any woman I know. Because of Kat, our children are the most gentle, kind children I know of. Kat is divorced. She has custodial care of her son, Dylan, and of her niece, Hanna. Both of our children are 8 years old and have been with our family, as it is now, one year each. I approached our relationship slowly, because I wanted to do right by the children. I now share custodial parenting rights to both children. Kat and the children live full-time with her mom and dad in their home. I live in an apartment complex for the elderly and disabled. My heartbreak is finding proper housing for our family. I am grateful to Kat's parents for housing my family. Kat's mother is in denial of her lesbianism, as is my mother. Out of respect, we do not show outward signs in front of our mothers. They see us as friends. In general, people are supportive of our family. The children have regular contact with all biological parents and relatives. We take care not to deny grandparents and relatives access to the children. We go out of our way to keep the lines of communication open. We make a special effort not to bad-mouth biological parents. We are still very much involved, hopefully for a lifetime, though we have a cordial, businesslike relationship with them."

Kat: "Our family includes me, Dale, my 8-year-old biological son, Dylan, and my sister's 8-year-old daughter Hanna, who came to us after a lot of turmoil in her own family. I am recently divorced. Both Dale and I are differently abled. Dale and I developed a friendship that sort of grew from there.

Family 17—Jim ▲▼▲ Gay Father—40—Massachusetts

"I am a gay male with two daughters, ages 17 and 13. I currently live with my husband of three years. We are run-of-the-mill people who have normal interests and activities. We are active, and we travel a lot with and without the children. Our younger daughter lives with their mother full time. The 17-year-old has just moved into her own apartment. Although the initial years were difficult, today I enjoy a fairly cordial relationship with my ex-wife without custody or visitation problems. Throughout the process of separating and beginning new lives apart, neither of us ever brought the children into our difficulties directly. Of that, I am proud and have taken great solace. The girls' mother has physical custody and there is shared legal custody. The kids go where they want, when they want. My younger daughter couldn't accept my partner's attention needs. She always used to get physically between us when possible. It took almost two years for her to relax. Now it's fine. My partner never had children around before and took about the same amount of time to adjust. The girls have regular contact with four parents, two biological parents and two step-parents. There is an excellent ongoing relationship with both biological parents. I have a very cordial relationship with my kids' maternal grandmother. She's met my partner and is very accepting."

Chelsea (Jim's 13-year-old daughter—Massachusetts): "I live with my mom. I consider my mother, her fiancé, my father, and my dad's husband to be my parents. I'm going to have a step-father after my mom and her fiancé get married. My dad is re-married, so it's like I have two extra dads. It's great to have lots of parents, and it's fun to have two Christmases, birthdays, and other holidays with each parent. It's hard sometimes when I don't want friends to know about my family, and I have to lie to them when they ask."

WHAT IS A FAMILY?   ▲▼▲   61

Family 18—Becka ▲▼▲ Lesbian Mother—44—
Washington State

"My family includes my son Tommy, my partner Caroline, Uncle Reggie, my mom, my dad, siblings, and their spouses and kids. Caroline and I had Tommy through artificial insemination with an anonymous donor. Tommy is now seven years old and has been with me since birth. He lives with me, and Caroline has him at least one night per week. She and Tommy have a very close and continuing relationship. We all do things together as well. We don't know his biological father, just that he is married, a father, and healthy. Tommy's grandparents love us and support us without reservation. We have experienced resistance from other gay and lesbian friends and support from heterosexual friends."

Tommy (Becka's 7-year-old-son—Washington State): "My family is friendly and nice to me. They are Mom, Grandma, Grandpa, uncles, aunts, and my godmother. My parents are my mom and my godmother. I call them Mom and Caroline. What makes my family different from other families that I know is they are different people. I've got four Indians in my family. We have lots of picnics and fishing. We go to sporting events and play sports. My family is really, really fun to play with. They are nice. They don't just stay inside. It's hard that most of my family lives far away. That's it."

Family 19—Sandra and Kelly ▲▼▲ Lesbian Mothers—
37 and 36—Ohio

Sandra: "Our family consists of two female adults and two teenagers. I gave birth to Miranda, who is now 17 years old, and Max, who is now 15 years old, when I was in a heterosexual marriage. I left the marriage more than two years ago because I thought it would be easiest on the kids. I moved out and let their father be the custodial parent, and I visited them on weekends for 16 months. When I was visiting them, they spent at least one night every week with me and dinner another night. I took them to school a couple of times a week, to the doctor, and to other extra things. We went to court, and Kelly and I have had the kids full time now for the last 10 months. They continue to have regular contact with their dad, but they have a very shaky relationship with him. They have not spent one night with their father in ten months, and he sees them about once a month. He begged for them when we separated, but he really didn't want them. Their relationship got worse and worse. He physically hurt Miranda several times. They both told a judge they wanted to live with me. Their dad's ego was hurt. He changed the locks on the doors to their home of eight years, wouldn't give them their furniture, and hadn't invited them back until very recently. We now live in our apartment. We've been looking for a condo or small house, but we want to stay in their school district because they are a senior and a freshman. It's expensive to live in this area."

Miranda (Sandra and Kelly's 17-year-old daughter—Ohio): "In my family, there's my mom. She's cool. I can talk to her. If I do something wrong, she may be angry, but she listens to me. Kelly, my mom's girlfriend, is very sweet. She's as genuinely my parent as any step-parent. She worries about us. My brother, Max, is kind, gentle, and hilarious. He's one of my best friends. Then there's my dad. He's just a big image. The person underneath is a jerk. My parents are Kelly and my mom. They take care of my brother and me. They provide a roof, food, love, time, and understanding. I know that they talk like they should. They sit down and present feelings and come to a compromise. It is awesome. I've never seen such a real friendship. I strive for what they share, but most people my age are fumbling for identities, values, and answers. The only disadvantage to having two same-gender parents would be to the people who would ignore or discriminate against us. It's their loss."

Family 20—Melissa and Trish ▲▼▲ Lesbian Mothers—
37 and 39—New Jersey)

"We are a loving family that consists of two lesbian mothers and one daughter. Our family was formed by love. Dawn
was from a former heterosexual relationship. She is fourteen
and has been with Melissa always. She lived with the two of us
for almost five years. She lives at home with us and has regular contact with both of us. She knows her biological father but
has no contact with him. He relinquished all parental rights
when Dawn was a baby. In the beginning of being a single parent, it was tough, but since we [Trish and Melissa] are together,
things are as normal as can be. Our parents are very supportive and are very active in Dawn's life."

Dawn (Melissa and Trish's 14-year-old daughter—New Jersey): "We're your basic nuclear family, just two moms instead
of one. My biological mother and her significant other, my
other mother, are my parents. My father has not been involved
in my life for six years."

Family 21—Denise and Alisha ▲▼▲ Lesbian Mothers—
33 and 34—New York

Denise: "Our family is made up of myself, my partner of 9
years Alisha, our 5-month-old daughter Zoe, and our three
cats. Alisha and I began dating exclusively nine years ago. We
moved in together eight and a half years ago and decided to
have a child two years ago. Initially, Alisha was reluctant to
have a child, but after spending more time with our friends'
children and after much discussion, we mutually agreed that I
would get pregnant using anonymous sperm donation. I gave
birth to Zoe in January 1996. We are currently in the process of
having Alisha legally adopt Zoe. Everyone in our life has been
very supportive. All of our parents view themselves as Abby's
grandparents."

Alisha: "There are two moms and our 5-month-old daughter in our family. Our daughter has been in our home with us since her birth. My partner, Denise, was artificially inseminated through an anonymous sperm donation program at a fertility clinic affiliated with a large public hospital. We know quite a bit about the donor, including his physical characteristics and health, the health of his immediate and extended family, his occupation and interests, his psycho-social history, current friendships and relationships, and his reasons for being a donor. We approached the process with a simple, albeit somewhat naive, desire to buy sperm and used the expertise of the clinic for the insemination. We were unprepared for the medical model approach to our situation. From day 1, Denise was a fertility problem just like anyone else. This was hard to get used to. Otherwise, the staff was very nice and accepting of us and the medical care was very good. I am almost through the process of adopting our daughter. Final adoption is expected in about four months. We gave our families one year's advanced notice of our plans to have a baby. Some took this opportunity to ask questions and talk to us about their concerns, which mostly concerned some of the issues our child might encounter. Though some concerns linger, we now have the support of family and friends. I have a good relationship with all of the grandparents. My parents are extremely excited and supportive of our family. I've been accepted into my partner's family, although I think there might be some difficulty in their seeing me as a co-parent. It will be interesting when my daughter calls me Mommy in front of them or their friends."

Family 22—Werner ▲▼▲ Gay Father—31—Austria

"I am a gay single father of my daughter, Anna, who is 3-1/2 years old. I lived with my long-time female partner, Katrina, until she died shortly after having given birth to our daughter. There was an intimate and loving relationship between us. Anna knows about her mother. Our family is just the two of us now."

▲▼▲

So, who decides who's family and who isn't? Clearly, families in today's fluid and still-changing society define themselves based on the very unique needs and circumstances that each of them faces.

It's All "Relatives" ▲▼▲ Creating Family Ties

2

But the eyes are blind.
One must look with the
heart . . .

Antoine de Saint Exupery,
The Little Prince

*M*y kid brother and I were sharing the back seat of the old Buick. Well, sharing might be an overly optimistic word . . . we were both occupying the back of the car, but there was a battle royal ensuing over seat territory as Dad drove through the hot, humid Northeast summer from our home on Long Island to our yet distant destination of Provincetown, Massachusetts. Everyone was

Alternative parenting challenges adults to create a healthy environment without the luxury of relying upon predetermined relationships. (John Clancy, Photographer.)

excited about our vacation, and our passion was hard to contain within the confines of the un-air-conditioned car. Mom began the day handing us books to read and pictures to color, but soon the tedium of the drive became unbearable, and we children lit into each other as only siblings do.

Mom slowly turned around, and pointed to a bright red line that wove its way through the hideous plaid upholstery that covered the rear seat. *"You,"* she said, glaring at me, "stay on *that* side of the line . . . and *you,"* she leveled with equally intense frustration at my brother, "stay over *there!"* Another family vacation had begun.

"Family" cannot be adequately defined by a list of who should be included or excluded. "Family" is much more a matter of what individuals share and how they congregate and interact with each other than it is a simple list of characters. Love, commitment, and nurturance are primary qualities that create and sustain family bonds. When we recognize the supportive emotional bonds that hold us in each other's hearts, we recognize family.

Family values has become one of the most bandied-about phrases of this decade. It is heard on the street, in the news media, in the halls of Congress, and just about anywhere else two or more individuals congregate. Two simple and apparently familiar words have been connected in such a way as to create incredible ambiguity that is so widely open to interpretation that the discussion most often offered revolves not so much around the reapplication of values to families but to a debate, over what, exactly, each participant means by the phrase. For the purposes of this discussion, *family values* will be used to refer to the mores incorporated by groups of individuals that transform their relationships to each other from a mere assemblage into a family.

In late twentieth century America, "family" has routinely come to refer to the immediate grouping of parents and their minor children. Some acknowledgment remains that grown children still constitute their parents' family, but it is clear that this is usually a secondary relationship once they have established families of their own. Despite this rather narrow conception of familial relationships, in reality, there are a myriad of family constellations living healthy, moral, and productive lives in this country today. More than half of them are considered to be "alternative" families in one way or another. Perhaps the family is headed by a single, divorced mother with Dad visiting every other weekend, or seeing his children only a handful of times a year. Perhaps it is Dad who has primary custody, and Mom is the visiting parent. In recent years, many single women have chosen to conceive without first establishing a committed relationship with another adult, and an increasing number of nonattached men are raising biological or adopted children. There are grandparents raising grandchildren, aunts and uncles raising nieces and nephews, and widows or widowers raising their children alone following the death of their partner. Due to a divorce rate that is currently well above 50 percent, many families have mixed and matched into "blended" families in which unrelated children are being raised by a biological parent and his or her second (or subsequent) partner. Many heterosexual as well as homosexual parents are raising children with their partners, although without the benefits or restrictions of a legal marriage. Some families still maintain ongoing and close interaction across generations with more than two generations living together. All of these families have values. All of these families are valuable pieces of the great American tapestry.

A common assumption about the gay and lesbian community has long been that because we do not procreate within the bounds of our romantic relationships, we do not create families. Thankfully, this misconception is beginning to fall away. For the millions of gay and lesbian parents and their children, the increasing recognition of their existence and value cannot come too quickly.

Gay- and lesbian-headed families remain suspect, however, to a significant portion of the heterosexual community and within segments of the gay and lesbian community as well. Questions abound regarding the mental health and the psychosocial/psychosexual development of children who are raised in minority family constellations in general and in gay/lesbian families in particular. Among the concerns raised are the following: Won't a child raised by gay parents grow up to be gay him/herself? How can a child succeed if there is no father/mother in the home? Will my child be teased for being different because I am gay? Are gays and lesbians emotionally capable of nurturing a child? Let me address these issues one at a time.

WON'T A CHILD RAISED BY GAY PARENTS GROW UP TO BE GAY HIM/HERSELF?

Ninety-eight percent of gay men and lesbians were raised by heterosexual parents.[1] Although the number of gays and lesbians is hotly disputed, some consensus exists for the incidence of homosexuality being between two and twenty percent of the general population, and the figure ten percent has been generally accepted by the gay and lesbian community. Studies of the incidence of homosexuality among the children of gay and lesbian parents reveal that the percentage is statistically identical to the incidence among children of heterosexual parents.[2,3] Based on statistical data, then, one would conclude that being raised by gay or lesbian parents is not a causative factor in determining the sexual orientation of an individual.

Aside from the question of incidence, one must ask the somewhat irreverent question, *"So what* if the child of gay or lesbian parents *does* turn out to be homosexual?" That the initial concern regarding the sexual orientation of such a child exists demonstrates the extent of homophobia in our culture. There is some validity to the argument that gay and lesbian parents would, indeed, present an environment in which a child's natural sexuality would more likely meet with open acceptance should s/he not be straight. As the families who contributed to this study clearly demonstrate, parents who are discriminated against because of their sexual orientation often raise their children to be more accepting of individual differences among people than are nonminority members of the general public. Conversely, some children of gay men and lesbians shy away from identifying with the gay and lesbian community because of the discrimination they have experienced in response to their parents' sexual orientation, and some homosexual parents hope that their children do not follow in their own painful footsteps.

HOW CAN A CHILD SUCCEED IF THERE IS NO FATHER/MOTHER IN THE HOME?

Many successful men and women throughout history, and certainly in our own time, were raised in homes without either a mother or a father. This fact does not in any way detract from the important role played in a child's life by a parent of the absent gender. Rather, it speaks to the flexibility of the human spirit. As a culture, we have come to identify our perceived normative experience as an ideal experience, perhaps even as the only healthy experience. Our psychosocioreligious proscriptions have been interpreted to mean that only children raised in a two-parent, heterosexual, preferably financially stable environment can succeed. To argue that such an environment is harmful to a child would be ludicrous. However, the converse argument that a child raised in a different environment would naturally incur harm is equally ludicrous.

Freudian psychoanalytic theory and Social Learning Theory (based on the concepts of social reinforcement and role modeling) both purport that children learn "appropriate" gender-role behavior by exposure to a parent who is of the opposite gender from themselves. The suggestion is, therefore, that children raised without an opposite-gender parent will remain immature in their own gender identity and gender-role behavior. Research comparing the children of gay fathers, lesbian mothers, and single heterosexual mothers consistently demonstrates that the children of gay or lesbian parents are indistinguishable in their social and psychosexual development from children of heterosexual parents.[4-6] "Children of transsexual or homosexual parents do not differ significantly from children raised in more conventional settings."[7]

In the 1940s and 1950s, John Bowlby was one of the earliest child development researchers to recognize the devastating effects on children when they were separated from a parent. His work with institutionalized children in postwar England taught us that human contact, love, and affection and attention to the emotional life of children starting in (or before) infancy are all critical to the healthy physical and emotional development of the individual. In fact, love without adequate food or shelter does more good than food and shelter without adequate love.[8]

A variety of delivery systems has succeeded at providing for the emotional needs of developing children. The nuclear family is one such system. Other successful systems are small group homes and the communal experience of the Israeli kibbutzim. Children fare well when they are loved and nurtured by adults who are consistent in their lives. The more loving adults that are present, the more a child can learn about life, love, and individual traits within him/herself and in others.

Single gay and lesbian parents as a group generally enjoy less support from their extended families than do single straight parents. It is also true that a relatively low number of homosexual single parents have ex-partners upon whom they can rely for help with their children. One of the unfortunate facts of late twentieth century American family life is that *most* partnerless parents are faced with at least temporary isolation and restricted incomes. Clearly, then, two parents are apt to be better than one. In homes with two parents, the economic resources of a family are likely to be superior to that of a single parent home. Two parents are also likely to be able to be more flexible with scheduling and will generally be able to relieve each other during times of stress. As unique individuals, two parents each provide their family with different talents, temperaments, and backgrounds. No one has yet demonstrated, however, that two parents must be of opposite genders, or biologically related to their children, in order to be effective in their task. The research on the children of gay and lesbian parents is consistent in its finding that there are no significant discernible differences in gender identity or gender-role behavior between children of opposite-gender parents and children of same-gender parents.[9-13]

Lesbian mothers face the dual challenge of establishing a healthy, positive self-identity as well as creating an environment in which their children can develop appropriately positive self-esteem. Although being a lesbian may culturally confer a nonnormative identity on an individual as a "not woman," becoming a mother reestablishes her as belonging to womankind. As mothers, lesbians, like their heterosexual sisters, often turn to their own family of origin for support. Many lesbian mothers also seek to establish ongoing relationships with other lesbian-mom households as a source of strength for coping with the difficulties of parenthood and with the challenges of the double minority status of being female and gay.[14]

Gay fathers face additional challenges in parenting their children. Due to biological realities, it is more difficult for men to become parents without women. Although sperm donation is simple, affordable, and available to lesbians, egg donation (via surrogate mothering) is complex, expensive, and not widely available. Most gay men who are not fathers from heterosexual relationships therefore choose adoption or coparenting with lesbian mothers as means by which to be fathers to children. Cultural bias often makes the adoption of a child, especially a young child, more difficult for men than for women.

In order to cope with the normal and extranormal stresses of parenthood, gay fathers turn to biological family, friends, and other gay or lesbian parents for social and emotional support. At least one organization that provides surrogate mothering for gay men, Growing Generations, in Los Angeles, California (see Appendix A), actively encourages custodial fathers and their children to maintain contact with birth mothers. Much like children of lesbians and known sperm donors, these children being raised by their gay dads will in fact know their biological mothers.

The truth is that parents are fundamental influences, but they are not the only significant adults in children's lives. Gay and lesbian parents, especially those who are raising their children in homes without parents of both genders, are generally critically aware of the need that their children have to develop relationships with adults of both sexes. Gay and lesbian parents typically provide a wide variety of opportunities for such relationships to develop. Many incorporate close friends as integral members of the "immediate" family. Children are often allowed or even encouraged to develop and maintain an ongoing relationship with their noncustodial biological parent or their sperm donor, when he is known.

Grandparents, aunts, uncles, and other extended family members often play a significant role for children of single parents or children whose two parents are of one gender. Drawing from the larger community, role models are often chosen from among teachers, clergy members, or Big Brother/Big Sister programs. The important element for the growing child is that an adult loves them, is available to them, and is willing to teach them about life.

WILL MY CHILD BE TEASED FOR BEING DIFFERENT BECAUSE I AM GAY?

The short answer is, "Probably . . . yes." Children tend to tell it like it is, and *any* difference is likely to be pointed out and used to schoolyard advantage. Your child will also most likely be teased for being too tall or too short, too smart or not smart enough, too heavy or too thin, for wearing glasses or braces, for having freckles, or for any number of other attributes that help to make her or him who s/he is. A more germane question might be, "How can I help my child cope with the inevitable teasing that comes from being different?"

Growing up is not always easy. There is a lot to learn in a relatively short amount of time. There are a lot of experiences that go into a childhood, and teasing, rightly or wrongly, is usually one of them. Children who feel good about who they are, where they come from, what they can do, and what they have achieved, are generally able to cope with reasonable teasing from their peers.

Gay and lesbian parents have a distinct advantage over other parents. We know at least one aspect of their identity that will present a challenge to our children at some time during their growing years. Knowledge is power. By being aware that the issue will arise, gay and lesbian parents can do a great deal to help their children deal with its effects. Primarily through teaching their children that they and their family members are good people with many attributes aside from their sexual orientation, gay and lesbian parents arm their children with a positive sense of self. Focusing on other aspects of their and their parents' identities and their family's heritage, children of gay and lesbian parents, like all children, learn that no one part of themselves is all of who they are. It is also critical for parents to teach their children that sexual orientation is a natural and healthy aspect of who we all are. Being gay or lesbian may not be popular, it may not be understood, and it may not be "average," but it is not bad.

Children may well be embarrassed by their parents' sexual orientation. They may also be embarrassed by a parent's playfulness in public, or the fact that a parent has a foreign accent. Being a good and effective parent often means teaching difficult lessons and facing uncomfortable truths about ourselves, our children, and the world in which we live. Children are resilient and tough. They can face challenges if they are given the skills necessary to cope with them. Many children of gay and lesbian parents believe that their "different" family experience has made them more compassionate than their peers from more normative homes. Having experienced overt or covert discrimination has given them a heightened sensitivity to individual differences and value.

All good parents want to keep their children from harm and strife, but all of us do confront difficult times in our lives. Ultimately, the child who learns to face and overcome adversity fares better than the child who never has an opportunity to develop his or her strengths.

ARE GAYS AND LESBIANS EMOTIONALLY CAPABLE OF NURTURING A CHILD?

Lesbian moms and gay dads have the same concerns, desires, fears, joys, and disappointments about parenting as do straight moms and dads.[15] A significant fallacy in thinking about sexual orientation is that one's partner preference is somehow emotionally related to procreation and child rearing. For women in particular, sexuality, whether homosexual or heterosexual, has only an incidental relationship to reproduction. Unlike other primates, human females are sexually available whether or not they are ovulating. The acts of sex, therefore, are not necessarily in concert with the process of reproduction. It is quite possible for a woman to become pregnant without engaging in sexual intercourse, for instance via alternative insemination. It is also possible, and even common, for a woman of child-bearing age to engage in sexual intercourse without becoming pregnant. Quite simply, there is not always an egg available whether or not sperm are introduced into the female body during sexual activity. Although heterosexual sex is not an activity completely unrelated to reproduction, for women the two are not necessarily tied to each other.[16]

Human male sexuality is somewhat more closely linked to insemination, since it is through the sexual climax that a man releases his sperm. Both straight and gay men have been known to engage in sex, however, without intending the behavior to result in a pregnancy.

Traditional psychoanalytic theory's proposed view—that homosexuality is one result of an individual's inability to resolve the Oedipal complex—suggests an emotional immaturity that may interfere with one's ability to care about, love, and nurture another human being. This conclusion may well have come from the fact that the only homosexuals seen by

Freud and many other early practitioners of psychotherapy were inherently unable to cope with their sexuality and the effects that being different wreaked upon their lives.

In 1972, the American Psychiatric Association (APA) dropped homosexuality from its list of psychiatric illnesses as described in the *Diagnostic and Statistical Manual*.[17] The APA found that many gays and lesbians were not at all dissatisfied with their sexual orientation and were living happy, successful, and full lives; or that their psychological difficulties were independent of their sexual orientation. Thus the earlier impression of homosexuals as emotionally immature individuals had to be reexamined.

There is no evidence that being gay or lesbian renders an adult incapable of offering love, support, and nurturance to children. On the contrary, the children of gay fathers and lesbian mothers are usually very much wanted, planned for, and provided for. There are no accidental pregnancies between lesbians, and no gay man has ever unintentionally adopted a child. Parenthood and homosexuality do not preclude each other emotionally in any way.[18–21] Indeed, some gay men and lesbians are so drawn to parenthood that they have attempted to survive straight marriages in order to parent children. As the number of options increases for gays and lesbians to parent without opposite-gender partners, perhaps these tragedies will be fewer in number. For men in particular, parenting children without a woman has not often seemed like a possibility, so many men marry despite knowing or suspecting that they are gay. The strains of such a relationship are not always surmountable, and many such marriages end in separation or divorce. As the children can attest, it is the breakup of the family, not dad's (or mom's) sexual orientation that causes them the most profound difficulty.

No longer does "family" necessarily mean one mom, one dad, and the kids. As the panoply of possible and acceptable family configurations expands, so does the need for conscious decision making about the types of relationships that we wish to develop with each other. Many children live with adults who are not their biological parents, or they live with one but not the other biological parent. Someone has to decide whether or not there will be a relationship with both the custodial and the noncustodial parent(s), and someone must further decide what those relationships will look like. Many factors go into making such decisions. What are the ages and capabilities of the children to understand the relationships? What are the belief systems of the adults about parenthood's rights and responsibilities? What are the laws in your state, province, or locality? How responsible are the adults involved? What are the children's wishes? Can your child legally have two parents of one gender, or can s/he have more than two legal parents? Ultimately, one would hope that the best interest of the minor children would be the compelling force in establishing familial ties. Rather than attempting to mold all families into a narrow "ideal," let us come to recognize and support the beauty in the variety of healthy and productive family models that do really exist.

The overwhelming volume of research on gay or lesbian parents and their children indicates that similarities to heterosexual families far outweigh differences. There are, however, some noteworthy contrasts, primarily relating to sources of stress and support for homosexual- and heterosexual-headed families. As already noted, the absence of emotional support from extended family, sometimes to the extent of estrangement, lends a burden to some gay and lesbian parenting that is not usually experienced by straight parents. While most heterosexual couples are encouraged by family to remain together, especially if children are present, the opposite is true of homosexual couples. Lack of support and understanding and varying degrees of intolerance from the general public are additional, common sources of stress for gay and lesbian parents and their children.

Creating a family is a complex endeavor. Even for the most traditional families there are questions to ask and critical decisions to be made about familial relationships. Which grandparent does one honor by giving the new baby his or her name? At whose home do the relatives gather for the holidays? Who stays home with the children, and who goes to work to provide an income? All families, gay or straight, single-parent, two-parent, or more, intact or not, are faced with such choices.

For families that are clearly nontraditional, the options multiply and the responsibility for active determination of familial interaction increases. The 1960's opened a door for individuals to "do their own thing." In the ensuing decades, the individuation from societal norms has grown to include whole families. Alternative parenting challenges adults to create a healthy environment without the luxury of relying upon predetermined relationships. It demands that decisions be made in areas of life in which other families can simply rely on convention. What are the decisions that allow gay and lesbian parents to create their own molds while sustaining the essential, nurturing qualities of family life? Let's look at some of the choices that are being lived by a group of quietly courageous families.

Family 1—Jeremy ▲▼▲ Gay Father—27—New York

"Since I was 13, I wanted to have a family of my own. Not so much a partner, rather kids. I worked as an aid at a day care center when I was 14 and did some babysitting. I could not, however, ever find a full-time sitting position because of most people's attitudes about men and children. Funny how it's perfectly okay for men to be fathers, but to be a day care worker makes people think of molestation! In 1991, after four years, I moved back in with my mother when my father died. She had always known of my desire to adopt children, and when I told her of my plans in 1993, she was pleased, at first. My mother and I are opposite sides of the same coin, she being a realist leaning toward pessimism, and I being a realist leaning toward optimism. She was quick to note that it would be difficult for me to adopt and raise a child when I was gay, Jewish, a heart patient, and single. When she found out that I was adopting an infant of color, I think she passed out. Again an interesting note that she had "dealt" with her gay son, but her gay son having an Black child was an issue. My mother is resilient, and when she laid her eyes on Micah, never again was a negative word spoken. It just shows you that prejudice falls to the wayside when you finally personalize it. I have really never had a relationship last more than a few months. I think it was this knowledge that made me pursue adoption by myself. If I waited for a husband, I'd never have gotten pregnant! There are reasons I have not had any long-term relationships. The biggest, pardon the pun, is that I am fat. In lesbian terms this is not an issue; in gay male terms, it is a sin! However, I was going to have a child by the time I was 25, and that was it.

"I have had no negative reactions to being openly gay with Micah. I do, however, choose the people in my and Micah's life very carefully. Micah has many gay tee-shirts like 'The mighty Morphin Flower Arrangers' and 'I'm the Prince, but my Daddy is the Queen,' all of which people find quite humorous.

"Micah is now two, and I find that I take on both roles of a traditional 'mommy' parent and 'daddy' parent. For instance, at a mixed group activity, I am more of a mommy as I play with the kids, make sure they eat, and watch them with the 'eyes in the back of my head,' as opposed to many of the heterosexual dads who stand around the grill, drink beer, and only get involved if there is baseball or football involved. The traditional dad in me has a firm grasp of discipline with my son, and that 'man's' voice that kids tend to respond to. It is a duty of any parent to teach right from wrong and to discipline through a method of reinforcement. It is important to respect a child's individuality, to instill social values, direct a child's activities, and to set firm limits when necessary with explanation of why this is important. I've rocked him to sleep, held him during illness, and begged God to make me ill instead of him when we would go to the hospital. Our lives couldn't be more perfect. Grandma is free to be a grandma, as opposed to a co-parent. Except for my surgeries, she has never had to do the getting up in the middle of the night or the 'doctor' stuff that are soooo fun. No, she can read to him and spoil him, then call me over when she is done.

"Not only is my biological family a source of strength to me, but so is the extended family. All of my friends and family are extremely supportive of my decision to adopt. The strongest family value that I was taught is one of communication. My father used to say, 'Unless we listen to each other, we have nothing.' In a healthy family . . . no matter what their needs are, family members are responded to with love, sincerity, and occasionally a 'care package of food.' It is through the family unit, however it is composed, that one connects to society. The family unit provides a connection to the past and a connection to the future. It is a place to build life-long relationships.

"To be a parent is the most gratifying act I have ever experienced."

Family 2—Alan ▲▼▲ Gay Father—46—Massachusetts

"We were married in October, 1972, two flower children very much in love. Being flower children, we were always around a diverse variety of real human beings: gays, straights, jocks, freaks, various ethnic and religious backgrounds. I once asked Margaret if she would still love me if I were gay. I was beginning to question myself then, but being brought up a strict Roman Catholic, I was not even allowed to consider my own inner feelings.

"Our darling daughter came into our lives many years into the marriage and changed everything for the better. Seven years later, our son was born after a romantic weekend on Block Island. The children still live in one home with both biological parents. The only other adult parental figure is Margaret's significant other, whom we see once a week. Our daughter kind of resents it sometimes, as she sees an extra parent. Our son likes it because he has a new playmate. Family and friends who know our situation are very supportive, and our relationship with the children's grandparents is the same as before. Maybe it's a little strained because of my being gay, but my father-in-law's brother is gay.

"Most of the men I date are married or gay fathers, so both sides know the situation with kids. The effect of having children on my relationships is 'so far so good.'

"A healthy family exists in a place or home where there is unconditional love, nurturance, and allowance for growth and individuality for all."

Margaret (straight mother . . . married to Alan—44—Massachusetts): "We were married in 1972. The children came along 8 and 15 years later. Both parents work and provide child care. I am the better disciplinarian. My parents are the only grandparents, and we keep in touch almost weekly. We have special feasts that we celebrate for Christmas, New Year's Eve, St. Patrick's day, and the Passover Seder. A healthy family doesn't keep secrets or make demands that the children keep secrets. People are allowed to be who they are."

Brett (Alan and Margaret's 15-year-old daughter—Massachusetts): "I discovered that my family is different about 3 to 3-1/2 years ago when we had a 'family meeting,' and my dad came out. Sometimes it's crappy being with my family, but I love them anyway. They trust me, and they let me have freedom and do things that most moms and dads wouldn't let their 15-year-old kids do. They love and care about me a lot too. Having my dad be gay can be challenging, but it doesn't really bother me. Any adult, gay or straight, who cares about you, loves you, and doesn't abuse you in any way gives you a healthy family."

Family 3—Rob ▲▼▲ Gay Father—53—California

"People in my life have generally been supportive toward my coming out, although my wife does not want my youngest daughter to encounter gay life at this age. My wife still provides most of the child care. I have my daughter every other weekend. Both of us discipline our children. I don't want my 9 year old to be aware of romantic relationships, as I have been separated less than a year, and she is having difficulty with the separation. I am open with my older daughter, but my son wants to know nothing."

Family 4—Samantha ▲▼▲ Lesbian Mother—33—Vermont

"We did not encounter any unusual problems in forming our family. Since the 'divorce' between Caroline and me, our son now lives in two homes. He has contact with his two parents, and I think my ex's boyfriend may be living with her. We both have a close relationship with our son. My parents are supportive from a distance. They send my son bonds, etc. My ex's mother hates me, and her father loves me. We do share phone calls and visits. We do not know our son's birth parents, as he was adopted from a Third World country. I used to work full time while my ex-partner took care of our son full time. Now I pay her child support. Both mothers discipline our son. I can't help but wonder if having our son affected our relationship, since my partner grew away from me. We experienced the same stressors as a heterosexual couple when one parent stays home. A healthy family stays together, works through problems, and hangs on the tightest when things are the worst. Never lose faith, hope, or trust."

Family 5—Linda ▲▼▲ Lesbian Mother—40—Utah

"When Donna and I first got together, we experienced homophobia from her children. Her 17-year-old son does not acknowledge us as a couple or a family. We met with some resistance in the medical community regarding alternative insemination for lesbians. Our ob-gyn was supportive to our efforts to bear a child, but her partners refused to perform the inseminations if they were on call. Nicolas' donor is unknown, so he does not know his biological father. We do have a full questionnaire that he completed including medical and family history. Two of Donna's children were also conceived by alternative insemination, as her husband had a low sperm count. The older children live with their father, but they have contact with Donna and with me. As for extended family, my mother is supportive of our family, but she lives several thousand miles away. My father is deceased. Donna's parents have disowned her, and they have not spoken for 10 years. I am the breadwinner, and Donna provides most of the child care. I also am home half-time. We both provide discipline for Nicolas, but I try to let Donna discipline her own children. Donna's children were a very divisive force at first. They tried to drive a wedge between us. Since they moved out, things have been better, but Donna is grieving over their loss. Nicolas has changed our relationship in many ways. We are less romantic and sexual, and have become more task-oriented and sleep-deprived. However, being his parents has really cemented our relationship as well. As a family, we've established some special rituals. We each kiss the baby good night every time he goes down, we like to read the paper together on Sundays, and we always eat together as a family. In a healthy family, the members love each other and treat each other with respect and love."

Family 6—Leah and Ali ▲▼▲ Lesbian Mothers— 40 and 42—Texas

"The biggest problem that we encountered in forming our family was the emotional stress over infertility, resolving this, and deciding on adoption. There was stress involved in seeking out agencies who would place a child with a 'single' parent. Adopting in this manner was most frustrating, since we see our family relationship as stable, loving, and very capable of loving and raising a child together. We all live together, and both Mom and Mama take equal child-rearing responsibilities for Jacob. We are fortunate that Leah met Jacob's biological parents and spent 2 hours with them. His birth mother has sent an album with family pictures of both her and the birth father. These will be very special for Jacob to have as he grows up. We agreed to send pictures and letters the first year. Through the adoption agency, they have sent gifts for birthdays and holidays. We have requested that no further gifts be sent because of our concerns that as Jacob gets older he may possibly be confused about his birth parents until he is capable of understanding his adoption. We do talk about them, using their names. He will always know he is adopted, and as an adult, if he chooses to seek them out, we will support that decision. As for extended family, my brother and sister-in-law are supportive and love Jacob very much. He has two cousins, ages four and two. Unfortunately, none of our parents are living, which makes us very sad in terms of Jacob's not knowing his grandparents. We have had a very positive experience with pre-school personnel and with our employers. We have chosen to be very open and honest with Jacob and those around us so that he will grow up with a positive and loving feeling about his family.

"Both moms work. Leah is an occupational therapist, and Ali is in academia. Jacob is currently in a private, Jewish pre-school for 6 hours daily. Until he was two, we had a wonderful nanny who continues to see him every couple of weeks to baby-sit since they have such a strong and loving relationship. Discipline is provided by both moms. It is very difficult to maintain and nurture our adult relationship, with an active 2 year old. Because we both work, we feel strongly that our time in the evenings and weekends is family time with Jacob. Romantically, we're exhausted! We do recognize these challenges, and we're trying to do more with each other like movies and dinner, but it is still difficult. Our family rituals include Friday night Shabbat dinners. The rest of the week, we also always have dinner together each night. As Jacob is getting older, Jewish holidays are beginning to play a more important role in our lives. A healthy family shows love, respect, encouragement, opportunities for growth, and does 'family only' activities on a regular basis."

Family 7—Lydia and Sari ▲▼▲ Lesbian Mothers— 43 and 42—California

"Our first child, Nathan, is Lydia's natural child via alternative insemination. Due to difficulties with a second conception, we chose to adopt our second child. Six months after we decided on adoption, we became the parents of a beautiful baby girl, Starr. Although only Sari and Lydia live with the children, Nathan and Starr have regular contact with three parents. Nathan's father spends every Wednesday afternoon and evening with us. Starr has spent time with her biological family, including grandparents and great grandmother, though she is too young to really know who they are. Her contact with these relatives will probably be on an annual basis from now on. She will, however, be told who they are and will always have access to them if she chooses. We want Starr to know who her birth parents are. We want her to know they chose our family for her to be a part of because they loved her and wanted the best for her. They knew they were too young and unable to care for her themselves. We want her to feel comfortable with who they are and to know she can contact them when and if she chooses.

"The kids have a good, open relationship with extended family. They really only have Lydia's parents as grandparents. Nathan is totally accepted as equal to their other grandchildren in their hearts and minds. Lydia's mother feels she is Starr's grandmother. Her father has never said anything one way or the other except for 'congratulations.'

"We think people are often surprised by our family. Some are warm, and some are curious, and some probably choose to avoid us, but we have never encountered any resistance.

"The kids have a variety of names for us. Sari is called Mama Sari, Sari, Mom, or Mama by Nathan. She is called

Mama by Starr. Lydia is called Mama Lydia, Mama, Mom, or Mommy by Nathan. We're not sure what Starr is calling her. We think it's Mama, but it could be Lydia. Nathan calls his father Daddy, Dad, or by his first name. Starr just smiles at him.

"Both of us work. Sari has her own business as an adoption facilitator. Lydia works for a law firm. Sari is home with Starr 2 days a week. The other three weekdays, she is in day care. Nathan is old enough to be in school during the day. We both discipline the children, albeit somewhat differently, but for the most part, we are in agreement on what is acceptable behavior, how to achieve it, and what to do when challenged by the children.

"We believe having children has brought us closer. Although it is love for each other that keeps us together, love of our family is a big consideration.

"As for romance . . . what romance? We have two kids! Actually, we really appreciate and enjoy the rare time we get to spend alone together. We have fun. The romance has changed somewhat. Now instead of sending flowers to show how much she loves me, Sari bought me a Volvo because it's a safe car. So the romance may not be as frivolous as it used to be, and it may be more of a practical style of romance, but it is still showing how much we love one another.

"Our special family rituals are eating dinner together each night, special holiday meals, celebrating all rites of passage, from Starr's first steps to Nathan's losing his first tooth. In a healthy family, each member is given respect, consideration, encouragement, support, and love."

Family 8—Carol ▲▼▲ Lesbian Mother—41—Kansas

"When my partner Rose and I were starting our family, we met with some resistance from friends, and, initially, from my mother, although we were careful who we told. We tried to 'screen out' those we thought would not support us. Many people whom we didn't expect to be supportive were. Our daughter is now 15 months old. Rose conceived her through alternative insemination, so she will never know her father. We do know practically everything about him regarding medical and family information and his interests. Drew lives with both of her parents. She calls me 'Mom' or 'Mommy,' and Rose is called 'Mama.' Now we get along very well with both of our daughter's grandmas. Both grandfathers passed away while Rose was pregnant. Rose and I both work professionally in counseling and social work. We have a daycare provider who now cares for our daughter along with her three kids. Both mothers discipline Drew pretty equally. Having a child has affected our adult relationships. We don't have sex as often, mostly because we're too tired. Some of it is the extra tension of raising a child. In non-romantic terms, it's changed a lot. We always have to think of our daughter, not just ourselves. As a family, we try to eat together for dinner. We have a family Christmas at one of the grandmas' homes. We're hoping to have another child the same way this year. In a healthy family, there is love, and everyone has the freedom to grow in their own direction, but they do so without growing apart."

Family 9—Jenny and Ann ▲▼▲ Lesbian Mothers— 33 and 38—Illinois

"Our donor couple (Jenny's cousin Laura and her husband Greg) wanted to let the rest of the family know our intentions of having a baby together. We wanted to wait until after conception, because we were afraid of the resistance and certainly didn't want anyone to talk them out of being our donor. When it was confirmed that Jenny was indeed pregnant, they made the announcement at Easter Sunday dinner. With 16 family members around the table, my grandmother finally broke the silence by saying, 'Hell, are you surprised? Laura and Jenny shared everything as children!' The laughter and the congratulations then filled the room.

"Co-workers knew that Jenny had conceived via alternative insemination. They were also supportive, as they thought it was such a '90s way to have a baby. Our gay and lesbian friends were incredible. They were as excited as we and came bearing many baby gifts!

"Our children live in one home, ours. Four-year-old Cait (the 'baby') calls Jenny 'Mommy,' and the man who 'helped make her' is called 'Greggy.' Our teenager calls Jenny 'Mom,' and both kids call Ann 'Boo-Boo.'

"Both moms work while Jo is in school, and Cait is in preschool. Since we're all gone during the day, in the evenings the family is together. We both discipline the girls, although Ann is sometimes more the enforcer.

"With a 4 year old who often times ends up in our bed with us, having children can hinder the romance every now and then. For the most part, the children bring us closer together, making each of us feel more loving and romantic. When we finally get the house to ourselves, it is like we are teenagers all over again! We believe the children make us more grateful for all the love within the household. We can't imagine our life together without our kids.

"On a different note, having the children makes our family more the norm. We aren't wild individuals with an inability to commit to a family. When someone asks how long we have lived together, and we say 12 years, they always seem shocked. For the most part, people seem to believe that this lifestyle is one that is usually not monogamous or family-oriented. We love being the complete opposite of that belief!

"We have dinner together every evening at the dining room table, and Cait always says the prayers. Jenny always sings to the girls when they are sleepy or not feeling well. We both tuck them in at night, and Cait always gives us kisses in our hands to put under our pillows. Jo used to take our kisses to school with her in her pocket, so she felt close to us. We take one day a week, usually Saturday, and make it 'Family Fun Day.' We all take turns choosing what activity we will do. Every time one of us uses bad language, Cait reminds us to say 'Oh Fiddlesticks' instead.

"A healthy family possesses the ability to communicate openly about anything, while supporting each other in a loving and nurturing manner. It's a family that has parents who are 'never too busy' for the important things and crises that come up in the lives of their children."

Jo (Jenny and Ann's 13-year-old daughter): "My parents are Jenny and Ann. I call them 'Mom' and 'Boo.' I guess when I was about six, I figured out other kids at school had dads. I don't know how I found out that my parents are gay. I guess I always knew. I know my mom talked to me about it when I asked questions. Knowing that they are gay has taught me to be honest about my feelings with them, because they have always been honest with me. The challenge about being in my family is to get along with my little sister and not argue. Love, kindness, and trust make a healthy family. Also, it is good to have a friendship with your family."

Family 10—Dee and Sherry ▲▼▲ Lesbian Mothers— 31 and 46—California

Dee: "Our boys know both their biological parents, although they live in only one home, ours. There is an ongoing relationship with their father as well. We both discipline the boys, although Sherry, their biological mom, does more of the face-to-face confrontation than I do. We discuss how we will discipline and how we will respond to different issues, and we always back each other up.

"In terms of our relationship, having kids around is another factor always to have to consider when making plans, say for a night out or to have company over. Because our kids are old enough at 17 and 15 to take care of themselves and make their own meals, it has been pretty easy to do whatever we would want to do anyway, except going away for a day or longer. We can't yet trust them not to have a big party. Sherry and I have a very solid romantic relationship, and most of the time, even when the boys are acting out, it hasn't negatively impacted our relationship.

"Our biggest family ritual is birthdays when the person having a birthday chooses a favorite meal and dessert. We also try to celebrate each birthday with each of our families when possible. We have recently started having a 'family meeting' sometimes on Sunday nights, though it's hard to be consistent because often one or both boys are not home. As teenagers who'd rather be with their friends than their family, the boys don't seem that interested in rituals, so we haven't created many.

"In a healthy family, people love each other and keep lines of communication open. The members are able to come up with solutions to problems of an interpersonal nature which arise, and everyone past toddlerhood has some responsibilities. There is a structure of discipline for the kids. Sometimes, the family does things together."

Sherry: "Occasionally, though more in past years, worry over the boys has been an emotional drain for me and has sometimes negatively affected my general receptivity to Dee. Working on parenting together has also strengthened our relationship.

A healthy family fosters respect for each other and appreciation of each other's individuality. There is trust and communication about what you think, want, and need. Members listen to each other even when they don't feel like it."

Family 11—Liz and Kathy ▲▼▲ Lesbian Mothers—
Both 32—Pennsylvania

"Our daughter, and our soon-to-arrive new child, live in one house with Mamma and Mommy. Both of us share in caring for and disciplining our daughter. During the day, while both of us work full time, she goes to a wonderful day care. Baby-sitting is usually arranged with aunts, uncles, and her grandmother.

"Now that we have a child, we have less time to socialize with friends, less time to spend private and romantic time together. There's less time to read, relax, shower, eat meals, and think clear thoughts. We find when we do have quick time together in the late evening, we are exhausted. There is less physical contact and less involved conversation. More of our conversations are about our child's day and activities than our own. Planning for everything is more involved.

"We go to church at least two to three Sundays a month. We read bedtime stories all together, we have regular family gatherings for special occasions such as birthdays and holidays.

"Members of a healthy family enjoy each other's company and spending time with one another. They are supportive of each other and can rely on one another for support and encouragement. Family members love one another unconditionally."

Family 12—Joyce ▲▼▲ Lesbian Mother—52—Hawaii

"My son is now twenty and has been with me since birth. He is from a brief heterosexual relationship during my 'bi' phase. He knows his dad and has regular contact with both of us. We both contribute income to the family. He has worked part time since he was fourteen and full time from age sixteen. When the kids (my daughter died when she was seven and a half) were little, a gay male friend did free child care one to two days a week while I worked. Both kids' dads also provided child care, as did other friends on occasion. I always disciplined the kids, and my daughter's father also disciplined her.

"Having children did affect my adult relationships. If my kids didn't like a woman I was dating, I wouldn't bring her around them, though that's rarely happened. My close friendships have tended to be with people who liked the kids. There were times I had to miss events for lack of child care.

"Our special family rituals are Winter Solstice, making Christmas cookies for our friends and family, and reading together most nights until Keola was ten or eleven. Until my son was sixteen, we went camping every Labor Day weekend with two other families. A healthy family is one in which each person is valued and respected for themselves, in which communication is honest and open, in which love is freely and frequently expressed, and in which there's room for change and growth."

Family 13—Roz and Stacy ▲▼▲ Lesbian Mothers— 22 and 23—Arizona

"Roz's daughter from her straight marriage is now 2-1/2-years-old and has been the daughter of lesbian moms for a little over a year and a half. Skye knows who her mother and father are, but she lives with her two mommies. She has regular contact with both of us. She sees her father on occasion.

"Stacy is the breadwinner in our home. Since Roz and Dave are still married, she gets an allotment from him, and his military pay each month. Roz stays at home with Skye and provides our child care. 'I love it!' She plans to work part time when Skye gets into preschool or kindergarten.

"Both of us and our single gay male roommate discipline our daughter. When her father is around, he does too, although he seems to be too harsh on her. It seems that it's a power trip with him. He figures he can't tell his wife what to do, but he can with Skye. Since he is in the Navy, he is gone a lot, and when he isn't on ship or overseas, he is in California. He takes leave days to come and see us, and last year, he spent our 'Christmas' (Winter Solstice) with us. He is not the good husband or father type right now. He stares Skye down and yells at her instead of talking to her and explaining things. He doesn't play with her but zones out on the TV. Then, as soon as he knows that Roz is mad at him, he is perfect and does everything right. When she's not mad anymore, he goes back to his same old stuff. He doesn't communicate, and he gets frustrated at everything. Roz says, 'I realized that I've spent the past 3 years trying to get him to change for me and Skye. I now realize that this is wrong He is who he is, and I can't expect him to change for me, because I know that I wouldn't change for him . . . I do still love him, but

I can't be with him. We are friends.' Skye knows who her Daddy is and loves him, but he scares her.

"Having a child affects us a lot. We hardly ever go out, and 90 percent of the time when we do, Skye is with us. On rare and special occasions, our roommate watches her for us. Since she is still little, she doesn't affect our sex life all that much, but we're sure she will as she gets older.

"As far as family members go, it's completely reversed from what it used to be. Stacy's parents accept Skye and Roz as part of their family. They introduce Roz as their other daughter and Skye as their granddaughter. Roz's parents, on the other hand, want nothing to do with Stacy and feel that their daughter is ruining her life by not being with her husband. They know about the three of us trying to have a relationship by living together and thought that it was completely wrong. Roz says, 'They think that in order to make a "real" family, I need to be with a man. They feel that if I satisfy Dave's sexual, food, sleep, housekeeping, etc. needs, then that will make me happy. Not so!!! I have not yet told them that Dave and I are through, though I plan on doing that when my mother calls and asks about him next.'

"We don't have many special family rituals. We try to spend quality time together and also get our own time too. Our biggest 'ritual' is putting Skye to bed. We play with her for a while, help her clean up and get ready for bed, then we read her a story. Sometimes she will 'read' us one, and we tuck her in to go to sleep. A healthy family is any set of people who are open, honest, sincere, caring, understanding, and who love and look out for each other, giving their time to each other.

"We are planning on getting married again this Spring. This time it is for the right reasons, at the right time. This time it is forever."

Family 14—Carole and Andrea ▲▼▲ Lesbian Mothers—
47 and 44—California

Carole: "People in our life have generally been supportive toward our family. We have a very good relationship with both moms' parents and with Alix's father's mother and her male companion. The latter have stayed with us when visiting. Both moms work full time in the medical field, and we both provide discipline. The children are in school, and our son goes to the Y after school.

"There is very little time for a romantic or nonromantic relationship, as Andrea and I have very little time alone together. Because we both work long hours, there is a need to spend as much other time with the children as possible. We celebrate holidays together . . . religious, patriotic, and any others we can find. People in a healthy family enjoy each other's company, show respect for each individual, maintain open communication, use appropriate discipline for children, and share in activities."

Andrea: "I also find that people have been generally supportive of us and that we have good relationships with grandparents on both sides. At home, having children does affect our adult relationship. There is no spontaneity and little time alone. What activities we do alone seem to be rushed. The children are a priority for both of us.

"A healthy family enjoys doing activities together, while allowing individual family members to have their own activities if the interest is there. Members feel comfortable in expressing their individuality."

Alix (Carole and Andrea's 13-1/2-year-old daughter—California): "I have two moms and a brother. I 'discovered' that my family is different from others when I was young. I don't really think there is anything challenging about being in my family. A healthy family loves each other and communicates with one another."

Jonathan (Carole and Andrea's 7-year-old son—California): "My two moms and my sister are my family. I like everything about them, except when my moms fight. What we like to do together is go to Mountasia, bike ride, and play games. People that don't fight and live in peace have a healthy family."

Family 15—Christine ▲▼▲ Lesbian Mother—60—California

"My seven grown 'children' know both of their biological parents, but they only have regular contact with me, their mother. When first served with divorce papers, their U.S. Marine Corps father asked for overseas duty and left within 3 weeks in an effort to stop the divorce action. At that time, divorce was not possible if the man was overseas. My lawyer worked fast! At first, my mother was extremely resistant to the concept of divorce and was never supportive of that decision, nor was she supportive of my decision to change religion. My siblings all agreed with her. My father claimed to be puzzled by my need for divorce, but he supported my decision. Over the years, there were occasional phone visits with my family and one 3-day visit from my mother as the children grew up. My ex-husband's family totally disowned all of us when I divorced their son. I felt bad about this, because we had had a good relationship until then.

"While they were children, my kids lived only with me. Now as adults, ages 29 to 38, they each have their own home. My female partners did live with us, and the kids called them by their first names.

"I've always worked for income, and each of my partners worked too. The children usually had part-time work once they were old enough. When child care was needed during the day, I paid a neighbor mother. Either my partner or I was home in the evenings. Then, as the children became old enough, they took care of each other.

"I was the primary disciplinarian, but the children were clearly informed they were to mind my partner when I was away. One partner had a young boy, just 1 month younger than my son, and she preferred that I provide discipline for him also. She was a 'dry' alcoholic and had not done a good job parenting prior to that time. Another lover had been a Marine and was a bit of a 'drill sergeant' at times. My son, a teenager at the time, resented that, and he never did like her. The girls got along with her fairly well. The youngest two, who knew her best, have always loved her. Several of the girls and I are still in contact with her. I still refer to her as one of my very best friends.

"Some lesbians have no desire to be around children, especially a family as large as mine, so they would not remain long as even friends. This was never much of a problem, however. People soon realized it was 'love me, love my kids.' Since the children were very well behaved, people usually did enjoy them. Members of a healthy family care about each other, support each other even when they do not agree; they are each encouraged to be as independent and free as is appropriate for their age. LOVE is the key."

Marybeth (Christine's 35-year-old daughter—California): "I found out my mom was gay as a volunteer at a hospital. I was in seventh grade. Soon after that, my mom's first lover, Agnes, came into the home with her son. Because of what happened with Agnes and me, I honestly never gave any of my mom's other female friends a chance. I saw no advantages.

"Being in junior high school and not knowing what gay is was hard. Up to that point, gay meant happy. Also, being raised by one set of rules, and then all of a sudden everything changed, and being expected to accept them was hard. As a teenager, you're already asking questions about sex, etc. A divorce in seventh grade and a lover coming into the house in eighth confuses a teenager. I wish everyone would remember what happened with Agnes and realize the hurt I have because of this.

"My mom and I haven't had a relationship since she 'left' me. She didn't come to protect me against Agnes and refused to come to my wedding, so she's let me down two times I needed her the most. I wish we were closer. The twins have the kind of relationship I wish my mom and I could have.

"My dad lives in England, and it's hard to keep up.

"Loving parents who do anything they can to raise the kids to grow up as responsible adults create a healthy family. Parents should teach their kids morals and values."

Jean (Christine's 29-year-old daughter, Tara's twin—California): "My mom is one of my best friends. I tell her more than I tell my twin sister. It's great having mom, mother, nurse, pastor, and friend all wrapped up in one.

"We were in the car, and one of the kids said that Mom was gay. I didn't believe them, so when we got home, everyone sat in the living room, and Mom explained. It didn't bother me then, and it doesn't bother me now. Seeing how some of my older sisters make a big deal that my mom's gay can be challenging. Who Mom chooses to sleep with is no one else's business but hers. If her soul mate is male or female, who cares? Just as long as she's happy!

"In our family, I like the honesty most of all. I don't shy away from saying how and what I feel about my family. I am proud of my mom and don't care what other people think. Communication, honesty, and willingness to listen make a healthy family."

Tara (Christine's 29-year-old daughter, Jean's twin—California): "I knew my family was different when I was in Girl Scouts, and other fathers had to take me to the father–daughter dinner with their daughters. I thought we were different because of the divorce. I think the challenges in this family are the same as other families, and that when people do find out my mom is gay, how they react, and seeing if they are still my friend or not. Being different is good as well as a challenge.

"I wish I were closer to my father. I wish it would be like the relationship I have with my father-in-law. I can talk to him about everything. I would like my relationship with my father to be open and honest.

"I really can't say that there are any advantages or disadvantage to having a gay parent, due to the fact that my mom is always there. I think the only thing I missed was having a dad, but I wouldn't call that a disadvantage.

"No matter what they do, I love all my family for themselves and not for what they have or have not done with their lives. I wish we all could get together and talk about Mom's being gay and how it really did affect our lives. Love, honesty, and openness make a healthy family."

Barbara (Christine's 38-year-old-daughter—California):"When I was a teenager, I wanted Mom to be like all the other moms I knew, NOT a lesbian. I wanted to change her. Now that I'm an adult, if Mom is happy, that's all that matters. It's her life, her God that she has to live with. She's always backed me up 110%, and I do the same for her. At least I would, but she doesn't need me to! At least that's the way it seems to me.

"I do know that we support each other, though not as well as we should. I wish we could get along better. A healthy family has love, caring, communication, thinking of the others before thinking of yourself."

Family 16—Dale ▲▼▲ Lesbian Mother—38—Florida

"We have an ongoing relationship with our 8-year-old children's noncustodial biological parents. We advise them of every decision we make on behalf of the children. We encourage the kids to remember their biological parents' birthdays and holidays with cards and gifts. The children's grandparents see me as Kat's 'friend.' I hit it off great with them.

"We are both on disability, currently looking for family housing. In the meantime, Kat lives with the children in her parents' home, and her mother provides child care without complaint. We keep our outings without the children to a minimum. We both discipline the children. We do not spank. Of course, Kat is physically most available to discipline them.

"Our lives revolve around the children. PTAs, school open houses, and pediatric appointments come first. We keep our outings with and without the kids to the daytime, because we both cannot drive.

"We are still developing family rituals. We are very affectionate. We take every opportunity to empower our children.

We talk and listen to our children. A healthy family has no secrets, a minimum of jealousy, and absolute honesty. Our children's grandmother and both of us have chronic illnesses. We never hide behind illness, though. If we don't want to do something or go somewhere, we say so. We say 'I love you' liberally to each other and to the children. We separate behavior from the person. There are bad behaviors, not bad people."

Family 17—Jim ▲▼▲ Gay Father—40—Massachusetts

"Having children was difficult at first. It's not something my husband Donald ever wanted. Now we seem quite happy. It also confuses people who know I'm gay when I mention my children. They get confused for a bit.

"Donald and I both work, and we both provide child care, but mostly me. I am the one who disciplines the kids.

"Our special family rituals are Tuesday nights out to eat with the kids, taking my younger daughter to soccer games and cheering her on, and watching movies together.

"A healthy family is happy people!"

Chelsea (Jim's 13-year-old daughter—Massachusetts): "I remember watching TV when my mom and dad called me into their room. He told me he's gay, and I really didn't get it at first. I forget how old I was. Does it affect how I interact with him? No, not at all.

"In a healthy family there is no hatred."

Family 18—Becka ▲▼▲ Lesbian Mother—44—
Washington State

"I'm the one who works, and both my partner and I provide child care and discipline for our son. I find that other lesbians run like hell unless they are mothers. In our family, we celebrate Halloween with the family next door, Thanksgiving with friends and family, Christmas with grandma and grandpa every other year, and the Gay Pride March.

"A healthy family is where the parents act like adults and take care of themselves in order to love, nurture, and care for the children—where the family exists to meet the needs of the children."

Tommy (Becka's 7-year-old son—Washington State): "The most interesting thing that ever happened because of who my mom is, is that I got to meet both mayors of our city. And the President gave me a high five. I have so many stories about my family! It would be really cool to know who my dad is. When I grow up, it will be me, my wife, and kids. I think my family now is pretty good, because we do lots of things together."

Family 19—Sandra and Kelly ▲▼▲ Lesbian Mothers—
37 and 36—Ohio

Sandra: "We're all much happier now that the two kids, ages 15 and 17, are living with us full time, although it's been very hard on Kelly. They don't ever stay with their dad.

"We both work full time. Kelly's a manager, so she has long hours. I work as much overtime as I can, because I make less than half as much. We went 6 months without child support which was very hard. As for 'child' care, we both listen, talk, and drive them *all* over. As the biological mom, I do most of the discipline. Kelly does if she feels she needs to. We talk about things as much as possible. I want and need her input. It's hard because she's stepping in pretty late in their lives.

"My parents live far away, and we have a so-so relationship. The kids' paternal grandmother calls them and is very good to them. She treats me and the kids okay, and Kelly too. Their grandfather doesn't want me in their home or for me to be mentioned. The kids aren't fond of him. Aunts and uncles are good to the kids and me.

"Parenting has been very challenging and wonderful. It's not what Kelly planned on. It's very hard, especially because they have not been visiting their dad at all. We don't have enough room because they were going to be visiting us, not living here full time when we move into this apartment.

"For a family to be healthy, there should be love, trust, communication, laughter, and anger sometimes. Adults should be loving and honest while giving support and guidance."

Miranda (Sandra and Kelly's 17-year-old daughter—Ohio): "Two years ago, my mom told my brother and me we'd be living with our dad instead of her. She'd changed her mind, and I was furious. She told me about Kelly. I believe my dad was scared, and he said he'd make a fuss about her being gay. She didn't want us to suffer, and she didn't want our peers to have to know. She didn't know how we would feel or how people, our friends, would react.

"I like the fact that there are very few heated arguments in our immediate family, the people I live with. We are able to discuss things calmly. My dad and I could never agree on anything. We always screamed at each other. We fought once a week at least. Otherwise I tried not to be at home, or I stayed in my room to avoid him.

"It's difficult in my family because it is obvious my dad is lonely, but I'm still angry about how he treated me. He's my father, and he's supposed to love, support, and guide me, but instead he was spiteful, critical, cruel, and destructive. In front of practical or complete strangers, he acted like a prince . . . funny, gentle, warm. How can I forgive him for being nice to them and harsh with me?

"I consider Kelly to be a second mom. She is sweet, patient, and wise. My mom is giving, understanding, and loving. My dad is too worried about what others think. He's selfish and mean, but I feel sorry for him because I bet he's lonely.

"A healthy family is one that is open and honest, trusting, unconditionally loving, supportive, and forgiving. A healthy family can sit down and discuss things, admit weaknesses and wrongs, compromise, and understand each other."

Family 20—Melissa and Trish ▲▼▲ Lesbian Mothers— 37 and 39—New Jersey

Melissa: "Dawn has lived in one home with Mom and Trish since we got together 5 years ago. Her relationship with her biological father is non-existent. Trish and I both work, and we both provide discipline. Dawn is old enough to be alone, but we both spend as much time as possible with her. Having a child doesn't affect our romantic relationship so much, and it doesn't get in the way non-romantically. We try to have dinner as much as possible together, watch videos, and we are starting to attend church.

"A family that cares and loves one another unconditionally and is willing to communicate is healthy. Also, families must support each other."

Dawn (Melissa and Trish's 14-year-old daughter—New Jersey): "In kindergarten, I guess, is when I saw not everyone had two mommies. We all get on each other's nerves majorly sometimes, but it's an advantage that there's always someone feminine to talk to. What I like best about my family is our closeness. What's challenging is determining who to tell and who not. My father has not been involved in my life for six years. I really honestly don't know what it would be like to have a relationship with him. In a healthy family, there is love and honesty and openness."

Family 21—Denise and Alisha ▲▼▲ Lesbian Mothers— 33 and 34—New York

Denise: "Our 5-month-old daughter has lived in the home with her two moms since she was born. She's too little right now to call us anything, but we plan to introduce the names 'mommy' for Alisha and 'mama' for me. We don't know her donor, but we have an extensive physical and psychological profile on him and his family.

"Both of us work, so we have a baby-sitter three days a week in the woman's home. I am home the other two days to take care of Zoe.

"How does having a child affect us? We spend more time socializing with parents and spend most of the evening talking about our children. Romantically, we go out a little less but not much. As a partnership, we are much closer, sharing more and working more as a team. Right now, bath time is our only 'ritual.'

"A healthy family is one that respects each other, allows one another time separately with the children, makes time for play, encourages the parents to have time away from the children, and accepts one another unconditionally."

Alisha: "We refer to each other as Mommy and Mama. When Zoe begins talking, she may pick up on this or create her own names for us. However, neither of us, bio-mom or not, will be called by our first names. Our daughter goes to a private sitter the three days a week we both work. We care for her all other times.

"At 5 months, discipline hasn't been a big issue! However, we've discussed discipline and how we plan to handle issues. We plan to approach it as equal partners, so neither of us is solely the good or bad guy.

"We include our daughter as another natural part of an activity, giving her the attention she needs and deserves but not focusing all of the attention on her. She has brought the two of us closer together, made us listen to each other and really understand our positions, and she has allowed us to learn more about each other's upbringing and value systems. We are now on a common journey, focusing our efforts on this mutual endeavor.

"We celebrate Easter, Thanksgiving, and Christmas in traditional ways. I'm a big promoter of special accomplishments and plan to mark major events, awards, concerts, graduations, etc., with appropriate acknowledgments such as parties and special outings.

"A healthy family is one that communicates openly with one another about any and all issues. A healthy family does things together but allows for separate relationships among its members. A healthy family has a rich sense of humor, a wide range of interests, and a social conscience."

Family 22—Werner ▲▼▲ Gay Father—31—Austria

"Anna lives with me and calls me Papa or Werner. One of her grandpas is her baby-sitter while I'm at work. We visit the other grandparents from time to time. We have a loving remembrance of Anna's mother. I am the disciplinarian, and I work to support my family. In addition to being cared for by me and by her grandpa, Anna goes to kindergarten. I don't think that having Anna has affected my adult relationships much, apart from a shortage of time as a consequence of child care. In a healthy family there is a loving, intimate relationship among its members."

▲▼▲

There is no single blueprint for designing the relationships among family members. Each family must and ultimately does find its own way in a complex world. Being or having homosexual parents is only one, minor aspect of family life, isn't it?

Parents and Children Together ▲▼▲ A Unique Bond

I have begun to plant thee,
and will labor to make
thee full of growing . . .

>   William Shakespeare,
>   *Macbeth*, Act 1, Scene 4

Parents and their children play a multitude of roles to each other. (Melanie Margolis, Photographer.)

I was a teenager dur-
ing the sixties. Right
around the time I
hit the big 'one-three,'
the Women's Movement
came to town, and the
world as we had all
known it came spinning
to its well-deserved end.
Dinner still appeared on the kitchen table promptly at six
o'clock, but as often as not, it popped out of a Swanson's box,
or it was Dad's special silver-dollar pancakes. Mom had returned to school to study literature and to find herself. One
evening, as she was carefully pulling back the foil wrapper
from a silver-toned tray, she turned to me and asked, "Now
that you're getting older, why don't we become friends? You
can call me by my first name. Wouldn't that be great?" I liked

the implied recognition of my impending maturity, and I gave serious, though only momentary, thought to her proposition. I think my reply startled her. Due to the events of the Second World War, my mother had largely been raised in foster homes far away from her own parents, and I believe she had lost much of her closeness to them during those unfortunate years. "No," I said, being somewhat careful to word the rest of it so she wouldn't be hurt by my refusal of her offer. "I have lots of friends. You're my mother. That's more special than just being another friend."

There can be no doubt that the relationship between parent and child is unique and powerful. Parents and their children play a multitude of roles to each other. Parents are children's caretakers and role models. They establish the values, opportunities, and boundaries by which their children experience the world. Children are their parents' joy and responsibility, objects of affection or of anger, sources of pride or perhaps of frustration. Children are often seen as a link between their parents and the future. The roles of being a parent carry with them requisite behaviors, rights, responsibilities, and sacrifices which are not necessarily rewarded in a timely manner. How many nonparents can understand that one droolly, gurgly smile is more-than-adequate compensation for months of diaper-changing, or that a single well-placed soccer goal is worth weeks of carpooling in the hot sun and heavy traffic? Hallmark doesn't stand a chance at topping the crayon-scrawled get-well card that appears under the closed bedroom door of a sick mother, and most parents would gladly forego a dozen roses in exchange for a fistful of wilted dandelions delivered with a dirty face wearing an ear-to-ear smile.

Being a gay or lesbian parent adds a dimension to the parent–child relationship. It is not an entirely unique dimension. Parents who are physically disabled, hearing-impaired parents, and celebrity parents have similar nuances added to the parenting role. All are different from mainstream expectations of who can parent well. Although popular opinion has questioned the parenting abilities of these groups, the objections generally do not hold up under informed observation or just plain common sense.

The job of a good parent is to understand and to support the needs of the developing child so that the child can grow up, be independently productive, and leave the parent behind. What are the myths that are associated with gay men and lesbians that suggest they are not equipped to fulfill the parenting relationship? What is the reality behind the myths? What are the real challenges that *do* exist in the relationships between gay and lesbian parents and their children?

MYTH: GAY MEN AND LESBIANS DON'T LIKE OR WANT CHILDREN

It is true that some gay men and some lesbians don't like children or want them around. This is also true within the straight community. The myth that homosexual people don't value children likely arose, at least in part, from an assumption that loving someone with whom one cannot procreate translates into not wanting children. Another possible source of this myth is the youth orientation that many people associate with the gay and lesbian community. In groups of young single people, regardless of sexual orientation, there is generally little emphasis on children. If one's focus were to shift to parts of any community in which individuals are older and more established in their lives, the desire to "settle down" and create a family becomes considerably more common and expected.

For gay men and lesbians, especially outside of heterosexual marriages, the obstacles of having and raising children are only now beginning to become more widely surmountable. The previous chapter discussed the variety of methods by which homosexuals are becoming parents. The reality that many of us go to great lengths to parent children indicates that sexual orientation is not a determinant of whether or not an individual likes or wants children in his or her life.

MYTH: THE CHILDREN OF LESBIANS AND GAY MEN WILL BE SEXUALLY ABUSED

Sadly, the incidence of child sexual abuse appears to be on the rise in our country today. No doubt some of the children who fall victim to sexually abusive adults are the children of gay men and lesbians. However, many sources of information strongly indicate that sex abusers are usually heterosexual men.[1,2] Women and gay men are not only known to show a low rate of child molestation, they also tend to display a stronger desire to nurture children than do straight men.[3]

Part of preventing child abuse, it seems, would be to acknowledge accurately where, and by whose hand the abuse occurs, and by using reliable predictors of abusive behaviors, not disproven prejudices. According to the Los Angeles County Department of Children's Services, predictors of abusiveness in adults include poverty, limited education, high stress levels, having been abused in their youth, and social isolation.[4,5] Abuse and neglect of children occurs in all strata of society. Ending it might well start by providing adequate support to all families in which they live, regardless of who those families are.

MYTH: LESBIANS AND GAY MEN ARE INHERENTLY UNFIT TO BE PARENTS

Beyond issues of abuse, in studies that examine the emotional and physical well-being of children of gay men and lesbians, there is unanimous agreement that these children are at least as stable and well adjusted as the children of heterosexual parents. Psychoanalytic theory, upon which much of our cultural bias is based, suggests that the children of homosexual parents should manifest problems in personality and psychosocial development. The facts of research, as well as observation, simply do not bear this out. There are no distinguishable traits between groups of children based upon the sexual orien-

tation of their parents.[6-10] The failure of researchers to find material differences strongly suggests that the sexual orientation of
parents is not a valid criterion by which to predict maladaptive
psychosocial development of children. The sons and daughters
of homosexual parents are as likely to make gender-"appropriate" choices of toys, friends, TV shows, and garments as are the
children of heterosexual parents.[11]

For children to develop into healthy adults, they need to
have their own individual uniqueness recognized and nurtured. The adults who provide such nourishment need not fit
any particular category. The stereotypical heterosexual,
two-parent home is only one of many possible environments
in which to raise healthy children. More important than the
number, gender, or sexual orientation of parents in raising a
healthy child is the ability and willingness of the parental fig-
ure(s) to support children's individual development according
to each child's unique needs and abilities.[12]

MYTH: THE CHILDREN OF GAYS AND LESBIANS WILL BE ENCOURAGED TO BECOME HOMOSEXUAL

Ninety-eight percent of gay men and lesbians were
raised by heterosexual parents, and several dozen research
studies since the late 1970s show no greater tendency by the
children of gay or lesbian parents toward homosexuality
than the children of straight parents.[13-15] We live in a culture
that is highly focused on and fearful of sex and sexuality. Although most of the emphasis is on heterosexual behavior,
and most of our established institutions, such as religion,
government, education, and advertising, actively promote
heterosexuality, there is significant apprehension that "normal" straight individuals will be "turned gay" if they come
into contact with gay or lesbian people. Even with all of the
societal encouragement to be straight and the concomitant
demonizing of homosexuality, roughly 10 percent of the population is identified as gay or lesbian. If the active support

and promotion of heterosexuality does not dissuade these individuals from expressing *their* natural sexual orientation, why would one think that an individual who is naturally heterosexual could be seduced into a denigrated and still socially dangerous sexual/affectional identity?

Theories and statistics are mere reflections of the real lives they purport to explain. The parents and children whose heartfelt responses are recorded below present a much more personal response to the myth of recruitment. Although most parents report that they would continue to love and support a child who came out to them as gay or lesbian, nearly every one of the respondents also says that they hope for their children that they are straight. Why would a gay or lesbian parent hope such a thing? The answer lies clearly, I believe, in the universality of parents' wishes that their children be spared hardship and suffering. No parents know better than gay fathers and lesbian mothers the difficulties of being a member of a scorned minority. No healthy parent would want such a fate for his or her child.

For the second-generation children, the children of gays and lesbians who are themselves homosexual, there may be a sense of normality as well as a sense of having let down their parents. Let them down? For the parents who feel that raising a child well means keeping him or her from the difficulties of being gay or lesbian, a second-generation child may indeed create a sense of having failed to do one's best. Other parents are delighted that their second-generation children can truly share in a unique world view. As with all parent–child challenges, communication about joys and disappointments is critical.[16]

Perhaps the day will come when sexual orientation will no longer be a source of discrimination. On that day, perhaps parents will dream only that their children find their own path without the need to worry that the child's truth will bring more challenge than the parents are willing to see them face.

MYTH: LESBIANS CANNOT PROVIDE PROPER HOMES FOR BOYS. GAY MEN CANNOT PROVIDE PROPER HOMES FOR GIRLS

John Bowlby was the first researcher of early child development truly to recognize children's undeniable need for love and affection. His observations of institutionalized children in England in the decades following the Second World War revolutionized the treatment of orphans and hospitalized children. Since his extraordinary work, and that of his professional descendants, psychologists have recognized that infants and children need to feel that they are loved by a parent or parent substitute who is available to them on a permanent and consistent basis.[17] The ideal setting in which this can be achieved is within a loving family. Ultimately, the love of a family provides children with two levels of benefit. Minimally, the family takes care of the child's physical needs for food, clothing, and shelter. On a deeper level, the child is provided by the family with a psychosocial environment in which to mature into an emotionally and socially capable adult.

From the egocentric perspective of childhood, each child experiences his or her own world as "normal" and adapts to the unique attributes of the personal environment in order to assure physical survival. When children are cared for by a parent or parents who love(s) them, mutually enjoyable and supportive relationships can develop. The overwhelmingly time- and energy-consuming demands of a young child, or even an adolescent, are most likely to be met in a healthy manner by adults who feel rewarded simply by that child's presence in their lives.[18,19] The tasks of parenthood are not gay or straight. They are based in love and sacrifice and can be performed regardless of a parent's sexual orientation.[20]

There have been communities of feminist lesbians who have demonstrated politically based difficulty in associating with males, including raising boy children, and the sons of these mothers have not always been treated well.[21,22] As political and cultural attitudes toward a patriarchal society have changed, there is considerably less anger in the lesbian community toward males. In fact, the reality of parenthood seems now to draw men and women together within the gay and lesbian community in a concerted effort to provide both male and female role models for our children.[23] For parents who feel they would do better raising a child of one sex than the other, adoption offers the ideal opportunity to make such a selection.

All children deserve to have a loving and supportive family. Gay men and lesbians who choose to be parents are, as a group, overwhelmingly motivated to provide emotional sustenance as well as physical care to their children. Children whose parents are consistent in their acceptance of their sexual orientation as well as their status as parents generally fare well in gay or lesbian homes.[24-26] There is simply no evidence, after decades of research, to support the contention that sexual orientation is fundamentally related to an adult's ability to parent.[27]

MYTH: CHILDREN SHOULD NOT GROW UP IN A SINGLE-PARENT HOME

The real myth here is that being a gay or lesbian parent means one is a single parent. Unfortunately, this myth is perpetuated within the legal system as well as in the eyes of many of our relatives and the general public. Even when there are two committed parents in the home, if they are of the same gender, each parent is considered to be single. This is probably because they are not legally allowed to marry, although they may wish to.

Certainly, some homosexual parents are single. Many, however, are partnered in relationships that are simply not recognized or supported by law, community, or family. In families where there is a same-gender coparent, there is also often a struggle to gain legal and/or community acceptance of the reality of the parent–child relationship.[28,29] An increasing number of states and counties are providing for some degree of legalization of the second parent's custodial status.[30] Gay and lesbian parents are frequently the ones to educate community institutions such as churches, synagogues, and schools by openly announcing that there are indeed two parents and that both adults are to be treated as such in regard to their children.

The difficulties of single parent households are not to be easily dismissed. Many are more likely to be economically disadvantaged compared to two-parent families, and discipline often suffers if there is not a responsible adult to supervise minor children whose parent must be out of the home to earn a living. These challenges are of valid and increasing concern to anyone who cares about the welfare of children. They are not, however, related to a parent's sexual orientation.

MYTH: CHILDREN ARE CONFUSED BY HAVING TWO SAME-GENDER PARENTS

Children are not confused by having two grandmothers, two grandfathers, or a multitude of aunts and uncles, cousins, or siblings. Why then would one presume that they would be confused by two moms or two dads? While it is true that children younger than about age seven have a fairly concrete and egocentric view of the world,[31,32] they clearly recognize and distinguish the uniqueness of each person and of each relationship. Perhaps having two parents of the same gender can help children to see the individual parent rather than simply assigning a role or label to Mom or Dad.

Children consider the adults who function as mother or father to them to be their parents. The adults also regard themselves as parents, whether or not a legal relationship is possible. Great emotional damage has been done to families when little or no recognition is afforded the relationship between children and their second mom or dad,[33,34] or when a parent's sexual orientation is used by the courts as an excuse to deny or limit custody or visitation.[35-37] Imagine knowing that you would never be allowed to visit or live with your mother or father again simply because of whom s/he loves! Thankfully, sexual orientation is becoming less of an issue in child custody hearings.

Homosexual parents and their children often face a great challenge in trying to define and establish a recognition of their real psychological parent–child relationships. The array of family structures in the gay and lesbian parenting community has led to a number of relatively (pun intended) novel relationships between children and the adults who parent them. Donor insemination and surrogate mothering may or may not result in a child knowing more than two parents. Second-parent adoption assures some measure of legality to the parent–child relationship, although it may entail at least temporary relinquishing of parental rights by a biological parent. Coparenting arrangements might even provide a child with three or four parents.[38,39]

Children who do not know one or either of their biological parents have differing reactions to this fact in their lives. Some have no desire to know the unmet parent(s), while others do wish for a connection. Children may canonize or demonize the unknown parent(s), depending upon their personal life experiences and individual temperament. As for anyone who has been placed in a custodial family through a closed adoption, the presence or absence of a need to know both biological parents is quite personal, and parents would be well advised to anticipate their children's future desire for information. Regardless of the official relationships, the hearts of children and parents are uniquely bonded.

SOCIAL ISSUES FOR PARENTS TO CONSIDER

Should I Be "Out" to My Child?

Coming out to loved ones seems to be universally difficult. For most of our friends and family members, however, our sexual orientation will realistically have little impact on their lives. For our children, this is not so.

When gay or lesbian parents who were legally married to opposite-gender partners choose to come out, their children's reactions are clearly age-related. In general, children of early elementary school age or younger are more distressed by divorce or separation issues if the parents choose to end their marriage than they are by their parents' sexual orientation per se. They generally fear that they will lose contact with one of their parents. This fear of loss is true as well when same gender parents separate. Older children, into adolescence and early adulthood, are more likely to be embarrassed about the parents' sexual orientation in response to social prejudice, or they may feel betrayed at having had the information withheld from them by a trusted parent.[40-42]

When children are born or adopted into a gay or lesbian family, the issue of coming out is somewhat different. These children do not associate their parents' sexual orientation with the fear of loss that accompanies divorce or separation. If they have always known that the parents are gay, the difficulty that they experience related to the information is likely to center around explaining a nontraditional family situation to peers, teachers, and others in the community.[43] If a child discovers the parent's sexual orientation as an uncovered family secret, however, there will indeed be a sense of having been distrusted or betrayed.

For preschool children, this is their life experience, and there is usually no significant anxiety. Once a child reaches school age, and particularly in adolescence, he or she may request that the parents become more discreet. How families make the decisions regarding the degree of parental 'outness' may well depend upon the level of social acceptance they expect in their locality. In general, the younger children are when they become aware that the parents are gay or lesbian, the fewer negative cultural influences have had time to take root and the more accepting they are of the news as just one more piece of information about their family.[44-46]

Sometimes the children of gay and lesbian parents are themselves homosexual. For these second-generation children, knowing about their parents' sexual orientation can be a tremendous source of strength and support. In general, children whose parents are honest about being gay feel much more secure about discussing personal issues, including sex and sexuality, with their parents. The parents' openness, self-assurance, and honestly engender the same qualities in their children.

Once parents have accepted their own sexual orientation and have taken the leap of coming out to their children, the parent–child bond is generally strengthened. Most children seem to want their parents to be happy. When they recognize that mom or dad is content, children respond positively to the information about the parent's sexuality. Older children in particular tend to appreciate the fact that a parent is being honest with them and trusting them with "adult" information, and this seems to carry more weight than the adolescents' feelings about the information itself.

What Will S/he Call You?

Unlike traditional families, gay and lesbian families do not have established names by which to designate many of our relationships. One of the most frequently asked questions when a couple brings a child into their home is, "What will s/he call you?" Many parents simply choose to be called Mom or Dad with their given name tacked on to the end. Some families choose to use Mom or Dad for a biological parent or primary adoptive parent, and the second parent is called by his or her first name. In some gay or lesbian families, an ethnic designation is used for one parent (e.g., Ima, the Hebrew equivalent of Mom), or a child-derived nickname may be used for one or both parents. The name game applies to extended family as well. What do the children call the parents of the nonbiological parent? The choices are personal and often reflect the degree of acceptance within the family of the reality that two same-gender adults and their children have formed a legitimate family unit. The reality of having to decide indicates just how new the growing phenomenon of gay and lesbian parenting is.

How Would Marriage Change Gay and Lesbian Families?

In most communities, a parent's homosexuality is no longer an adequate or automatic reason for him or her to lose custody of a child or to be denied the opportunity to conceive, to foster, or to adopt a child. Yet becoming and remaining custodial parents does continue to be more challenging and at times more tenuous for gay men and lesbians than for heterosexuals. Since homosexual relationships currently have no vehicle to establish universal legal recognition, gay and lesbian couples and their families continue to face the need to create alternative protections for their relationships, including for the parent–child relationship. Sanction of same-gender marriage would afford the legal recognition of gay and lesbian families that is needed to provide security to their children, especially in guardianship and custody-related situations.

IN THEIR OWN WORDS

Being a parent is not simply bearing a title. It is not necessarily conferred through genetics. It does not demand a particular sexual orientation any more than it requires a specific ethnic heritage. Parenting is a richly diverse and distinctive relationship that adults form and nourish with the children in their homes and in their lives. Parents and their children are above all each other's teachers of life. Their family experiences have much of value to teach us all.

In the words of the families below, one can feel the extraordinary connection between the parents and children. Each family's experience is unique, yet all of them have in common the bonds of commitment, respect, and love for each other.

Family 1—Jeremy ▲▼▲ Gay Father—27—New York

"I searched for self-acceptance in the egocentric world of the bars. The center of my existence for some time was me. With my son Micah, I view my life through his eyes. Before him, I never strived so hard to be unselfish.

Having started my career in education, I was able not only to observe, but also to assist children in adoptive families deal with problems that manifest naturally in almost any adoption. I prepared myself for Micah's adoption by taking a social service department training course and attending workshops for adoptive parents, and by reading books and other material on adoption. I tried to understand and empathize with the loss and attachment process, with the frustrations and joys that are part of the experience. I am also involved in a support group for single adoptive parents.

"I feel that it is through the family unit, however it is composed, that one connects to society. The family provides a connection to the past and a connection to the future. It is a place to build lifelong relationships. I feel that every child needs and deserves a family. A child needs the stability, safety, and commitment found in a loving family unit . . . The development of a child's individuality, his gifts, creativity, and talents are dependent greatly upon when and how the nurturing occurs. It is from within a family that a child learns social virtues and achieves the ability to relate successfully and positively to others. I want and need to be a family that has a child.

"I know the importance of having a loving, consistent, respectful environment, encouraging verbal give and take, and guiding and respecting my child. The most important thing in raising a child is for him to have a positive self-image that comes from being secure in knowing that he is loved and knowing what is expected of him."

Family 2—Alan ▲▼▲ Gay Father—46—Massachusetts

"I am out to both my children. My daughter is still very proud of me. My son does not yet quite comprehend 'gayness.' I truly think that they both realize that 'gay' is only one aspect of their father and not the whole picture, and that I'm still the same after all. Coming out to my children was not as bad as I anticipated. My daughter took it hard at first, but I'm still her dad. My son doesn't fully understand yet. Since I came out to them, absolutely nothing has happened to our relationship. In fact, my daughter is more tolerant towards people who are 'different.'

"My wife Margaret and I have a 7-year-old boy and a 15-year-old girl, and their gender does not affect how we raise them whatsoever. We raise them to be nonjudgmental, healthy, and happy. Hold no prejudices, and be yourselves. My dreams for my children are that they become and are happy with themselves, and that they be well adjusted to this ever-changing world.

"The children know the difference between hetero- and homosexuality, and they have been taught to save themselves for a special person when they understand love better in a mutual relationship.

"There are some issues related to my sexual orientation, but by having a gay parent, my children will not have to go through the years of anxiety and denial like I did. I feel that, because I'm a gay parent, I make my children's life experiences better, because I am not a stereotype. It's great watching and enjoying my 'little girl' grow and mature into a young lady and adult. We are both growing.

"If my children were to come out to me, I would only feel sad for them to have to experience the negativity of being gay.

"Both of our kids still challenge us. It's challenging trying to keep them on the right paths, observing them from babies to grown-ups. There is a lot more weirdness out there now than when I was their age."

Margaret (straight mother . . . married to Alan—44—Massachusetts): "Having a 7-1/2-year age difference between our children has enabled me to raise them as individuals. Gender has never been an issue. I dream for them that they will be happy with who they become and at peace with themselves.

"Our teenage daughter learned about sex and sexuality when she was seven and I was pregnant. We took out library books and videos and went through them together. Our 7-year-old son only knows that men and women can love each other or people of their same sex.

"My daughter seems to be heterosexual, as I am. We keep the communication open in matters of sexuality. She is closer to her father than to me. Probably because she and I are so much alike in temperament, she finds it easier to talk out her problems with her dad. We tend to lock horns first and then talk rationally. At this stage in their lives, their emotional health appears problem free. We believe in not hiding our emotions from each other, both good and bad. It's a family thing.

"If my kids came out to me as gay or lesbian, I would love and support them as much as I do their gay dad, perhaps even more. They're my own.

"The biggest challenge is knowing when to be a firm parent on an issue and when to hold back as a parent so that they can grow and learn for themselves. The rewards come when you realize that the decision to be firm or lenient was the right choice."

Brett (Alan and Margaret's 15-year-old daughter—Massachusetts): "I discovered that my dad is gay when he told us at a 'family meeting.' I don't care about it. It doesn't change how I interact with him. Yes, gay parents should be out to their children. They should discuss being gay with their kids.

"A good parent is a parent that loves you, trusts you, tells you the truth, and doesn't abuse you. Their role is to care and to love.

"The challenge it creates is if my dad has this guy over his house all the time, I wonder if the neighbors get suspicious."

Family 3—Rob ▲▼▲ Gay Father—53—California

"I have a grown daughter, a teenage son, and a 9-year-old daughter. Their gender doesn't affect me. However, my son resents me because I have been deceptive and separated from the family. As a father, I was more of the financial provider than the emotional provider. I dream for my children that they fulfill their own dreams.

"I'm totally open now about my sexuality. I came out when the older two were in college. My son discovered that I am gay by finding a correspondence on the computer. This was traumatic for both of us. It was difficult at first with both my daughters to come out at age fifty-two. My older daughter and I are closer now. She is becoming more like a friend. We're being open and having a more meaningful relationship. My son has severed our relationship and wants nothing to do with me. He only contacts me for money, though he avoids this also as much as possible. My younger daughter is fearful and has anxiety over abandonment. She lives primarily with my wife and receives psychological counseling. My daughter also has some difficulty in that my wife is overly protective. My wife does not want my 9-year-old to see anything gay. She has threatened me with a restraining order.

"Emotionally, there are some issues in our family. My older daughter has been fighting depression. My son is dogmatic and not open-minded. My 9-year-old has anxiety over being disabled by a physical problem with her legs and about abandonment. She also has an eating disorder.

"I love my children regardless of their sexual orientation. It would not be an issue for me if they were gay or lesbian.

"As a parent, I am challenged to be closer with my children, for them to know they are loved. My children turned out well with regards to being honest and having good character and good values. They are intelligent and personable."

Family 4—Samantha ▲▼▲ Lesbian Mother—33—Vermont

"I am a woman raising a 19-month-old son. That he is a boy doesn't affect how I am raising him. I hope for him to be happy, stable, and fulfilled. If he were someday to come out to me, I would love him, love him, love him.

"Being dumped by a partner when I have a child is particularly devastating due to our need still to interact as parents. It's very stressful.

"Watching my son grow, be joyful, and be silly are rewards of being his parent."

Family 5—Linda and Donna ▲▼▲ Lesbian Mothers— 40 and 49—Utah

"We are raising three boys and a girl. It's hard to say what effect there is from the kids' being the same or opposite gender to us. We try to raise them in a nonsexist way. I have to admit that since Donna and I are fairly 'butch,' we probably feel more comfortable raising a boy than a girl, although I desperately wanted a girl.

"We wish for them to be happy and to be mentally and physically healthy, to be able to make a living and be independent, and to have fulfilling relationships.

"We talk openly with the children about sex and sexuality. We teach them to respect and value all sexual orientations. We teach them that they will be accepted no matter who they are, though to be honest, I would accept their coming out, but would be disappointed and fearful for them. I think it's very difficult to be gay in this society, and for gay men, the health risks are great.

"Donna's children have always known I was gay. It was traumatic for them when she came out to them. After 3 years, one child doesn't seem to mind that his mother's gay, one has just begun to accept it, and the other still has no contact with us. After she came out to them, Donna's kids all moved out. I know they have heard negative things about us from family friends and the member of their Mormon church. Her kids live with their father. That seems to be working out okay. He is civil to us, although I've never met him face to face, even after 3 years!

"Our teenage daughter had intense conflicts about her mother's sexuality. She would write us long, abusive, expletive-filled letters about what she thought we were doing in bed, how vile we were, how her mother was going to burn in hell, etc. However, she has recently admitted to her mother that she has 'feelings' for a female peer, and they may actually be experimenting sexually, though we don't know for sure. The teenage boy is heterosexual. He seems most concerned that others not find out about his mom, because he is embarrassed and ashamed of her.

"Our daughter comes over for brief periods of time, several times a week. Until recently, her main interaction with her mother was to pick fights and try to talk her mother into getting back together with her father, or to express her feelings of being unloved by her mother. Recently, she has stated she's had a change of heart, and she feels okay about her mother's lifestyle.

"There are no custody issues right now. Donna went through a custody battle with her husband during which we had to be very closeted. Although she got physical custody, the kids eventually moved in with their father.

"Our 19-month-old, Nicolas, seems very happy and healthy. The 11-year-old boy and the 15-year-old girl seem okay emotionally. Our 17 year old is an 'All American' boy

who is doing all the 'right' things, but he still seems very conflicted about his mother's sexuality.

"Being a step-parent has been a great challenge. My position as parent is not accepted by society, and the children have
had a hard time accepting it. As far as rewards, I enjoy raising
children, guiding their development, playing with them, etc.
Raising my son has been a challenge just because caring for an
infant is so time-consuming, but I love watching him develop,
grow, and learn new things!"

Family 6—Leah and Ali ▲▼▲ Lesbian Mothers—
40 and 42—Texas

"Raising a 2-year-old child who is the opposite sex from
us is interesting, especially as he gets older and becomes more
and more aware of the physical differences!! Our hope is to
raise a young man who will grow to be emotionally healthy
and have a caring, loving, and nurturing attitude toward
women!

"Jacob is aware that there are some physical differences
between him and his mamas. We talk openly about the difference, and we also talk about his male relatives who have the
same parts as Jacob.

"We feel fortunate that Jacob will grow up always knowing about his family, although we're certain that down the
road there may be issues to work through. We recognize that
as Jacob grows up, there will be numerous challenges facing
him as part of this family. We are now hoping to instill a strong
self-respect and self-regard, so that he grows up feeling great
about himself, his moms, and the values about which he is
learning. We believe that a positive self-image and feeling
good about the things Jacob does will help him to grow up
now and forever with well-established self-esteem. We hope
that our son grows to be a self-reliant, healthy, happy child
whatever his sexual orientation. Whatever life brings his way,
we would be loving and supportive.

"We face the typical challenges of dealing with an independent 2 year old, but Jacob is the light of our lives. We cannot imagine our lives without him! He brings love, laughter, and enlightenment that only a toddler can bring to his family! His sense of humor, the way he communicates, and the joy he finds in life are incredible."

Family 7—Lydia and Sari ▲▼▲ Lesbian Mothers— 43 and 42—California

"We are raising one child of each gender. It doesn't really affect the way we are raising them. We want our son to be in touch with his feminine, intuitive side, and our daughter to feel proud of her strengths and know that she can do anything. We want them to be happy, feel loved, be honest and honorable, be proud of who they are, and reach their full potentials.

"We've taught our 5-year-old son, and will teach our 1-year-old daughter, that their bodies and its functions are good and normal, but some things are private. We've also taught him that his body is his own business, and that no one has a right to touch his body, and if that should ever happen, to let us know right away, and we will protect him.

"Nathan knows that we are partners, and we love each other, and we make up our family with two moms. Since he has a dad who participates in his life, nothing more in terms of our coming out to him has come up yet. If he were ever to come out to us, we'd be surprised, of course, but very supportive.

"We believe our children are very healthy emotionally as well as physically. We attend to all levels of their health. We also believe they feel good about themselves, they have great inner strengths, and know they are loved and supported by their family. We are very proud of our children and believe they feel proud of themselves.

"Every day is full of challenges, but those special rewards—a baby toddling up and hugging you around the knees, your son saying 'I love you, Mom,' watching our family grow—those special rewards make up the joy in our lives."

Family 8—Carol and Rose ▲▼▲ Lesbian Mothers— 41 and 31—Kansas

"We are two women raising a 16-month-old daughter. Rose is pregnant with our second child. We're trying not to stereotype Drew into 'girl' things, and we make sure she has exposure to balls and sports as well as to dolls and dresses. We dream for her to grow up healthy and successful, to learn to overcome prejudice, and to treat others as she would like to be treated.

"We hope that if Drew ever believes she may be gay, that she would feel comfortable coming out to us as soon as she knew. We'd ask what we could do, in her eyes, to support her.

"She is a very, very happy little girl who is open and loving to everyone. We hope we can teach her to deal with society effectively enough to remain happy and loving.

"Right now the parenting challenges we face are trying to figure out what's wrong when she cries, if it's really something we can and should fix, or if it's just a tantrum because she didn't get her way. The rewards are the smiles, the hugs, the kisses we get from her. Seeing her learn and discover new things and the excitement she experiences when she does are rewarding to us."

Family 9—Jenny and Ann ▲▼▲ Lesbian Mothers— 33 and 38—Illinois

Jenny: "We have a 13-year-old daughter and a 4-year-old daughter. We are raising them to be solid beings who are true to themselves. We promote strong self-esteem and praise in their individuality. We provide positive role models, both male/female and heterosexual/homosexual. Our dream for them is to find happiness and contentment in their adult lives, both personal and professional. Ann oftentimes says that she hopes the girls choose heterosexual lifestyles, because she doesn't want them to have the hurdles that a homosexual relationship can face. My argument is that ALL relationships have hurdles, and we can only pray that the road they choose is well placed with beautiful scenery along the way. I will support them no matter what. Their happiness is most important to me. Ann would also be supportive, although not happy.

"Jo, our 13-year-old, is well informed on the subjects of sex and sexuality. When I became pregnant with Cait, we explained conception, pregnancy, and childbirth to her. She watched a natural childbirth on video and was invited to be an active family member in the delivery room. Jo knows that sex is an expression of one's love for another, as well as a basic function of reproduction. She doesn't question her own sexuality. Jo often talks to me about her own feelings, and she feels at this point in her life that having sex is gross. She did ask what 'made' Ann and me gay. I explained that it was a personal choice for me, and Ann explained that she always knew she was gay. Cait at this point knows that she came out of Mommy's tummy, and that Boo-Boo cut her umbilical cord, which gave her her belly button.

"There was no actual 'coming out' day with our girls, as it is something that has always been. Jo began to ask if we were gay when she was 7 or 8 years old. She is fast to give thanks for having two loving parents. I once asked her if she was embarrassed having two female parents. Her reply was simply that out of all the children in her class, it was odd having two parents at all. I think I was prepared that my lifestyle would be a problem for my children, but it has not. The children, including nieces, nephews, etc., are more accepting than some of the adults in the family. With Cait, it again is something that has always been. When she tells a story, it usually is told like this, 'Once upon a time, there were three bears. A momma bear, a

Boo-Boo bear, and a baby bear.' The honesty in our family has always made us close knit and strong.

"Our biggest issues with Jo at thirteen are having a pimple and having nothing to wear for the Valentine's Day dance. Jo is comfortable with her sexuality and, right now, is expressing it through her wardrobe and hairstyle. She is so caught up in her issues, that she doesn't have time to think about her parents' sexuality and how it may or may not affect her. It is so much the 'norm' in our household, that I don't think it will ever become an issue.

"Jo and I are very close. We do everything together, and we always find time for hugs and kisses. She is not embarrassed to display her affection in public, and every morning when I take her to school, she kisses me good-bye before getting out of the car. We share secrets that Boo-boo would never understand. Ann and Jo are buddies. They take great pleasure in picking on Mom both verbally and physically if the mood strikes them. Ann and Jo do a lot of physical activities together, such as bike riding, karate practice, and softball. Although they are close, they do not engage in much 'girl talk.' Ann is very protective over Jo, and they often joke about how Ann will follow Jo on all of her dates when she is older.

"Our children have two loving parents. They have never witnessed verbal, physical, alcohol, or drug abuse in their home, and they have never witnessed their parents screaming and fighting. They know that they can crawl into our bed at night when they are scared. Our children have only witnessed honesty, integrity, and love . . . lots of love. I believe that their emotional health is outstanding, and it has not been harmed by the fact that they have lesbian parents.

"There is nothing in the world that is greater than my family! We are middle-class America of the '90's! My rewards measure from the hand-scribbled get-well card that my 4-year-old slid under my bedroom door when I was sick to the group hugs I get woken up with on Saturday mornings. My challenges are no different than any other concerned parent of today. I want to protect my children from the evils of the world. I realize I can't be at their side every minute of the day, and that has been a challenge for me personally. So, I arm them with information about drugs, unprotected sex, and peer pressure. Then I shield them with my love, and take a deep breath every time they go out the door. Doesn't every parent do the same thing?"

Jo (Jenny and Ann's 13-year-old daughter—Illinois): "I feel fine about my moms' sexual orientation. It doesn't bother me if they are or aren't lesbians. Parents should be out to their kids. They should be honest to their children. They should openly discuss it. Having lesbian moms creates no obstacles for me. I don't know about opportunities or challenges. I'm not always comfortable saying that my parents are gay.

"My mom is my mom, and Ann is my other parent. I love my parents even if they are gay. A good parent is someone who loves you unconditionally and someone who teaches you how to be a successful person."

Family 10—Dee and Sherry ▲▼▲ Lesbian Mothers— 31 and 46—California

Dee: "I have no idea if having boys rather than girls affects the way we are raising our children. Maybe I worry about them less when they are out at night than I would if they were girls. Maybe I would have more expectations of sharing mother– child confidences if they were girls. My dreams for them are that they become caring, productive members of society, that they can make the transition to adulthood without too much suffering and stumbling.

"I haven't taught them much overtly about sex and sexuality. They already knew a lot when I joined the family. I occasionally make references to the importance of condoms, etc. Once I accidentally told our 15 year old 'You can't have sex on

weekdays' when I really meant that I wanted him to be careful and use safe sex, and I also wanted him home on weekday
nights, but he was running out the door and didn't want to
talk about it. I got upset at his not listening to me, and I never
brought it up again. I don't know what he thought about it.

"The boys have asked us why they can't have girlfriends
spend the night if we are 'spending the night' with each other.
We have a policy of not outing ourselves blatantly, by kissing,
cuddling, etc., in front of their friends until and unless they become close friends of the boys' and are over a lot. Our primary
interaction with the boys is that we give them rides, we sometimes eat meals together, we take them shopping for clothes,
we assign chores, and we pay allowance when the chores are
done. Best of all, but infrequently, we talk about what's going
on in each other's lives together, usually at meals or in the car,
or during family meetings.

"If either of the boys were to come out to me, I'd be happy,
though not more or less happy than I am when they have heterosexual relationships. The part that would make me the hap-
piest is that they communicated with me about something
personal and important.

"Their emotional health isn't perfect, but it's getting better
as they get older, and I think their difficulties are due to normal adolescent contrariness, angst, and perhaps having to
cope with different, conflicting messages and norms in two
households, ours and their father's. I don't think that their
emotional problems have to do with our being lesbians.

"There are challenges having to deal with two kids who
don't really seem to want adults around, especially when I
didn't get to enjoy them as little kids before their adolescence.
Also, having to confront them in a disciplinary way is very
hard for me. The rewards are that I love kids, and here I got
two ready-made. It may be infrequently that I see a glimmer of
their unchecked playfulness or their growing insightfulness,
but it happens, and I relish those times. I have also gotten a lot
stronger emotionally by dealing with their adolescence than I
was before I joined this family."

Sherry: "It's hard for me to assess the effect of raising boys since I have nothing to compare it to, not having raised girls. I dream for my sons that they find a niche in which they are able to be fulfilled and use their abilities.

"I was outed to my sons as part of a custody battle. I talked to them about it whenever they wanted to, and they were comfortable with it until adolescence. I think they lost the sense that their parents were all-knowing rather abruptly, as my ex-husband and I strongly disagreed about my life. The were in their father's house for half the week and half at mine for a couple of years. Then they alternated 2 weeks at a time. For the last 7 or 8 years, they have been with me and visited their father less and less, mostly because they don't get along too well with him and especially with his wife. There are no longer any custody issues. Their father did sue for custody when they were very young, and it was a *very* difficult time.

"I've discussed with them how women are devalued in society, and I request respect when they talk to me."

Family 11—Liz and Kathy ▲▼▲ Lesbian Mothers— both 32—Pennsylvania

"We have a 2-year-old daughter and a new baby due in 6 months. We don't know the gender of the new one. We try to offer our daughter a variety of games and toys and books and not select gender-specific ones. We encourage her to play what she likes whether it be 'fixing things' or 'tea parties.' For example, we notice outside influences and society's pressure to wear, act, or play 'girl like' that we feel would be different if we had a boy. We intend to let our children wear, act, and play whatever they feel comfortable with. We dream for them to be happy and healthy, and for them to feel loved and supported in what they choose to do and who they are as people. We'd hope to be supportive no matter what their sexual preference and try not to have any preconceived notions of what that might be for them.

"Our daughter is loved dearly by her two moms and is a very happy and emotionally healthy 2 year old. We hope to help her learn to cope with many different situations and feelings and give her a foundation of strength and self-empowerment to handle the ups and downs that cross the path she chooses to take in life.

"Parenting challenges are to us such things as keeping perspective when things don't go as we expect or want them to. We need to exert extra effort in controlling tempers to help set an example for her of what's acceptable and healthy in expressing a variety of emotions. It's a challenge trying to balance a hectic schedule with work, chores, day care, and quiet time, and trying to find time to answer surveys, go to the bathroom, and eat an entire meal sitting down!

"The rewards are everyday things, from smiles, hugs, and kisses to being invited to join in the tea party. A reward is the bright face that greets us in the morning and watching our daughter grow and enjoy life in general. We love watching her treat others with compassion and in a caring way by taking a friend's hand or helping them with their coat or patting their back when they are sad."

Family 12—Joyce ▲▼▲ Lesbian Mother—52—Hawaii

"I had one daughter who died at age ten and a half from brain tumors. My son is now twenty. I consciously raised both kids to be free of gender stereotypes and limitations. My girl was very active, 'hell on wheels.' My son is also active but of a more mellow temperament. I've taught him to cook, plant and grow food, do laundry, clean, build things—all of it. My daughter was taught all that too. I dream that my son will find his life's work, whatever that may be, his direction in life, and go for it. I dream that he will be a kind, honest, and loving person, which he is! I dream that my daughter is at peace.

"I've taught my son everything about sex and sexuality, in a positive way, including safer sex, self-respect, and respect for others.

"It was easy to come out to my kids. My daughter was four when I came out, and she loved the woman I loved, so it was easy for her to understand. My son was born into it, and I just had to explain homophobia to him. He thought it was stupid!

"My son's junior high school years were difficult, because he was in such a homophobic school environment. I was less public at his request. He was fearful of being hassled and/or beaten up.

"When my son's dad was married, his wife targeted our son and was mean to him. This is something my son kept from me until later, so we had difficulties I didn't understand at the time. He was and is close to his step- and half-siblings and deeply loved his sister.

"My son and I cook and eat together, and we do yard work together. He has a girlfriend right now who really likes me, so the three of us have dinner and big talks about once a week. He occasionally comes to me to talk over his problems!

"I believe my son is an exceptionally understanding person because of his upbringing. He is compassionate toward others and is learning to understand himself. He is emotionally healthy.

"Being a lesbian feminist and having a son was a big challenge, and I think it has been positive for me and him. There were years when I resented being the disciplinarian. His dad is *not* a disciplinarian, although he's a lovely person. Another major challenge was my daughter's father being unavailable to her the first 2 years after we split up, to punish me. Fortunately, he came around, because they were very close, and she and I bumped heads a lot. Her death was my greatest challenge. Having foreknowledge and time to prepare for her death was very rewarding. Having her at home the last weeks and caring for her, her brother being able to be with her, the whole experience changed my life, and as hard as it was, I would say it was very rewarding. Seeing my son develop into a fine young man is also very rewarding. His love and affection toward me have always been my greatest reward. We have a loving, deep connection that got us through the rough years. Now our relationship is changing to adult-to-adult, which is delightful!

"All this said, I must say that if I had it to do over, I wouldn't have children. Although I've been active in my community and done a lot, I could have done a great deal more toward social change without the responsibility of children."

Keola (Joyce's 20-year-old son—Hawaii): "Some negative things happened because of my mother being a lesbian editing and writing in newsletters. Sometimes people would crank-call us or leave insulting messages on our answering machine. I was insulted at school a few times.

"I've met many very nice, supportive people who have helped me grow up to be an understanding, nondiscriminatory person, and shown me that love comes in many different ways and means. It has for the most part brought me closer to my mother and brought an understanding of her life to me.

"Parents should tell their kids if they are gay or lesbian. Make sure they know what it means and that there is absolutely nothing wrong with loving someone of the same sex or both sexes. Make sure they know that lots of people just don't know or understand what being gay or lesbian is and are often misled or told lies and bad things abut them. Sometimes it is safer not to reveal to anyone but your close personal friends that you have a lesbian or gay parent. Never let that hold you back from being and doing what you want."

Family 13—Roz and Stacy ▲▼▲ Lesbian Mothers— 22 and 23—Arizona

Roz: "I am raising my 2-1/2-year-old daughter the same way that I wish that I had been raised. If I had a son instead of a daughter, it would be the same way. My dream for Skye is to be healthy, happy, and loving. It doesn't matter what she does for a living, as long as she is safe and happy. That is all that matters.

"Since she is only two and a half, we haven't taught her much about sex and sexuality yet, but we plan to be completely open and honest about everything. We will explain everything, and hide or leave out nothing. She will be told about sex, sexuality, and babies, as well as diseases, as early as possible. As soon as we feel she is able to understand and deal with the information. I don't think there will be a problem coming out to her, since she has been raised in this environment. I don't know how I would 'feel' if Skye were to come out as a lesbian some day, but I would be completely accepting, supportive, and proud.

"We don't think that there will be any custody issues in the future. Her dad is pretty much a part-time father. Of course that could change.

"I feel that a lot of politicians are concerned about children of gay and lesbian parents. They don't need to be. We are normal, all-American families who love, nurture, and support our children. Contrary to popular opinion, it does not screw them up mentally, physically, emotionally, or any other way.

"The biggest reward that I get from being a parent is that I am both teacher and student every day. The biggest challenges are doing my best and hoping that I raise my daughter well, and that I instill morals, values, pride, self-respect, and principles in her for her to believe in and pass down through those that are close to her."

Family 14—Carole and Andrea ▲▼▲ Lesbian Mothers—
47 and 44—California

Carole: "We have a 13-year-old daughter and a 7-year-old son. I don't think their gender is an issue in how we are raising them. My dreams for them are that they should be emotionally healthy, secure, happy, and physically healthy. They know the basic facts of life. We've taught them that two people who care for each other is most important, not whether they are male or female, or the same or opposite sex. We've never really 'come out' to them. It's just the way they've grown up. If they were to come out to me, I'd be okay, very supportive.

"Our daughter knows her father but rarely visits his house. He is re-married with two stepsons and one new daughter. I think it is okay for her when she's there, but it rarely happens.

"For me, I think whatever emotional problems there are are related to my professional life and its demands. It's challenging trying to balance it all. The rewards of being a parent are sharing in our children's lives, activities together, and watching them grow and mature. Then there are the tender moments together that can't be described."

Andrea: "We have one child of each sex. It seems to make no difference in how we raise them, I just want them to be healthy and happy in their lives. They know the facts of life. Since they are growing up in a home with two moms, coming out to them is not an issue.

"It's rewarding to participate in the forming of a child's life, watching them grow and change. There are many special moments that I wouldn't trade for anything. It's a challenge not always having the support I could use that could make parenting a little easier. I have a very demanding job."

Alix (Carole and Andrea's 13-1/2-year-old daughter—California): "I found out my moms are gay when I was little. They never really sat down and told me. From what I remember, I kind of figured it out. It doesn't affect how I am with them. Gay and lesbian parents should be out to their kids and should discuss it openly."

Jonathan (Carole and Andrea's 7-year-old son—California): "I found out from my mom that they are gay. It's all right to have lesbian parents. I don't care. They should tell their kids about it."

Family 15—Christine ▲▼▲ Lesbian Mother—
60—California

"I am female. I have six grown daughters and one grown son. I do not believe their genders affected the way I raised them too much. I had been raised in a family that had little use for female children, thus I had to work through a lot of garbage as an adult. Thank you Mother and the Catholic Church. I did not wish my children to ever feel such a sense of being unwanted, uncared for.

"Since my children are now adults, they make their own dreams. I did hope that after high school, at least some of them would choose college. None did—at least not for a while. Years later, some are beginning to pick up classes in their own special interest areas. They now say they wish they'd gone earlier!

"Having grown up in a culture that did not even admit such words as sex and sexuality existed, I chose to be 180 degrees different. I have taught my children the facts of life as they truthfully are. As they progressed in age, we continued knowledge. They often brought their friends home to learn also, with parental permission only.

"My first partner, shortly after we were together, told the children that we were gay without my knowledge. She was angry at the time and did it that way out of spite. The kids and I had always had good rapport, so we were able to sit down and talk it over. It was a little scary for me the first few words, but then it just felt good and right to freely discuss this topic also. When the kids first found out, they held a 'family conference' without me and decided on their own that whatever made their mother happy was okay with them. Some have expressed not understanding the gay/lesbian lifestyle, but it has not seemed to change our relationship. As adults, some are closer to me than others, based on their own personalities."

Marybeth (Christine's 35-year-old daughter—California): "My dad was in the military, in and out of the house. My mom has had motivation, goals, and dreams, and she goes after them.

She put up with my dad to get her nursing degree to be able to raise seven kids. She's very unselfish. My relationship with my mom didn't change when I found out she was gay, only after a problem with one of her lovers. I didn't trust my mom the same after that. We were raised that being gay was wrong. Now, my mom is a gay minister. It's confusing. How can it be wrong one day, and then another day it's okay? Having a gay mom makes me look into religion differently. What's the truth? Also, there are times when I'm having trouble with my husband, and I wonder if it's 'my time,' if now I'm turning gay. My mom was married for 18 years. Because I was raised Catholic, I question my mom's choice. The biggest problem is the one with one of my mom's lovers. I question now if I could be gay because of her.

"Parents should be out to their parents, the younger the better. If the kids are older, understand they will have lots of questions. Honesty is the basis of trust. Tell the kids how and why things are. Explaining why and how this household is different.

"A good parent is sensitive, smart, and willing to bend. A good parent is someone who is willing to say, 'I am wrong' and someone who is able to love no matter what happens."

Jean (Christine's 29-year-old daughter, Tara's twin—California): "My mother's sexual orientation is none of my business. If she's happy, who cares who she sleeps with. My mom is still my mom, no matter what! Yes, parents should be out to their children and should openly discuss being gay or lesbian with them! Having a lesbian mom, I am better aware of people's feelings. I don't discriminate, because I know how it feels."

Tara (Christine's 29-year-old daughter, Jean's twin—California): "I love my mom for always being there for me and for not judging me for the mistakes I've made. My mom performed my wedding to my husband. I don't see my dad, who lives in England. When I was about nine, I asked my mom what I should call her. She said to use her first name, but that was too hard, so I just call her Mom or Reverend Mom.

"I was in the third grade when my oldest sister took all seven of us kids for a ride down to the beach, and she said 'Mom is gay.' I remember someone asking what that meant, and my sister said that it means she likes women and not men. Oh, is that all? We all agreed that it didn't matter who Mom sleeps with as long as she is happy.

"I remember when I started junior high, I told myself that I wouldn't tell anyone any more, because if people didn't know, maybe they would like me. The challenge for me was hoping people would not find out. When I was in the fourth grade, my mom's church, MCC, burned down, and I remember taking the article from the newspaper for Share Day. My teacher got so upset that I brought it in that he called my mom and told her that I was no longer to bring anything for Share Day unless he okayed it first. I didn't understand why, nor did I care until years later. I do also remember my teacher didn't like me any more. He wouldn't let me stand with him at lunch time. He really hurt me, and I couldn't understand why or what I did to him. I never talked to mom about it. I didn't know if she even knew I was hurt, but she did. I also remember that in sixth grade, a girl in my class yelled at me in front of my whole class at lunch time. I kept talking to my friend, I don't remember what the girl was saying. I just remember she ended it saying '. . . and at least my mom's not gay,' as if that was supposed to hurt me.

"I think the only opportunity that having a lesbian mom has brought me is that I am not a close-minded person. I do not judge people for their race, sex, or lifestyle. I feel all people are the same no matter what."

Barbara (Christine's 38-year-old daughter—California): "When I was fourteen, I found out Mom was a lesbian. She and her friend began sharing a bed. I'm sure Mom talked about it, but I don't remember for sure. It doesn't affect our relationship or how I interact with her. I love her no matter what. Gay and lesbian parents should come out to their children and discuss it with them when the kids can understand, but only tell them what they can understand.

"I think the only challenges of having a lesbian mom were of my own making.

"A good parent has good listening skills, patience, and is able to keep their mouth shut even though they feel they just 'have to' comment."

Family 16—Dale and Kat ▲▼▲ Lesbian Mothers— 38 and 37—Florida

Dale: "We applaud the local lesbian community in moving away from prejudice against boy children. We have a boy and a girl, both 8 years old and adopted, and we love them absolutely equally. I hope this doesn't sound crazy, but we are in love with each other, and we are in love with our children. My dream for my son and daughter is for lifelong health, happiness obtained in a legally, morally ethical way, not at the expense of others. I also dream of post-high-school education for them, college, vocational, or technical school.

"We do not lecture about sex. We answer no more and no less than the child asks. We try to get them together when we give the answer so one may not tease the other with it.

"It was very easy to come out to the children. I was out from the get-go.

"We approach the children's biological parents with an 'I'm okay, you're okay' attitude. Thank God they've been very cooperative. We make every effort to cooperate with them. The children are outspoken about their wishes to live with us. We have good communication with the biological parents. Our son is unhappy spending time with his father. Our daughter enjoys her father's company but not her mother's (Kat's sister). We have spoken to both children about the importance of maintaining family ties.

"We suspect our son will grow up to be gay. We are truly neutral on this. We worry about so many other things! I think the bottom line on our children's emotional health is teaching them to enjoy the journey as well as the goal. I encourage them

not to be reactive about perceived injustice by seeing bad behavior as an error. The Higher Power sees everything. Kat and
I being the best possible example is the secret to our children's
mental hygiene.

"Kat and I have been challenged to teach our children
personal safety without being paranoid. We are challenged
in making our children drug-resistant, because the biological
parents have a history of drug usage. We are seeking housing in an affirmative, pro-child neighborhood. Transportation issues and chronic illness on our parts frustrate us as
we strive to be the best parents possible. We take parenting
very seriously. We are rewarded by having sensitive, understanding children who sense our unconditional love. Our financial resources are so slim, but our love is beyond
measure. We rejoice in the privilege of being our children's
parents."

Kat: "I want my children to be healthy, whole individuals! I
will always love my kids unconditionally. If they are gay, fine;
I just want them to be happy and whole.

"If they have a question about sex or sexuality, they can
ask. I'll answer them truthfully and age-appropriately. Our son
was great when I came out to him! We were laying outside in
our driveway one night, and I decided to tell him. He had
questions that I answered, and I had questions that he answered. Our daughter was told by her mom, my sister. Since I
came out, our son has been more loving to me, but I think that
has a lot to do with his parents' divorce also. My son is not
thrilled going to his dad's, but he goes. My daughter loves going to her dad's.

"At this point, I'm pretty happy to say the children have
a well-balanced life. When they get older, who knows? All I
know how to do is love them.

"When it comes down to it, every day is a challenge. To
see them grow and mature daily, not only physically, but emotionally and spiritually, is a great reward. Even just seeing an
unexpected smile is great!"

Family 17—Jim ▲▼▲ Gay Father—40—Massachusetts

"I am a gay male with 17- and 13-year-old daughters from a previous straight marriage. I came out to them about 4 years ago and have been living with my husband for the past 3 years. I dream for them to be happy and productive well-rounded individuals who make a difference in the world. In terms of sex and sexuality, they've been taught that everything's okay within the context of responsibility, good judgment, and safe sex. It wasn't too difficult to come out to them. The separation and divorce, with the initial physical separation from them were problems. My sexuality never was high on the list of difficulties. I think I would have no problem if either of my daughters ever were to 'come out' to me.

"My older daughter has her own apartment which she shares with a friend. My younger daughter lives with her mother most of the time. There have been no issues with custody. There aren't really issues related to my being gay. Their friends all know, and my older daughter's friends, at least, seem very cool about it. I interact with my girls in a myriad of activities and levels.

"My older daughter was rebellious a year or so ago. She quit school, but she got her GED and a job and grew up fast, faster than I was ready for. Both girls have now adjusted and are very 'normal' I'm happy for them—that they're great children and seem very happy themselves."

Chelsea (Jim's 13-year-old daughter—Massachusetts): "A good parent is one who listens, is there, and just loves you. Should gay parents openly discuss it with their kids? It depends. All I needed to know is if he were gay. I didn't really need to know anything else. Having a gay father does create some challenges and obstacles. There are some people I don't want to know about it. When they call me at my dad's and ask, 'Who was that? That wasn't your dad.' I have to make excuses."

Family 18—Becka ▲▼▲Lesbian Mother—44— Washington State

"I find it challenging in raising a boy to deal with issues around sexism without taking away from his identity as a precious child. My biggest dream for him is that he will have joy.

"I have always been out to him, as he is the product of a lesbian relationship by alternative insemination. I currently answer any and all questions about sex honestly. Whatever his sexual orientation turns out to be, it's him.

"He spends time with his other mom, my ex. It's wonderful for him and a nice break for me.

"My son has excellent self-esteem. He's a great negotiator. He understands what his emotions are and deals well with them.

"My son brings me more joy than I ever hoped for. Parenting is a huge responsibility but well worth it!"

Tommy (Becka's 7-year-old son—Washington State): "I know my moms, but I don't know who my dad is. I think it would be nice—really, really cool to—know. It's kind of sad to have lesbian parents, but I feel okay about it. Yes, they should talk to their kids about it."

Family 19—Sandra and Kelly ▲▼▲ Lesbian Mothers— 37 and 36—Ohio

Sandra: "I dream for my son and my daughter to be happy, to be educated, to grow always, to be spiritual, to be givers and doers, to find people to share their lives—friends and partners, and maybe have children if they wish.

"I've taught them that sex is an important part of life to be taken seriously. I've taught them to be safe! Miranda was sexually active because of an abuse that made her feel ugly about herself. Then she went out the window at thirteen, went to a party, got drunk, had sex, and was 20 weeks pregnant before we knew. She gave birth at fourteen and gave her son up for adoption.

"Coming out to my daughter was pretty easy. It was harder for my son. It was shaky at first after I told them, partly because I was telling them I was moving out. Miranda was understanding. Max was blank. He withdrew some. If they were ever to come out to me, I'd be glad they could talk to me. It would be fine.

"Now that Kelly and I have the kids with us, we all share living space, we eat dinner together usually. Sometimes we watch TV, shop, go to dinner, go to the movies. There are never enough hours. We go to church. I take them to friends' houses, pick up their friends. We argue over the TV, the bathroom, the *phone*, their messy habits.

"I think they are pretty healthy, much better than the last 4 years of my marriage to their father. They are much, much, much better than when they were just with him. They talk, talk, talk to both Kelly and me. We've seen them both let go and talk about some pretty unhealthy things.

"Miranda's pregnancy at fourteen was very, very hard. I was going through the final stages of ending my marriage and coming out. I tried to be there for her, but my emotional health was not good. Kelly was just out of treatment for alcoholism. Everything was a mess. It was also hard deciding to move out and be on my own, not with Kelly even for 6 months. I spent most of my time with her, but I had a separate space to be with my children, so we could go slowly introducing them and Kelly. While their father still had custody, living away from them was a big challenge for me. The kids were angry and unhappy. It was a good separate couple-time for Kelly and me, but it was hard for the kids and me.

"I like my children. Most of the time, they are caring and nonjudgmental. The rewards of being their mother are many smiles, thank yous, I love yous, and their views on most things."

Miranda (Sandra and Kelly's 17-year-old daughter—Ohio): "I found out my mom is a lesbian almost exactly 2 years ago. She told me that, because it was the reason she was leaving us with our dad. He'd threatened to make that information public. My mom didn't think he'd be bad for us. He does love us in his own twisted way. She thought it'd be easier on everyone if she didn't put up a fight. She was staying in the same city, and we could see her almost every day until my dad started saying he wanted to agree to the times of our visitation.

"I think knowing has made me closer to my mom. Whether Kelly was with my dad or my mom, it is a difficult position for her to be in. She went from being single to being in a relationship and having two teenagers. She's good to us. She's easy to talk to, and we accept her just as she has accepted us into her life.

"My mom's being a lesbian doesn't bother me in the least. My mom deserves love, and Kelly gives her that. It is beautiful how affectionate they are. I feel that with the amount of violence and hatred in the world, no one has the right to get angry about whom someone *loves!*

"For the most part, gay parents should be out to their kids and talk about it. I think if the child is mature, then they will accept it. To me, it is just a detail, like the fact that my mom has dark brown hair. Children never really stop loving a parent, and although the issue may be difficult for some, eventually they will learn to deal with the information. Where they go from there is up to them.

"I have a strong and healthy relationship with my mom. I'm open-minded and mature. Not every situation is as positive as mine. I'm lucky. It's hard for me, because I'm still very angry with my dad for putting my mom down and for being cruel to me. He tried to say that because of my mom's sexuality, she was unfit, but it's he who is unfit.

"My mom's sexual orientation affected my relationship with my dad, because he would say awful things, and it made me sick with anger at him. My relationship has only become closer with my mom, because we had to stick together in the custody battle. Otherwise, my mom's sex is my mom's business.

"I think having lesbian parents creates a wonderful opportunity for me. I'm seventeen and establishing my sexual identity. If I ever have questions or problems, I know I can talk to both of them. I know, because we've discussed how I feel about them, and it was very comfortable. They're *real* people. A lot of kids look at their parents like heroes, and they can't see that they have problems. My mom has cried and hurt in front of me, and I understood her pain just like when I need to cry and hurt. I can. It's okay.

"A good parent is someone who is patient, wise, and empathetic, someone who can talk to their children honestly, someone who doesn't pretend to be something they're not. Kids can see through lies, and it only hurts to think that a parent can't talk to their own flesh and blood. Families are there to help you when you need it. You should be able to take advantage of that."

Family 20—Melissa and Trish ▲▼▲ Lesbian Mothers—
37 and 39—New Jersey

Melissa: "It's probably a little easier for me to raise a daughter. I dream that she will be happy.

"It was very natural to be out to her. It's all she's ever known.

"At this point, we've probably taught her everything we could have about sex and sexuality. There aren't really issues for her with our being lesbians. She just doesn't want it always to be her battle. I'd be fine if I ever found out she was gay."

Dawn (Melissa and Trish's 14-year-old daughter—New Jersey): "My moms are basically mellow, groovy people. I never 'discovered' that they're gay. That's just the way it was. I'm fine with it. Yes, parents should most definitely be out to their children, and they should discuss it openly. It doesn't play any role at all in my relationship with them.

"What makes a good parent is openness, love, and patience—lots of patience."

Family 21—Denise and Alisha ▲▼▲ Lesbian Mothers— 33 and 34—New York

Denise: "We have a 4-month-old daughter. I think her being the same sex as us will be easier. I dream that she will have a college education, preferably a master's degree. I wish for her to have a stable, fulfilling job, and for her to be happy, healthy, and to have an intimate relationship and many friends.

"She's just a baby, but she's got a wonderful disposition, crying only when wet or hungry. If she turns out to be gay, I would just want to make sure she was supported and sure herself.

"Being a parent requires that you have to remain very flexible. All plans are dependent on Zoe's disposition, her need to eat, or her need to sleep! I've also learned to be very patient.

"I've never experienced such profound and intense love in my entire life! When she looks at me in the morning and gives me a big smile, I just melt! I worry, however, that something tragic will happen to her."

Alisha: "I think raising a daughter will be slightly easier than raising a son, because we're starting from a higher level of commonality. It will encourage us to maintain the involvement of our male friends so that our daughter gets a male perspective. I dream that she remains healthy, happy, and loved, and that she develops dreams of her own.

"We haven't come out to her yet (she's only 4 months old), but it will be an ongoing process depending on her developmental stage. We will be honest and open with her. If she ever comes out to us, I would feel happy that she *could* and *did* feel able to.

"It's only been 4 months, but our daughter is so happy! Part of it is her own personality, and some of it is the happy, loving, content environment she lives in.

"Her full-face smile is a daily, and more often, reward that makes up for any challenges of temperament she presents us with. I sometimes stand over her crib while she's sleeping and smile or cry as I realize how much she has added to my life as an individual, a partner, and now as a parent and member of a family."

Family 22—Werner ▲▼▲ Gay Father—31—Austria

"I am a single gay male raising a young daughter. I live a great range of gender roles, not just one. I am both mother and father to her, now that her mother has died. I hope that her being the opposite gender from me has little effect on how I am raising her. My dreams for Anna are for a happy, self-confident life with warm and loving relationships with partners and friends.

"Anna is very sociable and independent. As a parent, I have learned to differentiate between what's more important and what's less so. I have learned to be patient and responsible. My rewards are just to love her, to take care of her, and to see that she needs me too. I get to see her growing and developing. I love to spend time with her."

▲▼▲

When I visit with these parents and children through the thoughts and feelings that they have shared here, I come away with an overwhelming appreciation for the love and respect that they give to each other. The children are truly loved and wanted, and their individual characteristics are deeply appreciated by parents whose own individuality may not have been so well tolerated as they themselves were growing up. The children also see and value the personal qualities that make their parents unique and special. They are living lives beyond the norm and are therefore developing an appreciation for the rights and needs of individuals, some of whom happen to be their parents.

Out and About in the Community ▲▼▲ When and How Do We Reveal Ourselves?

4

We do not want our ideas changed. We feel threatened by such demands, "I already know the important things!" we say. Then Changer comes and throws our old ideas away. (The Zensufi Master)

Frank Herbert,
Chapterhouse: Dune

... gay and lesbian parents instill a sense of family and personal pride in their children. (Melanie Margolis, Photographer.)

I sat crouched between the hedge that ringed our large backyard and a fragrant lilac bush. I remember bands of sunshine and the sweet scent of new blossoms surrounding me as I waited to be found by "It." I must have been about 8 years old, and the neighborhood kids were embroiled in a game of hide and seek. The foliage provided a pretty good camouflage. From where I sat, I could see "It" running around the yard, occasionally uncovering a friend who would then run at top

▲▼▲ 153

speed to touch "home" before being tagged. But I don't seem to have been visible myself. I guess I had chosen my hiding place well, so well that I soon began to wonder if I would ever be found and brought back into the fold of friends. Hiding began to feel lonely, and I found myself wanting to be discovered yet knowing that by the rules of the game, coming out of hiding could mean losing.

For many gay and lesbian parents, coming out of hiding presents a risk of loss not entirely unlike that of the children's game. The world is certainly more gay-friendly than it was even a handful of years ago, but it is far from being universally safe. Even if we as adults feel confident about identifying ourselves, when coming out means exposing a child to possible censure, ridicule, or physical harm, one does take pause to reconsider the consequences.

Coming out is not a one-time act. It is an ongoing and daily series of decisions about how to dress, what jewelry to wear, how to cut one's hair, what words to use in regard to our relationships, what acts of affection to engage in publicly, which photos to place on our desks at work, which bumper stickers to put on the family car, and whether or not to allow the neighbors into our homes where they may see books or magazines lying around. It is deciding whether or not to petition or apply for domestic partnership benefits at our place of employment and choosing how to identify the adults who wish to attend a parent–teacher meeting in a child's school. Sometimes staying hidden feels safer than exposing our real selves. Sometimes staying hidden feels stifling and unnatural. Sometimes it is not possible to stay hidden, and we must find a way to handle the repercussions of being known in all of its fearsome or wondrous manifestations.

Just as coming out does not happen all at one time, it does not need to happen everywhere. Venue-specific decisions have to be made. Most of us do not live in communities that are so tiny that all of our business is known every place we go. Few of us even live any longer in close proximity to all of our relatives. Each arena of our lives begs an individual choice about whether or not to reveal ourselves or how much of our truth to expose. The implications of being out within the extended family are quite different from those of being out to a best friend. Being out to co-workers is not the same as being out to clients or to the boss. Being out in a support group is not the same as being out in our places of worship or to our pediatrician. Being out to the neighborhood is not like being out in the gay and lesbian community. Being out to adult friends is not like being out to our children's friends or to the friends' parents. Being out to family, to friends, to strangers, to school personnel, or to landlords each carries different risks and different rewards.

When gay and lesbian parents, or their children, decide not to come out, they are allowing a protective buffer to exist around themselves by virtue of society's general assumption that parents are straight. By not revealing parental sexual orientation, many hope to blend into their social environment and thus to protect themselves from the scorn that they anticipate will come if they were to be seen as outsiders. What good parents wouldn't seek to maintain a shield of protection around their children? If anonymity is safety, who wouldn't choose to remain hidden?

What loving parent, on the other hand, would seek to teach his or her child to be dishonest, fearful, and ashamed? For the children of gay men and lesbians, coming out personally or as a family carries the serious risk of being seen by peers as being different, and yet the act of revealing the truth about one's family may well be the most emotionally freeing act of a child's or parent's life. Yes, there are risks with which straight families do not need to contend. There are also prospects for emotional and spiritual development that are not always available to other families. Learning to face fears, becoming an advocate of compassion, taking pride in one's heritage, standing up for the value of one's family and its individual members, and discovering compassion in others are all opportunities for growth that are afforded by the process of coming out.

There is a vast difference between fearing negative conse-quences and anticipating them. When we make an informed decision to stay invisible out of a realistic presumption of dan-ger, we are engaging in valid discretion. But if we remain clos-eted out of fear, what lessons are we teaching our children about self-respect and honesty? As with so many of parent-hood's difficult choices, the decisions of whether and where and how far to come out when children are involved call for the most careful examination of parents' motives.

It has long been known that gay and lesbian families pro-vide environments that are as psychosocially healthy for chil-dren as are comparable straight families. When studies have matched gay- or lesbian-headed families with straight families of similar qualities of socioeconomic status, adult partnership involvement, and the number, age, and gender of children, no significant *intrafamilial* factors were found to create differences in the children's development.[1-5] The only factor that has been seen to create notable difficulty for the children of homosexual parents is continuing rejection and misunderstanding on the part of extended family and of the general community.[6-10] With this in mind, gay and lesbian families are wise to consider carefully the possible impact on their lives that would be en-gendered by coming out.

The comfort and safety of being out depends greatly on the open-mindedness of the people with whom you share your life. Individuals, families, and communities each have their own degree of openness and flexibility. While it is true that many Americans are still uncomfortable to a greater or lesser degree with the concept of gay and lesbian parenting, the numbers are shifting dramatically as more national as well as personal attention is being paid to our families. According to a recent *Newsweek* study, "almost half of those polled felt gays should not be allowed to adopt, although 57 percent thought gays could be just as good parents as straight peo-ple."[11] People who love you, trust you, and feel that they know you reasonably well are more likely to change their views about sexual orientation than they are to change their feelings about *you* when you come out to them.

Sometimes, even when we come out, we are not recognized. The public's assumptions about parenthood and sexual orientation are often so ingrained that people can't quite fathom what they are seeing or hearing. A lesbian couple I know tells a story of an encounter with a stranger on the street. The couple was with their infant daughter, one mother handing the child to the other, when a woman came up to admire the newborn. "Which of you is the mother?" they were asked. "We both are," was their simultaneous reply. The stranger looked confused and asked again, receiving the same answer. She looked at the mother who was not holding the baby and said, "Oh, I know. You must be the aunt." Two mothers simply did not fit her paradigm of how the world works.

For gay fathers, single or in a couple, the stereotypes are even more pronounced than they are for lesbian mothers. Strangers simply do not understand why men are pushing a stroller, and even relatives are known to wonder how these dads will take care of their young children. In at least one instance, a nurse refused to release a newborn to her adoptive gay father, even though he had legal adoption papers with him, because she did not believe that he could be the girl's parent.

Children are known to be pretty accurate barometers of their parents' attitudes and emotions. If they are presented with information about their family, whether it is about ethnicity, race, or sexual orientation, they will react to the information with about as much comfort and acceptance as their parents do. I am the eldest child of two Jewish survivors of the Nazi Holocaust. When I was young, I attended schools and lived in a neighborhood in which I was among predominantly Christian children whose parents had been born in America and had always lived lives of relative safety. I learned by my parents' and grandparents' examples to view my family as special and to regard our background as a source of strength and pride. When I was teased for being different, I hurt, but I also recognized that my tormentors acted out of ignorance and prejudice, not out of truth.

When gay and lesbian parents instill a sense of family and personal pride in their children, the children are not only able to face an ambivalent or even hostile world with self-respect, they also tend to feel more compassionate toward other minorities. They know first-hand what it means to be misjudged, and they learn to see the essence of the people with whom they come in contact rather than simply responding to external appearances or simple labels. Learning early that the world has cruel corners is not necessarily a disadvantage, as long as the child is equipped with appropriate coping strategies and the strength of self acceptance. Children who are able to rise to one challenge are better prepared to handle other difficult circumstances in their lives.

An increasing number of large corporations, such as IBM and the Disney Company, are offering domestic partnership recognition and benefits to unmarried couples, including gay and lesbian couples. If you work for such a company, being out at work should be relatively comfortable. If, however, your place of employment is not supportive of its gay and lesbian employees, outing yourself and your family at work may not be so safe or so easy. Many gay and lesbian parents and their older children are out nearly everywhere else in their lives, but they choose to protect their livelihoods by remaining invisible at work. One wonders how many co-workers are keeping similar secrets.

Anyone who has been to school knows that the schoolyard can be a threatening place for children who are different. Especially for young adolescents, peer acceptance is a critical factor in children's self-esteem. Teaching children to respond positively when others are cruel, or simply careless, is a powerful vehicle for creating self-assurance and an atmosphere of understanding among school-age children. Simply helping a child to respond to hurtful jokes or remarks by stating that such comments are not true and make them feel bad can often cause others to rethink their words. Although we would all like to think that teachers are going to be supportive of the children in their classrooms, this is sadly not always so. Teachers, like all people, are subject to their own experiences, misinformation, and prejudices. Talk with your child's teacher and other school officials about your family. Spreading truthful information is still the best way to thwart ignorance. The staff at your child's school may or may not be open-minded about your family. Be prepared to suggest that they view and use the videos *It's Elementary*[12] and *Both My Moms' Names Are Judy.*[13] It may not be easy, but perhaps you will open doors that have been shut for too long.

There are many types of neighborhoods in which gay and lesbian families live. Some are openly accepting of differences among their residents, and others are not. Only you can judge your own community. You may be surprised, though, at how well your family is accepted if people know you, and you are in general a good neighbor. People who live in more liberal urban areas, especially in the Northeast and California, are more likely to find acceptance of gay and lesbian individuals and families than are those who live in other areas.[14] Like all preconceived ideas, this is not universally true, and you may find pockets of acceptance in even the most conservative areas. In general, the more personal and accurate information people have about gays and lesbians, the more likely they are to view us as "just folks" and not as strangers to be feared or changed.

Are you comfortable inviting new friends or neighbors into your home? Do you find yourself turning gay- and lesbian-related books around on the shelf so that the bindings don't show, or do you just "let it all hang out"? Do your children hesitate to ask friends over, or do their friends suddenly have a change of plans after they or their parents find out about your sexual orientation? Dealing with friends and neighbors certainly presents challenges for gay and lesbian families that straight families probably don't even think about. As in other areas of life, honesty may well be the best policy in preventing or correcting awkward social situations. Staying hidden is always a choice, and it may be the right one for you. If potential visitors seem reluctant to join you in your home, or to have you in theirs, consider asking them what they find unsettling, and then be patiently open to answering questions or offering information about yourself, your family, and gay and lesbian issues in general. You may just have created an opportunity to turn fear and misunderstanding into comfort and acceptance.

It's always hardest to tell a difficult truth to the people we value the most. While few of us care much if a casual acquaintance chooses not to associate with us for who we are, such rejection can be devastating when it comes from a loved member of our family. Not only does the initial dismissal hurt, but relatives are people with whom we will always need to deal, even if the "dealing" is through avoidance. For this reason, many gay men and lesbians, parents or not, have the most difficulty coming out to parents, grandparents, siblings, and other close relatives. Homosexual parents do not wish to see their children rejected or treated unfairly by grandparents or aunts and uncles, so they may keep their sexual orientation secret. What does this do to the children they are trying so hard to protect? Of course, every family situation is unique, but for the most part, secrecy of any sort strains relationships. If your children feel the need to hide a part of their family truth from loved ones, can they ever really accept that part of themselves?

To paraphrase a modern truism, "stuff happens." Children cannot be insulated from hurtful situations, no matter how much their parents would like to keep them from such experiences. How do gay and lesbian parents help their children respond when life throws them a batch of lemons? At home, the lessons can begin quite simply and very early in a child's life by sharing information about prejudice and ignorance. Even toddlers can understand that people hurt others when they are scared or uninformed. From the time babies first interact with other children, they can be taught to be nice, to play fair, and to respect differences among people. It is not rude or inconsiderate to notice that someone looks or sounds different from you, but it is inappropriate to mistreat them because of the difference. Teaching children to take pride in their individuality and in the uniqueness of their family helps them to weather the unkind remarks and behaviors of others.

Just as maintaining silence creates stress, opening communication builds closeness and understanding. Talk with your children about being out. Whatever their age, they are sure to have experiences, ideas, and feelings about disclosing your sexual orientation that are personal and possibly quite different from your own. Understand also that depending on their age, personality, and other factors, they may change their mind from time to time about being out. Discuss with your children ways that they might respond to unkind remarks or to inaccurate comments that they may overhear. Being prepared ahead of time is much more empowering than thinking later of what one could have said!

There are an estimated six to fourteen million children living with at least one gay or lesbian parent in the United States today.[15,16] Many of these children are helped to feel less different and less isolated simply by knowing other, similar families. Being aware that there are many kinds of families is also a great help to children who feel separated from peers for not being part of the mainstream. Creating a personal network of family and individual friends is a powerful way of helping children feel more accepted in their world. No one likes to feel like an outsider. We all want to know that we are essentially acceptable to others, and children who come from nonmainstream families may need to see that they are not the only ones.

If you do not know other gay or lesbian families in your area, you may begin by contacting a wonderful organization called GLPCi (Gay and Lesbian Parenting Coalition International) or COLAGE (Children of Lesbians and Gays Everywhere) (see Appendix A) Many fine local support or social groups are also in existence around the country. They may be sponsored by churches or synagogues, by local gay and lesbian centers, or by local gay and lesbian parents. If you cannot find an appropriate group in your area, why not start one? All it takes is getting the word out, and you can do that safely by using e-mail, a voice mailbox, or a P.O. box address for correspondence, if you do not feel comfortable using your own phone number or address.

Another way of creating a base of self-acceptance and an understanding of our diverse social fabric is through books, videos, and other media that address gay and lesbian family issues or that teach about other cultures (see Appendix B).

There is plenty of material available for all ages and virtually all ability levels. The Internet is also burgeoning with gay and lesbian interest groups.

Everyone has a story to tell. Tell yours, and inform others. Listen to others to learn for yourself about all the diversity that our growing community has to offer.

Family 1—Jeremy ▲▼▲ Gay Father—27—New York

"When I was working to adopt Micah, I was out in my community, my town, but not in the new adoptive world. I had so many strikes against me as a gay, single, Jewish man, I had to weigh which desire was stronger—to be true to myself, my community, and friends, or to become a parent. The two goals are often mutually exclusive. I decided not to offer information that I am gay. I didn't feel that it was relevant to whether I should be a parent or not. No one ever asked specifically, but still, not saying anything was an issue for me.

"I didn't get a lot of support from my community. I knew gay parents, and I knew of a few gay men who had biological children, but I didn't know any gay men who had adopted. When I did hear about men who had adopted, they typically adopted older children. Gay men who adopted did so as a couple. I wanted to find another single gay man who had adopted. There is a myth in our community that we cannot adopt. I run into gay men all the time who say bluntly, 'I always thought about adopting and just thought it would be impossible or illegal'."

Family 2—Alan ▲▼▲ Gay Father—46—married to Margaret, straight mother—44—Massachusetts

"I don't believe that the neighbors know that I'm gay. I am out to my wife, children, in-laws, the pastor of my parish, and to several close friends. Our daughter's boyfriend knows. I'm not out to my co-workers, my stepmother, and my brothers and sister. There's no particular reason. I will come out to them eventually. Our children's' schools do not know. We do prepare our children to deal with homophobia.

"Our friends are some of our co-workers, people from work, and friends of Margaret's significant other. We choose them by common interests in politics, religion, and general outlook. Some are gay, some are straight. We meet them at work, church, our children's' schools, and through outside activities.

"The children socialize mostly with their peers, neighborhood kids, and cousins. As a family, we spend social time with each other, my wife's significant other, and at church activities.

"I belong to a gay fathers support group and to two AIDS groups. Three years ago, I joined the Gay Fathers of Greater Boston after seeing my first therapist's advertisement on Pride Day. She told me about this organization and gave me a contact person to call."

Brett (Alan and Margaret's 15-year-old daughter—Massachusetts): "My friends are a wicked lot of people that are like me. To meet friends, I just get up all my courage and start talking to them. Then we're friends. Bam! Like that. Do they know about my dad? Uh, no. I'm not out about this at school or at church. I don't really talk about it, because it's not really the hot topic of our conversation. There are people at my school that are wicked homophobic. They say all faggots should be shot. That pisses me off. I just shrug it off because they are the stupid ones that can't understand that everyone's different. I try to explain that gay and lesbian people are the same as us. When people make comments about my family, I tell them to shut up. I am out to my boyfriend of 11 months that totally understands and still likes my dad just as much. I don't belong to any support groups."

Family 3—Rob ▲▼▲ Gay Father—53—California

"I am out to my neighbors, to my child's school, and to just about everyone I know now. Only my father, who has

Alzheimer's, does not know. I have not been rejected by many people. There have been no issues with school personnel, although my daughter was teased by other kids. School personnel at her Jewish private school were made aware of this. I choose my personal friends based upon their character and values. They include both gay and straight people. I've met new friends in gay-support and social groups and during travel. Previous friends are from school or were met socially in my marriage. My kids socialize with their own friends, relatives, and friends of the family. As a family we see my sister's family, my mom, and other relatives.

"My son is homophobic, as is my wife. My older daughter has no problem with it. My 9 year old is scared of gay life because of the effect it has had on her life."

Family 4—Samantha ▲▼▲ Lesbian Mother—33—Vermont

"Although my neighbors know that I am a lesbian, they react with benign neglect. They don't talk about it. I am out to my co-workers and staff at work and to friends and family. I am not out to my medical patients because it's not an appropriate discussion unless I am asked. I find that I feel a connection with certain people. My friends are both gay and straight, and I meet them at work, in the neighborhood, and at social events. I attend gay and lesbian support group meetings occasionally, bimonthly. My 19-month-old son interacts with children of my friends and with a cousin. As a family, we socialize with other gay and lesbian parents, hetero couples, and singles."

Family 5—Linda and Donna ▲▼▲ Lesbian Mothers— 40 and 49—Utah

"We are out to 'everybody.' The neighbors seem very accepting, and there has been no problem with the children's schools. I'm [Linda] a psychologist, so I'm not out to some of my clients. They might not be accepting, and our therapeutic relationship might be disrupted. However, most of my clients either know or suspect I'm a lesbian judging from their comments.

"We choose friends on the basis of how interesting and unconventional they are, their mental health, and how supportive they are of my choices. They are mixed gay and straight. Many friends are 'ex's.' Some are former students, most of whom are married with children. Others are professional colleagues. Our children socialize with neighborhood friends and kids at school. As a family, we socialize with other lesbian couples with children, mainly. We don't socialize as a family very much, due to time constraints and Donna's lack of interest. We do belong to the lesbian parents' support group, the Human Rights Coalition, NOW, etc.

"We've prepared the children to deal with homophobia by talking with them about others' potential reactions, and telling them to tell their friends that their mothers' sexuality has no bearing on their own."

Family 6—Leah and Ali ▲▼▲ Lesbian Mothers—40 and 42—Texas

"Some of our neighbors do know that we are lesbians. All who do know have been very friendly, some more than others. One who found out initially that we were moving in, went to our next door neighbor, whom we had not yet met, and asked her what she was going to do about her new neighbors. Our neighbor said, 'What do you think? I'm going to treat them like new neighbors!' The day we moved in, she came over with a beautiful new plant to welcome us! The neighbors behind have a 5 year old and a 2 year old. They're very friendly, and the kids play with our 2-year-old son.

"Jacob's school knows that we are lesbians, very much so. We made the decision even before becoming parents that schools would know about our family. We interviewed several pre-schools. All directors were open about our family. Our current pre-school has asked us to do an in-service for their staff about gay and lesbian families. They have been very open and supportive. They love Jacob, and they are great with both of us as well. Jacob wants us to say that he likes the food at school!

"We are out to our families, friends, and just about everyone. Ali is more openly out at work. All know there, including probably a few students. Jacob and Leah attend all faculty functions with Ali. Leah is out at work, but not quite as openly. She's out with immediate co-workers, and most teachers know she has a child. Some know or suspect there is a significant other. Leah is an Occupational Therapist in a public school setting, and it is more difficult and risky to be totally open, but as Jacob gets older, this too shall pass!

"We base our friendships on common interests and likeability. Our friends are mixed. There are lots of straight friends who do and don't have children and are supportive of us. We also have lots of gay friends with and without children. Outside of school, Jacob plays with primarily children of other gay and lesbian families. He does also play with our neighbors' two children and the 3 year old of a heterosexual family who we're friends with. As a family, we socialize with other gay and lesbian families and friends from both of our jobs. One Sunday each month, we meet to socialize at a pot luck with our gay and lesbian parents group. One Saturday evening each month, this same group has spun off into an issues discussion group, without children, to discuss various concerns and issues that we face daily and in the long term.

"At Jacob's young age, we have begun talking lots about different kinds of families, and we are beginning to instill in him the fact that his family is special and wonderful. As he gets older, we'll continue to address the issue of homophobia and how we can best prepare him for the challenges.

"The family issue in terms of having two moms has been easier than we thought. We've had very positive experiences with most of the people we have come into contact with. We never make our 'lifestyle' an issue. We are simply a family raising our young son. It becomes easier as life goes on to deal with the public and those around us, since so many people have been so supportive."

Family 7—Lydia and Sari ▲▼▲ Lesbian Mothers— 43 and 42—California

"We are out to everyone. Usually we don't advertise, and we don't hide. We were on the front page of the *Los Angeles Times* and did a nationally broadcast Maria Shriver 'First Person' TV show. I think we are pretty much out to the world.

"I'm sure there was some talk among the neighbors, nothing malicious, just, 'Hey, did you know?' I don't know that the children's schools/day care treat us in any special way because of our special family. I think they treat us with respect because of the type of people we are and because of the type of children we are raising.

"We choose our friends by how we relate to one another and what we have in common. They are gay and straight people whom we meet at work, through other people, other parents, wherever. The kids play with other kids that they have fun with.

"We have belonged to and did attend a lesbian parents and their children group but haven't for a while. Sari has hooked up with a gay and lesbian parenting group, and we have attended functions with them. I think the most important part these groups play is in support, especially for our children.

"We've told Nathan that there are all different types of families, some have a mom and a dad, some two moms, some one mom and no dad, some just a dad, some two dads, some kids live with uncles, aunts, grandparents, etc., and that he is very lucky because he has two moms and a dad and lots of 'uncles,' 'aunts,' and cousins, etc., who love him. When he gets a bit older, we will discuss the fact that some people don't think you should have two moms or dads who love each other, but at this point, it's a bit premature. He also has friends with same-sex parents so he won't feel so isolated."

Family 8—Carol and Rose ▲▼▲ Lesbian Mothers—
41 and 31—Kansas

"We haven't told the neighbors outright, but we haven't hidden it. Whether or not they know probably depends on if they want to acknowledge it or not. They haven't treated us differently. Drew isn't in school yet, but her day-care provider knows that we are lesbians, but both her mother and father are gay, so it wasn't an issue at all. Since Drew was born, I've [Carol] been out to my mom, some relatives, and most of my staff where I work. I'm not out to my boss, though she has the same 'clues' as everyone else in the office. She's always treated me as a friend, but she has also voiced her disapproval of 'those' people. We're not out to several relatives, mainly because my mom's afraid of what they would think—of her probably.

"Our friends are friends because of their intelligence, similar likes and dislikes, and their openness to diversity. They are mixed gay and straight people whom we meet at work, church, lesbian groups, and through other friends. Drew's friends are day-care children and some of our friends' kids. Our family friends are other lesbian families, Rose's sister and brother-in-law, some single lesbian and straight women without kids. We belong to a lesbian mothers group and to a local lesbian group.

"We've tried to teach Drew to stand up for herself, but at 16 months, there's not much to do yet about dealing with homophobia."

Family 9—Jenny and Ann ▲▼▲ Lesbian Mothers—
33 and 38—Illinois

"Our neighbors are very accepting. We are especially close to the neighbors to our left. They spent New Year's Eve with us, and we interact with them on a daily basis. She refers to us as 'the married women next door.' We believe that our daughters' schools know too. We didn't walk into the school with our lesbian T-shirts, but we did present ourselves as a couple. We are both active in the school activities that involve our children. On parent–teacher night, we attend together. No one has ever asked about the relationship, but they refer to us both as the parents. The school personnel treat our children wonderfully. I think they are appreciative of all parents who are a part of their child's education.

"We are out to everyone close to us, including co-workers, friends, and family. People we may associate with for one reason or another do not necessarily know. We see no reason to introduce ourselves to everyone we come into contact with as Jenny and Ann the lesbians. In casual conversation, I [Jenny] may refer to my spouse, and if I'm asked who that is, I don't hesitate to say, 'Her name is Ann.' As I've stated before, we don't lie about our lifestyle.

"Friends are people with common interests and scruples. This does not include sexual orientation, as we have personal friends who are quite heterosexual. Our circle of friends is definitely mixed. We meet them at work, at gay and lesbian dances, civic organizations, and through other friends. One of our closest friends oftentimes refers to herself as homophobic! We tease her about her confusion of our lifestyle. Our children socialize with children of our friends, neighborhood children, and classmates. As a family, we get together with family friends, couples both gay and straight who have children. We go boating, camping, roller skating, on picnics, and take day-long trips to surrounding areas.

"We have just recently become involved in GLPCi (Gay and Lesbian Parenting Coalition International), and we are looking for local support groups to join."

Jo (Jenny and Ann's 13-year-old daughter—Illinois): "I have a lot of friends, including Mom, Boo-Boo, and Cait, my sister. I meet friends at school, from other friends, and the kids of friends of my parents. Only my best friend knows that my moms are gay. She thinks my parents are cool. I'm not out at school. My classmates think I live with my mom and my aunt. Everyone in my family knows, though. My grandma asks me a lot if it bothers me. I think it is uncomfortable for her. I'm also not out at church. It is something I choose to keep to myself. If your parents are gay, then people think that you will be gay, and that gay people are perverts and will molest children. When I hear someone make a prejudiced remark like that I react with sadness, and I feel that the person making the comment isn't very smart. I usually ignore it. I can't control what people think or say. I know that they are not educated about the facts. When people ask me questions, I'm truthful about it; I try to answer their questions as best as I can.

"I don't belong to any support group for kids of gays or lesbians, but we are planning to attend a conference this summer, and I can't wait."

Family 10—Dee and Sherry ▲▼▲ Lesbian Mothers— 31 and 46—California

Dee: "Our neighbors know. In fact, the neighbors we share a wall with in our duplex are gay men! We were worried that when we moved to the suburbs after living in San Francisco, we would have to be more closeted, and people would be prejudiced against us, but we have been pleasantly surprised. Everyone is kind. There has been no outward disapproval or discrimination. One neighbor, who has since moved, was even very excited about our trying to get pregnant. She asked us often how it was going and gave us things her son had outgrown.

"Our 17-year-old son is out of school, but the 15-year-old's principal knows because she is a friend of ours from church. We're not sure if his teacher knows. In the past, we have come out on the forms for school. School personnel have not always been professionally neutral about this. At a previous school, and with school authorities in general, there have been problems. We've had counselors imply to our son that our lesbianism is somehow detrimental for him, a cross he has to bear, or an explanation for his maladaptive acting-out because as women we cannot offer him enough discipline.

"We are out in most aspects of our lives—to family, friends, co-workers, and to church members. I am not out to my patients at work or their families, because I am afraid it would jeopardize our professional relationships. I feel conflicted about this.

"I have many friends from all of the activities I have been involved with in my life, high school, college, grad school, all past jobs, lesbian groups, church groups, etc. I guess I choose mainly by common interests and enjoyment of people's personalities.

"We have more straight friends, by chance, because of several factors. Most of my friends from before I came out are straight. We are the only gay people at our church, and work friends are often straight. The boys' friends are other teenagers and extended family members. The kids join us sometimes when we get together with our families.

"We continue to attend the group in which we met, a mostly lesbian group called 'Not Your Ordinary Christian Women's Support Group.'"

Sherry: "I am out at work and everywhere. We are not obviously out to the kids' friends. My good friends are a few lesbians I have known for years, and some family members and a couple of people I work with and enjoy spending time with. Also, I count some of Dee's friends as my own as well. As a family, we join together for dinner when Dee and I have friends over.

"We talked with the boys about homophobia when they were young. They know it firsthand, because their father and his family were vocally homophobic. It is not much of an issue for them now, but it was an embarrassment to them around the ages of twelve to fifteen."

Family 11—Liz and Kathy ▲▼▲ Lesbian Mothers—
both 32—Pennsylvania

"The neighbors we communicate with know we are lesbians. Our closest neighbors, including their teenage children, are fantastic neighbors and very supportive of our family. We have a good relationship with them and get together regularly. We don't know our other neighbors.

"We are out at our daughter's day-care center. We encourage them to ask us questions if they'd like. We also offer occasional literature regarding children from gay or lesbian households. They are very supportive. The teachers have all seemed to respect us equally as parents. They are supportive of differences in our family from most others at the center and recognize our two-mom family. Most teachers so far seem open, willing, and interested in reading material we offer them from gay and lesbian parenting organizations about day care and our families.

"We are out to all of our co-workers and bosses, the day-care center, doctors, extended family, friends, neighbors, and at church. We are not out to clients at work. We don't share personal information with clients in general, as our personal life is none of their business and has no bearing on the work we perform for them. If any of them ever ask, we would tell them the truth, but it very rarely is an issue.

"Our friends are a mixed group of gays and straights. They are people with whom we have things in common, enjoy spending time with, and have similar interests. We meet them at sports, church, day care, and through old friends from college, etc., introducing us to new friends. Our 2-year-old daughter socializes with her grandmothers, cousins, uncles, aunts, friends, and classmates. As a family, we get together with friends from church, day care, old friends made at college, sports, etc., and we spend lots of time with our extended family. We also belong to a group called 'Philadelphia Family Pride.'"

Family 12—Joyce ▲▼▲ Lesbian Mother—52—Hawaii

"When the neighbors found out, they moved from ignorant homophobia to friendly acceptance and, in one case, close support. All my neighbors are straight. When my children were in elementary school, the school knew that I was lesbian. My son wanted that information private in junior high and high school. The school personnel were fine toward my son except in kindergarten. I think his lesbian teacher was paranoid of being outed. Their attitude toward me was a little uncomfortable in some cases, okay in others. Now I'm out to everyone in my life!

"My friends are primarily feminist women—both lesbian and straight. I choose them by mutual values, interests, and trustworthiness. My closest feminist friends I've met working in domestic violence. Other friends I've met through lesbian and gay events and mutual friends. My son's friends are his peers, former classmates and surfing buddies, long-time family friends, his older step-siblings, and his younger half-brother. As a family, we socialize with my son's dad, dad's current girlfriend, and the above-mentioned siblings and their families.

"From the beginning, I told my children the truth of myself. I raised them around openly lesbian and gay, good people and explained that some people were prejudiced, and that they could choose who to tell or not. I do belong to gay/lesbian support groups."

Keola (Joyce's 20-year-old son—Hawaii): "Having a lesbian mother affected me when I was young only because other kids at school were told by their parents or by other kids that gays and lesbians were sick or bad people. I would always hear kids making jokes or putting down gay people, thinking it was funny. I didn't want them to know my mother was a lesbian. I thought they might tell everyone in school, and I would be teased, made fun of, or even hurt. As a young boy, I felt sometimes like I would have to keep my friends away from my mom. They might find out and tell everyone.

"The other kids got even worse as teenagers. Still, they were instilled with feelings of hate towards gays and lesbians by friends and relatives. There was always a joke or insult with the words gay or lesbian. Some guys in my high school were even beaten up because they were gay. Sometimes just being quiet and not doing anything to help them made me feel like I was somehow letting my mother down.

"On the other hand, I didn't know how many girls at school were lesbians. I couldn't tell them apart from most girls. Now I know that there were many lesbian and bi girls that went to my school.

"I think, as I have grown older, my feeling have changed a lot for the better. I've learned to accept my mom's sexuality and not fear the consequences, be they good or bad. I've learned that trying to hide her orientation from friends or others makes me feel like I'm dishonoring her and myself. If my mother's being a lesbian somehow makes people not want to be my friend, then it's their loss, not mine."

Family 13—Roz and Stacy ▲▼▲ Lesbian Mothers— 22 and 23—Arizona

Roz: "I'm not sure if our neighbors know. We haven't actually told them, but I'm sure that they see what goes on in and around our house. We hide nothing from anyone. If they know, there has never been any kind of reaction. The only thing is that the teenager across the street made some derogatory 'faggot' comment to our roommate who is a gay man. We all talked to him, and there hasn't been any trouble since. I plan to tell my daughter's school that we are a lesbian couple when she gets into school.

"Both Stacy and I are out to everyone. We feel there is nothing to hide or be ashamed of. Why shouldn't it be like any 'straight' couple? We are more discreet around certain family members, though. If they can't accept us as we are, then they lose out on knowing and loving some good people.

"My friends are mixed straight, bi, gay, and confused. I choose my personal friends the same way everyone else does—common interests, personality, fun to be with, common views and morals, things like that. Most of my friends, I've met through my roommate or Stacy's jobs. Others I've met at bars, clubs, or they are friends of friends.

"Unfortunately, my daughter Skye doesn't have many children to socialize with. None of our friends have kids, and since she is home with me most of the time, she really doesn't play with other kids all that much right now. Stacy's brother and his wife have a son about 10 months younger than Skye, so she plays with him.

"We don't socialize much as a family either. Occasionally, we have a friend or two come over for dinner or something. We do spend quite a bit of time with Stacy's family, though.

"No, we don't belong to any lesbian support groups, but I wish that we did. We feel that we need to be more active in the community, but when it comes right down to it, we either don't have time, money, or there are more pressing obligations to attend to.

"As Skye is only two and a half, we really can't prepare her for anything like homophobia yet. I feel that if we raise our daughter with self-respect and to know that someone's sexual preference does not affect their job performance, family values, or any other abilities, I think she will do just fine. Hopefully, she'll be as proud of us as we are of her."

Family 14—Carole and Andrea ▲▼▲ Lesbian Mothers— 47 and 44—California

Carole: "I don't know if our neighbors know that we are lesbians. It's never been discussed. They know we all live together as a family. We've never had a problem. We don't socialize much with them, but this may be due in part more to work schedules. My son's school does know, and there's never been a problem. We've been accepted.

"I'm out to my parents and siblings, lesbian friends, and a few other straight friends. I'm not out to professional colleagues or to patients due to the nature of both our positions in the medical profession. There are concerns about homophobia affecting our jobs and referrals. There's no reason to bring any issues of sexuality or sexual orientation into this setting. It is difficult, however, not to be open about my family and significant other.

"My friends are both gay and straight and are chosen by shared interests, ease of communicating, and likability. We meet through work and some outside activities. The children mostly socialize with school friends. As a family, we socialize with our families and other families that are both gay and not gay.

"I don't belong to any support groups now, although I have been in a professional lesbians group and briefly in some lesbian parents groups.

"Fortunately, homophobia has not been an issue for our kids. They know about our family structure and that some people are intolerant of our lifestyle. We try to discuss tolerance in general toward people of all kinds."

Andrea: "I'm also not sure if the neighbors know. It really doesn't come up. Everyone is generally friendly. My daughter's school does not know.

"I am out to my immediate family, parents, aunts, and to other friends in the gay community. I'm also out to a former straight best friend. I'm not out professionally. I'm in a management position in a Catholic hospital, and my partner is an M.D. in the same hospital. I feel there would be consequences for each of us if we were out in our professional setting.

"Our children socialize with friends from school and softball activities. The family gets together with both sides of our families and with other friends who have families.

"I feel we prepare our children to cope with homophobia by talking openly about how people may feel about same sex relationships."

Alix (Carole and Andrea's 13-1/2-year-old daughter—California): "I can't really name all my friends, but they're mostly from school or softball. They don't know about my moms' sexual orientation. I'm not out about this at school, and I don't talk about it with people. I don't know why not. I'm not sure if my grandparents know, but I think so. I've never mentioned it.

"I sometimes hear people call gay people or lesbians fags. I don't say anything. I just deal with it. I try not to let it bother me. I'm never asked any questions about my family or my parents, unless it's about my mom and dad getting divorced.

"I don't go to any support groups for kids of lesbian or gay parents."

Jonathan (Carole and Andrea's 7-year-old son—California): "When someone asks about my family, I say nothing. Some people don't like it when people live together like that. I don't know who says that. I don't say anything back to them. I don't worry about what other kids think about us."

Family 15—Christine ▲▼▲ Lesbian Mother— 60—California

"I have been out at home and at work since 1972, though I am sure there are sometimes people who just don't see. Usually, there seems little reaction at all among the neighbors. Occasionally someone might have a few questions for their own information. During the years my children were growing up, their friends were at our home frequently. I was not aware of any problems with their parents. The children outed me at school and any time someone did not seem to know! I never felt any difference from school personnel. Most I had known for years before coming out, but there seemed no change after that.

"Due to my primary interest in church, my friends are people who have a sense of their own spirituality. We would have similar moral beliefs. Since I am also a registered nurse, some of my friends are of the medical field also, but the religious factor still seems to hold true. They are a mixed group, but with a heavy percentage being gay. I meet them at church, at the hospital, or at conferences relating to one of these. I also do befriend my neighbors, who are usually straight. Both my work areas are with gay and lesbian people. There's little opportunity to meet too many straight people. I enjoy the company of straight people too, when the opportunity arises.

"My kids socialize with their own friends, mostly straight, but they do have some gay friends too, probably about the percent of gays in the area. Now that they are grown, we don't really socialize as a family. During their younger years, between work, school, and raising seven children, socialization was not usually done as a family. We did go on camping trips, etc., as a family, but not usually with others. We had a large enough number with just us.

"As a pastor, belonging to and attending meetings of gay and lesbian support groups simply falls into part of my job description. I also speak to college groups on topics such as 'Homosexuality and the Scriptures' and other related topics.

"In preparing my children to deal with homophobia, I have given them much information, but most of all, I hope I simply provided them with an example at home of all the things a homosexual is not. They've had times when school friends had things to say, but my children were always supportive of me."

Marybeth (Christine's 35-year-old daughter—California): "Most of my friends are foster parents and others who need help with housework or in other ways. We meet mostly at church or at foster-parent meetings or gatherings. They know about my mother's sexual orientation. My in-laws also know about my mom. I only talk to my dad's aunt, and she knows. I have no contact with any other family members. At my church, the choir members know, but I don't think the parish needs to know. I only talk about it if the subject is brought up and in a situation that it seems okay.

"The AIDS issue is a big misconception. The other one is that gay couples don't stay together the same as heterosexual couples do. It makes me angry and want to educate them. How is being gay so different? I've always turned the other cheek or changed the subject. I respond to questions about my mom openly and honestly.

"Do I belong to any support groups? I never heard there was one."

Jean (Christine's 29-year-old daughter, Tara's twin—California): "My friends are my mom, my husband, my day-care parents, my in-laws . . . people I meet through business, school, places I lived, and through my husband. They know about Mom. I'm also out to my extended family, through work, and at church. When and if it comes up, I do talk about my mom's orientation. I am not ashamed of her.

"The misconceptions I've heard about gays and lesbians are that they have sex all the time, and if they have children, they will raise them gay, which in our family is totally not true! I get mad! I don't think it's fair! How do I deal with homophobia? Well, my husband doesn't like it, but when it comes up, I simply tell him that it's none of his business. I get pretty upset. When people ask about our family, I tell them the truth. I am not ashamed, and I answer questions that people have. I don't belong to any support groups. Why should I?"

Tara (Christine's 29-year-old daughter, Jean's twin—California): "I consider my mom, my husband, my sister, my twin, and people who are honest my friends. I meet them at work, church, or through other friends. My close friends know about my mom. I've been out about it at school, with family, and at work. When I go to church, it's at MCC Christ Chapel, and they don't seem to care. I talk about mom's sexual orientation sometimes, but not with people whom I know who have closed minds. The misconceptions that I hear are that when gay people raise children, they will grow up and become gay or lesbian. I don't pay attention to prejudice. I think they all just have closed minds. I do try to educate people who listen. I listen to their point of view. I answer questions the best way I can. I don't have any problems with homosexuality."

Barbara (Christine's 38-year-old daughter—California): "My friends are my husband, two of my sisters, and two people I see often, both child-related. One is the mother of kids I take care of. The other is a lady down the street, but we met through our kids. We've found a lot in common the last couple of years. My friends are usually my kids' friends' parents. Only two of my very close friends know that Mom is a lesbian. As a teenager, I was embarrassed that my family was so different.

"I do day care in my home. The one mother who is my friend knows about Mom. None of the others do. It's none of their business. I really only talk about it with my two close friends, my husband, and our kids.

"People think that gays and lesbians cannot be good parents. I know from my own life that it's not true. I get mad! I get hurt! Mostly, I just try to ignore it. I'd like to tell them that everyone has the right to live their life the way they want to.

"When people ask about our family, I give as much or as little information as I feel they have the right to know.

"I've never heard of any support groups for kids of gay or lesbian parents."

Family 16—Dale ▲▼▲ Lesbian Mother—38—Florida

"When people are unsure who you are, they are insecure, but when you are open and honest, they feel more secure. I live in an apartment complex for elderly and disabled people. My neighbors in my apartment complex and in my neighborhood know I am a lesbian. Ironically, I was mistreated more when I was half in and half out. I answered questions from two 12-year-old boys in my neighborhood and people on the bus. This is my opportunity to open minds. Many of the people who mistreated me, I suspect of being lesbians themselves, even though they are living heterosexual lives. Amazingly, senior citizens handle it well! When I came out, all kinds of sincere friends came forward.

"I suspect everyone at the children's school knows. We do not come out to them, because we fear they may take it out on our children. The school personnel are very professional. I don't think they're used to my aggressively advocating for my children, but that's me as a person, not because I'm a lesbian.

"I'm out to everybody except school and pediatric personnel, but I'm not 'in your face' about it. I'm not out there, because I fear they would take it out on the children. I have experienced many times people who say they're cool about it only to discover them stabbing me in the back later. If someone did that to our children, we would go ballistic! I have agreed with our parents and grandparents not to be published in mainstream newspapers or magazines while they're still alive.

"Our friends are mixed, all races, nationalities, ages, men, women, lesbian, gay, bisexual, and transgendered. We look between the ears, the most important part of a person, not the surface. We choose friends who have common interests as us, who are gentle, kind-hearted, who love children, and are committed to making this a better world for all. We meet our personal friends through volunteering for non-profit gay organizations. In the future, we hope to start a social group for lesbians and gays who are parents.

"Our children socialize with each other. Dylan was best friends with the boy down the road before he moved in with Kat at his grandparents'. As a family, we socialize with relatives. Due to physical challenges, we are 'transportation handicapped.'

"I volunteer for the lesbian/gay hotline one night a week. Due to health reasons, I have taken a leave of absence. Kat and I continue to attend two social groups for older lesbians.

"We have emphasized to our children that frank discussion of sex or sexual orientation is not well tolerated in this culture. We ask them to keep it within the family . . . ask us questions and avoid discussions with outsiders. We don't want to be accused of 'recruiting' others to the gay 'lifestyle.'"

Family 17—Jim ▲▼▲ Gay Father—40—Massachusetts

"Our neighbors almost certainly know. We had an outdoor wedding with gay pride stickers on cars. There has been no apparent reaction. We keep to ourselves naturally, as they do, but all is cordial enough. My partner's ex lives next door and is our really good friend. I am out to everyone, although I don't know if my daughter's school knows. I'm not overly concerned either way. Strangers don't know. I don't announce it upon introductions. When it's relevant, it comes out somehow.

"I choose friends by personality and common interests. My best friends tend to be gay women and a few gay men. My friends are mostly gay but certainly mixed. We've met at my Unitarian Universalist church. My brother is my best friend. He just came out this month, although I assumed he was gay.

"My daughters socialize with individuals from school, the neighborhood, and work. Family socializing is occasional visits to my parents' home, church once in a while, and with our neighbor who was my husband's partner and our best friend.

"I support and am a member of local gay support groups and the Boston Gay Fathers Group.

"The girls and I talk about homophobia from time to time. My life is a good positive role model. My straight and gay friends are good role models as well."

Chelsea (Jim's 13-year-old daughter—Massachusetts): "I mostly meet my friends in school. Only my best, best, close friends know my dad is gay. I'm not out about it. I don't really talk to people about it. With my grandparents and extended family, it never comes up. When I hear someone make a prejudiced comment or joke, I never say anything. When someone asks about my family, I say my mom's remarried, and so is my dad. I don't belong to any support groups."

Family 18—Becka ▲▼▲ Lesbian Mother—44— Washington State

"Some of my neighbors do know I'm a lesbian. They're very supportive. My son's school is also very supportive, almost solicitous. I'm out to everyone who cares. I'm not out to patients who do not ask or who are not gay or lesbian.

"My friends are mixed gay and straight. I choose them according to mutual interests. We meet professionally and through other friends. My son socializes with anyone he wants to. As a family, we socialize with other families with or without children.

"My son and I have open discussions around the issues of homophobia and all kinds of bigotry."

Tommy (Becka's 7-year-old son—Washington State): "I have a lot of friends, boys and girls. I've heard other kids teasing gays and lesbians. I don't say anything back to them. Well, no, I don't worry about what people think about my family. I don't know what I say when they ask about us."

Family 19—Sandra and Kelly ▲▼▲ Lesbian Mothers— 37 and 36—Ohio

Sandra: "I'm sure the neighbors know. They were cool towards us at first, but they're okay now. We haven't said much, except that we were looking for a condo to buy together. I'm more concerned about when we buy a home. Miranda is very open, really too much, to total strangers.

"The teacher and school counselor who know both offered to testify on our behalf in the custody hearing. The teacher came the day of the trial but didn't have to testify because once the female judge talked to the kids, it was decided that we would get custody. I've had some negative stuff from a secretary who refused to send me report cards, etc., when I was not the custodial parent, and even months and months after Miranda and Max lived with us full time. She wouldn't call here or send mail here.

"I am out to my children, my parents, my three brothers and three sisters, my pastor, and all my close friends. I'm not completely out at work, because Kelly and I work in the same department. We are careful, but everyone knows. It's just not talked about by some.

"Kelly is not out to her parents and family, so we aren't really a couple to them. We're sure her mom knows, but Kelly can't step over that line yet. Buying a home may force the issue. Sometimes it's hard.

"I am close to several people at work and one good friend from high school still. Kelly's closest friends are her former partners. We also have some old 'couple' friends. Our friends are gay and straight. We meet them through church and work. The kids' friends are from school.

"We get some gay literature from various organizations. We've thought of joining a Lutheran support group, but we work very long and odd hours. It makes it hard to attend meetings.

"We talk with the kids about homophobia a lot! We went very slowly with Max. My brother said something to make him not look at Kelly and me for weeks. He was upset and angry. He seems to have worked it out."

Miranda (Sandra and Kelly's 17-year-old daughter—Ohio): "I have lots of friends of all ages and walks of life. I meet people in class, at work, at parties, at concerts, through other friends. I just talk to them. I'm out about my mom except for at work, because it is unprofessional and could make work uncomfortable. Mom and I work at the same college. Some people are close enough to know, but work is work, and there are some different issues involved there. Our managers know. I'm out at school to both students and teachers, and I'm out to family.

"My mom went to the church my dad grew up in, and it is difficult for all of us to feel comfortable there. He decided to out my mom to mutual friends from church before my mom had the chance, but none of them were upset about it. They were, however, angry at my dad, because he was trying to turn them against my mom. We are presently looking for a new place to worship.

"I do talk about mom's sexual orientation. If I overhear someone at school saying something derogatory, I jump into the conversation. One of the misconceptions I hear people say is that there is incest in families with gay or lesbian parents. If someone tells a joke about gays or lesbians and it's funny, I laugh. If it is offensive, vicious, or cruel, I say something about it offending me.

"Dealing with homophobia depends on who is homophobic. If it were my boss, I might say that I have gay/lesbian family members but not say who specifically. I'd say please not to say things in my presence. Usually I try to educate people.

"When people ask about my family, I answer them honestly, to the best of my ability.

"I don't attend support group meetings, partly because of school and work. My time is limited, and I don't have a car. I will some day."

Family 20—Melissa and Trish ▲▼▲ Lesbian Mothers—
37 and 39—New Jersey

"Our neighbors know, and everyone is fine. A few people we're not close with, but being lesbian isn't the issue. We just don't connect. Dawn's school is very accepting, mostly. We're out to everyone.

"We have straight and gay friends whom we choose for things we have in common. Most of them are childhood and old friends. The newer ones are our neighbors. Dawn's friends are from school and from the neighborhood. We belong to the Gay and Lesbian Parenting Coalition International (GLPCi), and we get together with people at their functions."

Dawn (Melissa and Trish's 14-year-old daughter—New Jersey): "My friends are people from school basically. I meet them by casually starting a conversation and agreeing to hang out sometime. They know about my moms. I'm out about it at school, and in my family they all know. I do talk about it with people. Some of the prejudices I hear are names like 'fruitcakes,' 'queens,' and 'butches.' When I hear them, I normally cut them short. People's homophobia and their prejudice is a part of my everyday life. When people ask about my family, I answer them. I don't belong to any support groups for kids."

Family 21—Denise and Alisha ▲▼▲ Lesbian Mothers— 33 and 34—New York

Denise: "Most of our neighbors do know that we are lesbians. Most are friendly to us. Since Randi's birth 4 months ago, several neighbors have surprised us with their support. They've bought us gifts and come over to see the baby. I am out to my parents, all friends, most of my extended family, and most of my work colleagues. There's not one particular person I'm not out to. It's more a degree of openness in certain settings, for example at work and with neighbors. We don't hide who we are, but we don't kiss in the yard, for example.

"Most of our friends are gay and straight people we have worked with over the years, people from graduate school, or new friends met through a gay and lesbian parenting group. These are the people we socialize with as a family.

"Zoe is only 4 months old, but she has two 'friends' whose mothers are gay and one 'friend' who is the child of a work friend.

"We belong to a gay and lesbian parenting group in our city called 'Lambda Family Circle.'"

Alisha: "We've never hidden anything from our neighbors, but they've never asked me directly, nor have we made a big announcement. My guess is that some have figured it out, others don't have a clue, others don't pay any attention. Most neighbors have been nice. Others don't acknowledge us, or anybody else for that matter. There's been some confusion now that the baby is here. It seems to have made our family situation very clear to a few neighbors, who are fine, but it's more confusing to others. In fact, within a week or two of bringing our newborn daughter home from the hospital, one neighbor asked if we were baby-sitting the baby. The funny thing is that we got the exact same questions 4 months later!

"I'm out to just about everyone I know including family, friends, and co-workers. When Zoe is in school, they will know too. The only place that I'm rather protective of my personal life, not just sexual orientation, is at work. Most colleagues, including my boss, know about my family. Peripheral staff don't necessarily know, as a protection against the gossip mill or threats to my career. However, I do not lie if asked directly.

"People I choose to be personal friends share my main interests and values. They are honest, loyal, deep friends. I expect a lot from a true friend, therefore, my circle of close, personal friends is small. My larger group of friends is mixed, including men, though I prefer the commonality of experience and outlook of my lesbian friends. We meet at grad school, through other friends, and in the gay and lesbian parenting group.

"Though I feel we have maintained the majority of our friendships, we've gravitated toward our friends, gay and straight, who have children. Right now, Zoe 'socializes' with the babies of our friends.

"We belong to the Lambda Family Circle, a gay and lesbian parenting group.

"We plan to be open and honest with our daughter about our family and to be realistic about the issues and difficulties she may face as a child with two mothers. We will expose her to diverse families and situations so that she can see all sorts of 'different' kinds of families. There are also some great books that we will share with her when she is of an appropriate developmental stage."

Family 22—Werner ▲▼▲ Gay Father—31—Austria

"I do not think that my neighbors know that I am gay, since there's no personal contact between us. I am generally out in public and to my friends and some relatives. There are a lot of people with whom I don't talk about my sexual orientation, however. My friends are both gay and straight. I meet them nearly everywhere . . . at university, on journeys, at work, during outdoor activities like mountain hiking, at parties, and through societies. I also belong to local and national gay and lesbian support groups, and I do attend meetings and activities. Anna plays with her cousins, with the neighborhood kids, and with kids from her kindergarten. As a family, we socialize with our relatives and friends.

"Till now, my daughter at age 3-1/2 has not experienced homophobia. I am preparing her to deal with it in the future by her experience of loving relationships with my partners, who are her friends too. Further, I try to prepare her by reading specific children's literature. I want to talk to her about homophobia in the near future."

▲▼▲

When I was in high school, we had a dress code that prohibited girls from wearing slacks to school. On the day before winter vacation one year, all the girls wore slacks. We figured that if there were enough of us, the administration wouldn't hold us to standards that we believed were outdated. It worked. When we returned to school in January, the dress code had been changed.

Perhaps some day enough gay and lesbian people will be known, and being homosexual will carry no more stigma and no more danger to our children than having blue eyes or black hair, or wearing slacks in school. In the meantime, each of us must make daily decisions about when, where, and how to share sensitive information about ourselves, our parents, and our families in general.

To Be or Not to Be?
Sexual Orientation Is Not a Choice

5

"The journey to the Temple of the Sun requires more than a boat . . . It is a journey on many levels," she said calmly.

> Moyra Caldecott,
> Guardians of the Tall
> Stones

I *was no more than 7 years old. As I sat in yet another doctor's waiting room, eager for my parents and my younger brother to emerge from the door that led to "the office," I entertained myself by reading a popular children's magazine. You know the one I mean.[1] It has stories and jokes and pages where you have to*

. . . sexual orientation is only one aspect of any well-developed personality . . .

find the hidden faces of presidents in the trees and flowers of a barnyard scene, and it has the "Can you find the bunny that doesn't fit with the other bunnies?" page. At first glance, of course, all the bunnies appear to be identical. One must look closely at the minutest of details to find the one that doesn't fit the others' mold. Nearly thirty years later, I would come to realize that I was the errant bunny. Having come to that realization, I also came to locate many, many other "misfit bunnies," and in finding them I now understand that we are not misfits at all. We simply fit a different picture of how bunnies can be.

What creates the "different" bunnies? No one really knows for sure, although many over the years have offered their thoughts and beliefs about it.

WHAT IS SEXUAL ORIENTATION?

The most useful, realistic definition that I have ever seen refers to homosexuality as "an unchosen, lifelong, irreversible state of being in which the individual is attracted sexually to one's own sex, rather than to the opposite sex."[2] This is an explanation that addresses feelings and personal essence, whether or not these emotional responses have ever (or yet) resulted in overt behavior. I was a lesbian long before I acknowledged having crushes on other women. In fact, I consider myself to have been a lesbian long before I had ever heard the word. It is simply who I am and who I have always been.

When we speak of sexual orientation, we are referring to one of four aspects of human sexuality (sexual orientation, biological sex, gender identity, and gender role).[3] It is the aspect that is about who an individual finds sexually attractive. Who turns your head, and who stirs feelings in you? These are automatic physiological and emotional responses to another human being and are not the result of conscious choice or decision making. Homosexuals are sexually and emotionally attracted toward members of their own sex, heterosexuals are attracted to members of the opposite sex, and bisexuals are attracted to members of both sexes.

Biological sex (also referred to as gender), another component of human sexuality, refers to the physical equipment, hormone levels, and the X or Y chromosome combination with which an individual is born. Most people are clearly biologically male or female. On occasion, the genitals are incompletely or incorrectly formed, and a newborn's biological sex is unclear or may even appear to be the opposite of what genetic examination of the X and Y chromosomes indicates. Our physiology, however, is not related to who we find sexually attractive.

A third element of sexuality is a person's gender identity. Gender identity is the psychological feeling of being either male or female. Gender identity may or may not match biological sex, and it is unrelated to sexual orientation. Lesbians are women who are attracted sexually to other women. They feel like women and usually have the biological attributes of women. Gays are men who are attracted sexually to other men. They feel like men and are generally biologically male. Transgendered people, sometimes called transsexuals, have one set of biological characteristics, but feel as if they are really members of the opposite sex. Some transgendered people are gay, lesbian, or bisexual, while some are heterosexual.

The final piece of sexuality is the social sex or gender role that an individual adopts. If a person behaves as males are expected to behave within a given society, s/he has adopted a male social sex or gender role. If the behavior of an individual is that expected of females in the society, s/he has adopted a female social sex or gender role. Some common expectations in our culture are that males are aggressive and wear pants, and females are sensitive and wear dresses.

The social role that an individual plays is not a direct function of biological sex, although it is practically determined by the gender expectations placed on an individual by virtue of the appearance of his or her genitalia at birth. Most biological females take on female roles, and most biological males adopt male roles, but this is not always the case, and sex-role behavior is not necessarily an indication of an individual's sexual orientation. Katharine Hepburn wears pants and is heterosexual. Rock Hudson was known to behave in very stereotypically masculine ways and was gay.

The role that an individual plays in social situations is often a product of socialization in conjunction with an inner sense of comfort in the behaviors. We all know sensitive men and aggressive women, but our responses to individuals who embrace opposite-sex characteristics are telling of our deeply ingrained social expectations. It is usually acceptable to us if a woman wears pants, but what happens when a man chooses to wear a dress? Our culture is more accepting of women and girls who adopt a masculine role than of men or boys who embrace feminine behavior.

Sexual orientation is determined early in life, and it is separate from sexual behavior. An individual can decide to engage in or not engage in any behavior. Even if I have an extraordinarily strong urge to eat ice cream, I am capable of deciding not to. This decision may lead to an uncomfortable sense of deprivation and perhaps even to an intense focus on ice cream, but as a rational being, I am not compelled to act on my drive. Expressing oneself through *behavior*, therefore, is a matter of personal choice. Sexual *orientation* is not a choice and cannot be changed even through intensive effort.[4,5]

Much like being left- or right-handed or ambidextrous, individuals are gay, straight, or bisexual. Earlier generations were taught to write with the right hand regardless of their natural handedness. It can be done, but such instruction does not usually translate into people performing other manual tasks with their nondominant hand. Anyone, gay or straight, can choose to be celibate, though few decide to deprive themselves of satisfying such a basic biological need as sexual gratification. Although a homosexual person can even choose to engage in heterosexual behavior, it would be no more natural or satisfying to the individual than if a heterosexual were to engage in homosexual behavior. We can only choose whether or not to live with integrity as our true selves, or to live in denial of who we really are.

HISTORICAL AND CULTURAL INFLUENCES

Estimates of the incidence of homosexuality range from roughly 2 percent to slightly over 20 percent of the overall population.[6] The wide range in the figures is essentially a product of variation in the research methodology and definitions of homosexuality that have been used by various researchers. There has been little consensus among researchers on the definition of "homosexual." Some include only individuals who have engaged in homosexual behaviors, while others include subjects who report physiological, emotional, and/or erotic feelings for members of their own gender.

The continued stigma attached to homosexuality also affects subjects' responses to researchers' questions.[7] When people are asked about behaviors rather than feelings or ideation, the numbers are low, because we do not always act on all of our urges. In studies in which the researchers are identified with an orthodox or fundamentalist religious or political group, the numbers are low, because most gay and lesbian people fear condemnation. In studies in which subjects were asked to respond orally or without anonymity, the numbers are low, because gays and lesbians have learned that it is generally safer not to out ourselves to strangers. On the other hand, when subjects were treated with respect for their privacy and in studies in which homosexuality is defined as a condition of nondeviant thought, feelings, or behavior, the numbers rise dramatically, coming close to estimates from the animal kingdom and from societies in which same-gender sexuality has been considered to be acceptable. The gay and lesbian community generally uses a figure of ten percent.

Western cultural identification of the nature of homosexuality has been fraught with controversy in recent centuries. Where conservative religious belief has a stronghold, homosexual behavior was, and often continues to be, conceived of as a sinful, unnatural act. Along with societal and scientific advances of the mid-nineteenth century, homosexuality became viewed primarily as a mental disorder and to some extent as a conscious antisocial choice. Either perspective is, of course, damaging to gays and lesbians (and to their children) as individuals and as a group. Modern secular thought regards homosexuality as an inherent psychological orientation. With all of the social, legal, and emotional stresses that plague gay people, it seems illogical to most gays and lesbians that a sizable portion of the dominant society continues to consider sexual orientation to be a choice. We simply do not understand why anyone would imagine that we choose to belong to a group that is so consistently maligned and threatened.

Homosexuality was listed by the American Psychiatric Association as a category of mental illness until the 1972 release of the Association's *DSM-III* (*Diagnostic and Statistical Manual of Mental Disorders: III*),[8] the "bible" of psychiatric diagnosis. In 1975, the American Psychological Association officially supported the change.[9] By 1989, the revised reference in the *DSM-III-R*[10] to homosexuality classified homosexuality as a disorder "only if accompanied by the client's personal distress regarding his or her sexual identity." In the 1994 *DSM-IV*,[11] the most recent edition of the manual, "persistent and marked distress about sexual orientation" constitutes the only reason to diagnose homosexuality as a mental or emotional disorder.

The jury is still out on the nature/nurture debate of modern psychology's attempt to quantify and understand sexual orientation. There seems scant evidence that sexual orientation is largely a result of poor or inappropriate parenting. There are, however, some gay and lesbian individuals who do turn for affection to members of their own gender following traumatic experiences with the opposite sex. Since not all individuals who experience such negativity choose to live as gay people, it does not appear to be very useful to view this as necessarily causative.

I have wondered from time to time whether we aren't perhaps reversing cause and effect. What if a child's inherent homosexuality is reflected in nuances of behavior and attitude that result in a parent–child interaction to which the parent (or teacher, or other authority figure) reacts in ways that are inappropriate to that child's best interest and safety? What if straight Daddy or Mommy is subconsciously threatened by a child who does not adopt heteroaffectional responses to the parent?

To date, only a handful of data have been collected to address the causality of homosexuality, or the causality of heterosexuality for that matter. Scientific study within this decade offers evidence that *suggests* that some gay men possess a gene on the X chromosome, inherited from their mothers, that is related to homosexuality.[12] Other theories regarding hormonal influences on fetuses and differing brain structures in gay and straight men have been suggested, but reliable and reproducible studies are not available. Data collected historically about pregnancies from decades ago or from men who have died of AIDS leave unclear the role played by disease or other medical complications.

THE ROLE OF PARENTS

What we do know is that being raised by gay or lesbian parents does not cause anyone to be homosexual any more than having straight parents causes a child to be heterosexual. The comfort level of discussing and expressing sexual orientation in gay and lesbian homes probably enables homosexual children to express this natural orientation more openly than gay or lesbian children in straight homes, however, so the incidence of gay and lesbian children coming from these homes may appear to be slightly higher due to a higher tolerance of personal differences. A possible genetic link to male homosexuality may also account for slightly increased numbers of sons of gay fathers who are themselves gay, although the clearest suggestion of genetic causality comes from a 1993 study of chromosomal material that can only be inherited from one's mother.[13] There is generally no difference in the psychosexual development of children based upon parental sexual orientation. The largest correlation of relatives sharing homosexual traits occurs between siblings, especially twins, not between parents and children.[14]

As noted earlier, both social learning and psychoanalytic theories assume that children need two opposite gender parents in order to establish healthy gender identity and sexual behavior.[15,16] However, direct study of the children of lesbian mothers in comparison to the children of single, straight mothers indicates that there is no difference in the children's development of gender identity or gender-role behavior. The lesbian mothers tended to be more flexible in their choices of toys for their children, but children from both home environments chose similar toys, with boys being more likely to use gender-specific toys than girls.[17]

When there is no father in the home, lesbian mothers are more likely than straight mothers to provide male role models for their children. However, children do not necessarily model their gender role behavior on that of their parents or other adults. Children naturally turn to their peers as primary examples of acceptable gender behavior and are more likely to follow peer examples than adult role modeling.[18,19]

Some children of gay fathers or lesbian mothers express concern that they may themselves grow up to be homosexual. In general, these young people are fearful that they will be targets for other people's homophobia. They may have experienced difficulty in coming out to peers about their parents and are concerned about not being accepted if they are also gay or lesbian.[20,21] The majority of children whose responses are included in this study, as well as the preponderance of information available in the literature, indicate that sons and daughters of homosexual parents feel freer to explore their own feelings than do children of straight parents. The children of gay fathers and lesbian mothers understand that there are many possible healthy expressions of sexuality, and they are usually more concerned with the personality and personal goodness of a potential mate than they are with their partner's gender. Although most are straight, they do not consider any one sexual orientation to be superior to any other.[22,23]

PERSONAL EFFECTS

Individuals generally become aware of their sexual orientation quite early in life. When they enter adolescence and begin to realize an interest in sex and sexuality, most individuals can identify whether they are attracted to boys, girls, or both. Most gays and lesbians recognize their affinity to same-gender individuals by adolescence or in their early adulthood.[24] Some say that they were aware, at least of being "different" from their peers, by the age of three or four.

As noted earlier, 98 percent of gay and lesbian people were raised by straight parents, and the children of gay and lesbian parents follow roughly the same percentages regarding sexual orientation as the children of straight parents.[25,26] In order for individuals to accept their own sexual orientation, whether homosexual or not, they must reach a level of personal congruence between the way they view and value themselves and the way they believe other people view and value them.[27] How soon gay or lesbian people come out after realizing their sexual orientation depends largely on the degree of acceptance they expect to find for homosexuality in their social environment. Some are so homophobic themselves, or fear that their loved ones will be, that it may take years or decades to acknowledge their true sexual orientation.

Children who prefer to play with opposite-gender toys or to engage in opposite-gender activities are expressing a natural personal preference. Not all tomboys grow up to be lesbians, and a boy who plays with dolls may be gay, or he may become a straight man who knows how to be sensitive and nurturing. Many gay men and lesbians played very happily with gender-"appropriate" toys as children and continue to engage in gender-congruent activities as adults. Gender-specific play is probably more accurately viewed as a reflection of emotional temperament and social interest than of sexual orientation per se.

While none of us grows up in a vacuum, a characteristic as basic and inherent as sexual orientation is not susceptible to influence by social or other environmental factors. We may be capable of modifying our behavioral expression of our sexuality, but sexual orientation is immutable. In reality, sexual orientation is only one aspect of any well-developed personality, and it is rarely given much emphasis when people describe themselves.

The parents and children below discuss the varying effects that being gay or lesbian has had on their lives. For some it has created difficulties, for some it has not. All of them accept it as part of their identity and have developed some degree of strength from being different from the norm. For most of these families, the parents' homosexuality has been more of an issue for outsiders than it has for family members.

Family 1—Jeremy ▲▼▲ Gay Father—27—New York

"My earliest memory of anything to do with my sexuality was when I was about 5 years old. My father caught me in his room in front of the full-length mirror with a towel wrapped around my head. I spun around imagining I was "Diana" changing into Wonder Woman. My relationship with my father went downhill from there. Even though I have aunts and uncles on both sides of the family, I seem to have been the only one who turned out gay. I was one of those children who knew I was gay but never had the word. The rest of the world knew I was gay and had the word. I suppose every family should have a pioneer to be proud of.

"As parents, we are in a unique and frightening position. There is a population out there who would kill us and take our children merely because we express a sexual orientation that differs from the norm. I am a single, gay, Jewish, white male raising a black adopted son. That statement alone is enough to make people see red across numerous socioeconomic and cultural lines."

Family 2—Alan ▲▼▲ Gay Father—46—Massachusetts

"I always felt I was different as a child, but realization after many years of denial came when I was an adult over 40 years old. For years I was involved in drinking, and coming back from a Christmas party in 1992, I was pulled over by the State Police for drunk driving. Margaret had called them. She went to pick up our daughter and told the desk sergeant to leave me in jail. I can honestly say that was a literally sobering experience for me. Three months later, Margaret and I had the most wonderful dialogue in the 18 years of our marriage. We talked until 3 o'clock in the morning. She asked me if I were gay. I told her, 'Yes, I think I am. Let us talk about this.' She said there was no problem with this, because we can still raise the kids and live in the same house, but after the children are grown and out on their own, we will get a divorce. We will always have each other because we have known each other for more than half of our lifetimes. Margaret confessed afterwards that she watched the 'Joan Rivers Show,' 'Oprah,' and 'Phil Donahue' where they had one partner coming out to a spouse or a spouse that was gay, and it was scenarios of this nature that got her thinking about me and my self-destructive behavior. We are now and always will be the absolute best of friends, just like we were in the beginning of our relationship years ago.

"The children know that when the bedroom door is shut, they must knock first. I don't hide my sexuality or flaunt it either. I have my wife and my dates. I'm not looking for a long-term relationship."

Margaret (straight mother . . . married to Alan—44—Massachusetts): "I knew I was straight in my early teens. Now I am with my husband and with my [straight male] significant other. Our sexuality is neither hidden nor blatantly flaunted."

Brett (Alan and Margaret's 15-year-old daughter—Massachusetts): "I'm straight. I like guys, and I'm comfortable with who I am. My parents' sexuality doesn't affect me any.

"I am a teenager, a dancer, a regression person, a person who dyes her hair blue, green, red, and purple, a punk rocker, an individualist. I like going to Coffee Kingdom, listening to Chuckle Head, Green Day, Fudge Tunnel, Marilyn Manson, Alice in Chains, and skateboarding and playing the electric guitar.

"What do I like about myself? I like my eyebrows. They're perfect. And I like my sense of humor, my good imagination, and my kind personality. I don't like that sometimes I'm a bit of a hypocrite. Also, I'm kind of shy, but I don't dislike that much.

"Sometimes I worry what other people think about my family."

Joey (Alan and Margaret's 7-year-old son—Massachusetts): "I'm a person. My hobbies are arrowhead collecting and bottle caps. What's special about me is I have two beauty marks. Sometimes I wish I could change into a girl."

Family 3—Rob ▲▼▲ Gay Father—53—California

"At some level, I knew it even as a child. My sexual orientation is perceived as the reason for the separation from my wife. In actuality, that is only one of the reasons."

Family 4—Samantha ▲▼▲ Lesbian Mother—33—Vermont

"I have been aware all of my life. I became definite over the last 10 years. My ex-partner struggled with this, and apparently has joined the other team! I was in a committed, monogamous relationship for 7 years until our break-up. Now I'm single. How often does a woman make a commitment to another woman, have a child, and then leave her for a man? Talk about identity confusion! I now know about lesbian divorce!"

Family 5—Linda and Donna ▲▼▲ Lesbian Mothers— 40 and 49—Utah

"I [Linda] have known ever since I was a child, but I didn't really come out until my late twenties. Our sexuality affects our children in that we socialize primarily with lesbians and lesbian couples. Since becoming a parent, I have been monogamous with Donna."

Family 6—Leah and Ali ▲▼▲ Lesbian Mothers— 40 and 42—Texas

Leah: "I was aware as young as 9 or 10 years of age that I was different and had attractions to girls and women. My first sexual experience with a woman was at age seventeen."

Ali: "I 'discovered' I am a lesbian during and after college.

"We hug and kiss, and usually when Jacob sees this, he says either, 'Happy home' or 'Happy home hug.'

"We have continued to remain in a committed, monogamous relationship and will celebrate 18 years in June."

Family 7—Lydia and Sari ▲▼▲ Lesbian Mothers— 43 and 42—California

Lydia: "I've always been attracted to both men and women; I just didn't know the name for it. When I was in college, two women moved into a guest cottage on the property where I was living. They were both young and funny and bright and attractive, and there was never a question in my mind as to what their relationship was. As I got to know them, and they became more comfortable and expressive around me, I had the opportunity to observe firsthand a healthy, loving, alternative relationship, and it made it very easy and comfortable for me to act on feelings I had for women.

"We have been in a monogamous relationship for 10-plus years. It has had its ups and downs, but we have chosen to stay together and work through the difficult times because we love one another. We have both learned and grown tremendously in this time. I believe we've grown even more during the time we've been parents. We have to be more responsible for our relationship. It is the foundation of our children's lives."

Sari: "I believe that my childhood abuse issues left me with a profound mistrust of men in general, and so my rescue was found in women. I believe that if a gentle, loving, and nurturing man had entered my life before Lydia, my love and life would have taken a different course. Actually, on some level, I am attracted to men but feel much more comfortable on a spiritual level with women. Overall, my sexuality has been on the back burner for most of my adult life. One day, I hope that will change. I am not too sure how, though I am hopeful."

Family 8—Carol and Rose ▲▼▲ Lesbian Mothers— 41 and 31—Kansas

Carol: "I've known as long as I can remember. It finally hit me in junior high that not everyone was like this, and it wasn't the socially acceptable orientation. I stopped feeling bad about it in high school.

"Since becoming parents, the relationship is harder, but I think I've gotten stronger. I've always been with Rose since becoming a parent. We continue to show affection to each other, even when Drew's there."

Family 9—Jenny and Ann ▲▼▲ Lesbian Mothers— 33 and 38—Illinois

Jenny: "As a child growing up, I was always the prissy little one. I knew I was a girl, and I was proud of it. I guess I always knew that I liked boys. I never even considered the alternative, not even in play. I became sexually active when I was 16 years old. I was attracted exclusively to men, until I met Ann. She sparked my curiosity, and I was extremely attracted to her. Up until that point in my life, I had never contemplated a sexual relationship with another female. I have been in a monogamous lesbian relationship now for 12 years, so I guess I discovered my current sexual orientation when I discovered Ann."

Ann: "I have a bit of a different story: I was always the 'tomboy' in my family. I remember about the age of five, wearing a dress to an Easter party and feeling quite out of place. I begged my mother for a suit and tie like my older brother. As a youngster, I never allowed my hair to grow long, and whenever my mother insisted that I wear a dress, I would wear jeans beneath it. I remember having a crush on a neighbor girl when I was 9 years old. By the age of thirteen, I was positive that God had made a terrible mistake. I wore Ace bandages on my chest in an attempt to keep my breasts from growing. At the age of seventeen, I 'tried' sex with a male. The act made me feel like a queer. That was my one and only attempt at a 'normal' life. I always knew I was different, but that experience confirmed the fact that I was indeed a lesbian.

"Our sexuality is expressed openly in our household. We don't lie or try to hide things from our girls. We focus on the pure love that is shared by two consenting adults.

"I was married to Jo's father until Jo was 17 months old. Since that time we have been committed to our relationship together. Cait is the product of lesbian love!"

Jo (Jenny and Ann's 13-year-old daughter—Illinois): "I am heterosexual. I feel just fine and dandy about that. My moms' sexuality has no effect on mine. I am my own person.

"I am a girl who is nice. I am thirteen, and I go to middle school. I'm pretty. I like dance, music (all kinds), and I like to go to the mall. I love art! What I like about myself is that I'm nice to everyone and kind, and I have great eyes, and I look good with my new 'Friends' haircut. I don't like that I'm kinda chubby, I think.

"I don't worry about what other people think about me or my family."

Family 10—Dee and Sherry ▲▼▲ Lesbian Mothers— 31 and 46—California

Dee: "I was twenty-six when I suddenly and finally put the pieces together and realized I was a lesbian. Even before I had had any relationships with women, I felt I finally understood who I was, and it made me feel very strong and happy.

"The boys (ages 17 and 15) know we are sexual, though we don't discuss it unless they ask questions. One of them has gotten into our sex toys once that we know of . . . We are very affectionate with each other, and the boys see that. We hold hands in the car, and we kiss and hug a lot at home. I've been in this relationship since I've been a parent."

Sherry: "I discovered I was a lesbian when I went to college at age eighteen. I started having dreams about my roommate. I went to a supportive counselor (pre-Stonewall), with whom I fell in love.

Since I've been a parent I was first with my husband for the first 6 years. Then for 2 years I had a lover who did not live with us. I was single for about a year, and then I had another lover who lived with us and was very involved with the kids. My next lover of 2 years did not live with us or like kids. I was single again for a year. Since then, I've been with Dee."

Family 11—Liz and Kathy ▲▼▲ Lesbian Mothers— both 32—Pennsylvania

Liz: "The summer before college, I discovered a number of people I knew and liked were lesbians, and I finally realized I was attracted to women in the same way they were.

"I'm not sure what role our sexuality plays in the family's life, as it's just such an integral part of our family. I guess the effect is in the fact that our 2-year-old daughter plays with two moms in the doll house at school, and we have to spend a little more time explaining our family and wondering what the reaction will be to our doctors, teachers, parents, etc., than typical heterosexual couples do.

"We have been in a committed, monogamous, long-term loving relationship for 10-1/2 years, the last two of which we have also been parents."

Family 12—Joyce ▲▼▲ Lesbian Mother—52—Hawaii

"At age thirty, I fell in love with an old college friend who'd come to visit during the time my marriage was ending. My daughter was four at that time. My son was not yet born. I've had several sweethearts over the years. The kids always knew, but never were we sexual in front of them. They saw hugs and kisses, yes, but nothing more.

"I had one off and on, increasingly bad relationship with the woman I came out with. We lived together with my daughter for about 6 months early on, then for 9 months with my son at the bitter end, when he was ten. Another woman sweetheart lived with my son and me when he was six for a year, and another lived with us for 9 months when he was fourteen. He liked them all. I've dated a few other women over the years.

Keola (Joyce's 20-year-old son—Hawaii): "My mother's being a lesbian has shown me there are many different paths of sexuality, and they are all wonderful. I myself am straight, and it's right for me. Sometimes when I was younger, I wondered if I would be gay because my mother was a lesbian. As I got older, I found that I had sexual feelings for girls and not boys. So, in my personal experience, I found my own sexual path knowing that all the other options were there, and they are all fine and dandy."

Family 13—Roz and Stacy ▲▼▲ Lesbian Mothers— 22 and 23—Arizona

Roz: "I was fourteen, Stacy was fifteen. We were each other's first same-sex partner. I think Stacy had been slightly aware way before fifteen, though. I was very confused. I had been with guys before her.
"We plan to raise Skye to be open to anyone and everyone, no matter what sex, sexual preference, race, color, religious background, or anything else. As far as I see it, Having same-sex parents is a sort of a gift, a blessing. It opens you up to help you grow. As far as being parents, our sexuality doesn't matter."

Family 14—Carole and Andrea ▲▼▲ Lesbian Mothers— 47 and 44—California

Carole: "I discovered I was a lesbian in postgraduate school. I have a lesbian sister and discussed sexuality with her. That increased my awareness in myself. Interestingly, a number of lesbian women sought me out as a friend before I was aware of my own orientation. I think being gay has limited our socializing as parents and our integrating our personal and professional lives. Andrea and I have been together continuously since I became a parent."

Andrea "While going through a difficult time in my marriage, the opportunity presented itself to become involved with a member of the same sex. Carole and I are out to a limited number of friends, and we are not out at work. This limits socializing in a professional setting.

"I was married during my daughter's first year of life. Otherwise, we have been together since my daughter was a year and a half old."

Alix (Carole and Andrea's 13-1/2-year-old daughter—California): "I'm Alix. The things I'm interested in are softball, going to the movies, and being with my friends. I like that I'm athletic. I don't like that I can be too shy at times. I don't really ever worry about what other people think about me or my family.

"I don't know about my own sexual orientation. I haven't thought about it, but I find a lot of guys cute. I feel fine about it. My moms' sexuality has nothing to do with mine. I'm not allowed to date yet anyway."

Jonathan (Carole and Andrea's 7-year-old son—California): "I'm a smart little boy. My hobbies are being a couch potato and watching my sister play Nintendo. I don't know what's special about me, but there's nothing I would change. I don't know if I'm gay or not."

Family 15—Christine ▲▼▲ Lesbian Mother—
60—California

"I was about 37 years old and involved in classes to become a registered nurse, studying to be able to afford a divorce and raise my seven children. At one psych hospital, the instructor said to stay away from a particular patient because she was a lesbian. I was CURIOUS about this person, and of course, I made a beeline to meet her.

"Even now, some of my children express they 'don't understand' my sexuality, though they have all expressed a desire that I be happy. Some are quite comfortable with my lifestyle. ALL will attend occasional special events involving me at my Metropolitan Community Church. They attended Sunday schools at a Metropolitan Community Church for a number of years."

Marybeth (Christine's 35-year-old daughter—California): "I am a parent and foster parent, so kids are one of my main interests. I also love music, choir, and needlecraft. I like that I want to help others. I am mostly independent and don't need someone else to make me happy. Because I like to help others and make them happy, I sometimes put myself last.

"I believe that I am heterosexual. I mostly feel fantastic about it, but having sex with my husband is few and far between. My mom's sexual orientation has very little to do with mine. I am what I am."

Jean (Christine's 29-year-old daughter, Tara's twin—California): "I'm the youngest child of seven kids, a twin. I enjoy children, motorcycle riding, and reading. I'm a good mom and wife. I also am open-minded and caring. I'd like to change my weight. I don't worry about what others think about me or my family.

"I am totally 100 percent straight. I love having sex with my husband, and simply, it's no one's business! What effect does Mom's sexuality have on mine? None."

Tara (Christine's 29-year-old daughter, Jean's twin—California): "I am my mother's sixth child, the older of a set of twins. I love spending time with my husband, writing, spending time doing things around the house, and children. I like that I'm open and honest, though I dislike that I'm too much so. I love to learn, and I like my looks most of the time. I dislike that I'm a slow learner and that I have low self-esteem.

"I questioned my sexuality once, but that's all it was. I think all people do."

Barbara (Christine's 38-year-old daughter—California): "I am Barbara, wife, mother, friend, daycare provider, sister, and daughter. The order of these isn't always the same. I enjoy kids, cooking, needlepoint, romance novels, and the beach, the ocean. I'm a kind person with a big heart. I care about people. I'm good with kids, a great cook, and I do a good job with my needlepoint projects. I don't listen very well, and I tend to make bad snap judgments. I doubt myself. My self-confidence isn't always very strong. Sometimes I do worry about what people think about me or my family.

"I wondered A LOT if I was going to grow up and be a lesbian. I went out of my way to prove that I wasn't. I slept around with men quite a bit to try to prove to myself that I was 'normal.' Now I know I'm heterosexual, and I'm comfortable with that. It's right for me."

Family 16—Dale and Kat ▲▼▲ Lesbian Mothers— 38 and 37—Florida

Dale: "I knew I was 'different' since I was 4 years old. Even my brothers picked up on it saying, 'She's different.' I asked, 'How am I different?' They answered, 'We don't know how you're different, but we know you're different.' When I was 12 years old, I knew I loved women when I identified with the man kissing the woman rather than the other way around when I watched movies. Also, when I was twelve, my neighbor caught me ogling his wife.

Kat and I casually hug and kiss in front of the children. We have shared age-appropriate books on gay and straight sexuality with the children. We answer every question—no more, no less.

We are committed for a lifetime, because we want to 'drop roots.' It takes time to achieve true intimacy. In our opinion, we feel children should not see an endless parade of lovers. How would they learn trust and intimacy?"

Kat: "I am still questioning my sexual orientation. I was always a 'tomboy,' but I was attracted to men. I'm very open and decided I needed a change! I've always been interested in emotionally strong women."

Family 17—Jim ▲▼▲ Gay Father—40—Massachusetts

"I always knew I was gay. I came out at age 37. I met Donald 2 weeks after coming out and have been with him for the 3 years since. We do everything any other family would do."

Chelsea (Jim's 13-year-old daughter—Massachusetts): "I love soccer and being with my friends. I like to listen to music in my room, and I like to write. I like that I'm really good at soccer, and I have a great sense of humor, at least that's what my friends say. I don't like that I can be convinced very easily.

"I'm normal, I guess, and that feels fine. My parents' sexuality has no effect on mine."

Family 18—Becka ▲▼▲ Lesbian Mother—44— Washington State

"I 'discovered' I was a lesbian on my 21st birthday. A friend showed me. My sexuality is my business. My orientation is my family's business. Since my son was born 7 years ago, I've had two divorces."

Tommy (Becka's 7-year-old son—Washington State): "I'm a kid. I like to play and watch sports, play games, play with my friends, and I like school. I'd like to be eighteen or nineteen, so I could play college football. What's special about me is that I was born under a lucky star.

"I know that being gay or lesbian means a woman is married to a woman, and a man is married to a man. I don't think I'm gay."

Family 19—Sandra and Kelly ▲▼▲ Lesbian Mothers—37 and 36—Ohio

Sandra: "I was about 20 years old and pregnant with Miranda, but I had such a negative view of being gay that I thought those things aren't me. I didn't act on my feelings for about fourteen years. Kelly was about twenty-four when she first fell in love with another woman.

"I was married to Miranda and Max's father and in only that relationship until I met Kelly about 3 years ago."

Miranda (Sandra and Kelly's 17-year-old daughter—Ohio): "I love to sing and dance, and I write poetry. I want to study psychology and possibly become a psychologist. I love talking to people. People fascinate me. I like that I am loving and compassionate, that I am intelligent, patient, fun, understanding, sexy, and that I am genuine. I don't like that I procrastinate, but who doesn't? I also dislike that I'm forgetful and too trusting. My confidence fluctuates, and I have trouble saving money.

"I worry about what people think of me sometimes, but I definitely do not worry about what people think of my family. I have doubts about myself, but I know for sure that my immediate family members, who I live with, are *wonderful* people!!

"I call myself bisexual. I feel it's too early to limit my options. I'm young enough that I'm still sorting all of that out. My 15-year-old brother is straight. I'm unsure how I feel about my sexual orientation. I think for me, my attraction goes past sex, race, height, weight, etc. I am looking for someone that I connect with, someone I can talk to, whom I can respect, whom I can spend time with and be myself with. Whether I will fall in love with a male or female does not matter.

"I had had dreams about girls and boys, and when my mom came out to me, I felt relieved. It opened the door. I felt I could ask questions. She doesn't tell me I have to choose. It is okay for me to be whatever I want. My mom loves me no matter what."

Family 20—Melissa and Trish ▲▼▲ Lesbian Mothers— 37 and 39—New Jersey

Melissa: "I probably knew since I was small, but after Dawn was born, I knew for sure. During my pregnancy, I accepted my being lesbian.

"Since Dawn was born, I've had three relationships of a couple of years each. My current relationship with Trish has been for almost 5 years."

Dawn (Melissa and Trish's 14-year-old daughter—New Jersey): "Who am I? I'm still searching for the answer. I like drama and reading, and I like my basically friendly nature. I don't like my physical weight. I try not to worry about what people think about me or my family. I'm very open.

"I'm bisexual, maybe. I have no problem with it. My parents' sexuality has no effect on mine."

Family 21—Denise and Alisha ▲▼▲ Lesbian Mothers— 33 and 34—New York

Denise: "I began liking girls in eighth grade, but I didn't realize it and come out until age twenty. Probably the biggest impact will be on Zoe's school life once she gets older. Since becoming a parent, I'm still with Alisha!"

Alisha: "It took me from about age nineteen when I first began to explore my sexuality to about age twenty-five when I met my current partner to become comfortable with being a lesbian and to cope with my family. Denise and I have grown closer in our mutual effort to provide care for our daughter. We will be honest with our daughter about who we are."

Family 22—Werner ▲▼▲ Gay Father, 31—Austria

"In retrospect, I discovered my sexual orientation in early childhood. I've been aware of being gay since puberty. Then I learned my capability to love a female person too, although I define myself as gay. My sexual orientation plays a natural role in our family life. It is clear to my daughter, who until now has not been affected by others. I had a loving relationship with Anna's mother, Katrina, until I was widowed. After a long time of mourning, I had several short-term relationships with men. Now I am in a several months' long relationship with Erich.

"Anna knows just what she asks for about sex and sexuality. Up till now, she knows about loving relationships (gay and straight). Childbearing is a usual question now, but she doesn't ask about sexual activities apart from kissing. Being out isn't a problem. I never tried to hide it. I have come out to my daughter by everyday life since her early childhood, so it's natural to her. She does not understand homophobia yet. If Anna were ever to come out to me as a lesbian, I would be somehow happy, but I wouldn't mind for her to come out as straight. In other words, essentially whatever she is will be okay."

▲▼▲

Sex and the nature of sexual orientation is such a hot-button issue in our culture that one would expect it to have been studied and analyzed more, perhaps, than any other topic. It is, however, also a largely taboo subject, and so factual information is scant.

The personal anecdotes of these families about the effects of parental homosexuality on their lives is quite telling. Despite the apparently widespread belief that gay men and lesbians are not appropriate role models for children, the families headed by gay and lesbian parents seem to be doing a fine job of raising well-adjusted children. The children are mostly comfortable with their own developing sexuality, and almost all of them feel quite free to grow into whomever they naturally feel they are. Their primary concern about their parents is that the adults feel happy and satisfied.

For the adults, coming out in a homophobic world presented many challenges and difficulties from which they would like to shield their children. For the children, their unique families are allowing them to see beyond stereotypes in themselves and in others and to understand that sexuality is only one aspect of anyone's being. It is striking to me that the only true source of pain for children of homosexual parents stems from the intolerance of outsiders.

God and Goddess ▲▼▲ Religion and Spirituality in Gay and Lesbian Families

6

In order to take control of our lives and accomplish something of lasting value, sooner or later we need to learn to Believe. We don't need to shift our responsibilities onto the shoulders of some deified Spiritual Superman, or sit around and wait for Fate to come knocking at the door. We simply need to believe in the power that's within us, and use it.

Benjamin Hoff,
The Tao of Pooh

*I*t was late autumn, but in south Florida, the insects were biting. The 4-year-old felt a sudden sting in his right heel, but he was having

There are now religious organizations that . . . recognize the divinity in all human life . . . (Steven Jay Porus, Photographer.)

fun and playing hard, so he just ignored it. He let the shock and the pain subside and continued to run and shout and laugh with his friends. That night, after "Batman," and after macaroni and cheese, and after all the bubbles had drained from the bathtub, he folded his hands together and thanked God for his day. He asked for blessings for his parents and his grandparents, and he listed his friends as well, trying to think of as many names as possible in order to forestall the in-evitability of lights out. The boy's mom sensed a hesitation in his prayers, and she thought to say, "You know, it's okay to ask for something for yourself if you want." The boy thought for just a moment before he challenged the Almighty with, "Hey, God! What's the deal with the fire ants?"

Good question. What's the deal with being bitten in the heel by tiny, hidden creatures that leave you stinging? What's the deal with making the world appear to be lush and nurtur-ing and safe, only to have it turn around and cause pain in some of your most sensitive places? Most of us were taught from early childhood that there is a God who will protect us, sustain us, listen to our sorrows, and heal our wounds. We learned that God's home was a safe haven for us in times of trouble as well as in times of joy. It was years later, when we came to understand that we loved people of our own gender, that we began to learn that in God's home and in God's name, we might well be bitten in the heel by tiny, hidden creatures that left us stinging.

Many feel the sting and conclude there is no God. Others remain confused, and they feel separated from their own faith. Still others examine the stinging foot and ask how to in-tegrate this new experience into their lives. Harold S. Kush-ner, in *When Bad Things Happen to Good People*,[1] uses the story of Job to present us with the concept that God does not set out to cause us pain, but He does ask us to challenge ourselves to use our pain for growth. It's easy to see why gay men and les-bians choose to leave the now-painful religious institutions of our childhood. It is somewhat harder to understand the drive behind resolving the conflict between our negative experiences of organized religion and our personal senses of spiritual integrity.

Even for those adults, whatever their sexual orientation, for whom the struggle to define an acceptable expression of spirituality is relegated to one of life's back burners, the presence of children in their lives forces the issue. When one's children begin to ask about God, parents discover that they need to get answers. For gay and lesbian parents, finding answers that comfort rather than disquiet their children and themselves is often a challenging proposition. How do you reconcile mainstream religion's animosity toward you and your family while holding true to your inner knowing that who you are is good? What *is* the deal with the fire ants? What do they help us to know about ourselves, and what can they encourage us to learn about God?

THE ORIGIN OF THE SPECIOUS

Religious fundamentalists of all denominations adhere to a definition of homosexuality as a perversion of sinful and unnatural *actions*. Many people of the cloth continue to preach the inevitability of God's wrath on sexually active gay and lesbian people, and they instruct their homosexual followers to heal their sins through self-control and self-condemnation. Celibacy is a very valid choice for an individual to make for him or herself whether for spiritual or other purposes. For an outside entity to impose such constriction on anyone can hardly be construed as a sign of acceptance.

Gay and lesbian people are lay members of religious institutions, and they are members of the clergy. Rose Mary Denman is a lesbian whose personal struggle illustrates the conundrum which many religious homosexuals face. The Reverend Ms. Denman was serving in the United Methodist Church when that body passed a rule that homosexuals could not be ordained ministers. Her personal and professional challenge loomed large. How could she preach truthfulness to her congregation while hiding behind the lie of the closet? She was brought to trial by the Church on August 24, 1987, though not for being incapable as a minister. She had served as an exemplary minister. The charge against her was simply that she was a lesbian, which now made her ministry a violation of Church law. She was found guilty by the United Methodist Church, and subsequently transferred to the Universalist-Unitarian Church, where her sexual orientation did not exclude her from the clergy.[2]

Traditional Christianity and Judaism have purported to "hate the sin but love the sinner." Many faithful gay and lesbian followers of Judeo-Christian doctrine have struggled with the question, "Is lying more or less of a sin than homosexuality?"[3,4] We are taught to be truthful. We are taught that being gay or lesbian is unnatural, yet we know that it is natural for us. If we live as gay people, we commit one transgression. If we hide our sexual orientation, we are in essence living a lie. However, most Jews and Christians seem to end their religious studies in early adolescence, so perhaps we do not have an adult's understanding of our religious heritages. Like children who are learning that the tooth fairy is not real, maybe we should take another look at the stories we have been raised to believe.

Large numbers of mainstream Methodists, Presbyterians, Lutherans, Mormons, Baptists, Catholics, Episcopalians, Jews, and followers of other faiths and denominations are taught that the book of Leviticus calls homosexuality "an abomination," and the story of Sodom and Gomorrah is commonly interpreted as a condemnation of same-gender sex. Both lessons are widely taught, and both are lessons taken out of context.

The prohibition against men sleeping with each other as they would with a woman appears along side of and on par with the admonition not to mix wool and linen and the instruction to stone one's unruly son in the town square. Are our religious institutions preaching selective piety? Within the context of the historical era in which the laws were recorded, Judaism was replacing the local pagan faith of the Middle East, and the new religion sought to replace ritual temple sex with other forms of worship. The prohibition is more likely to be a warning against worshipping as the locals did than an interdiction against sexual expression of love between committed partners.[5]

In drawing lessons from the tale of the destruction of Sodom and Gomorrah, why are we not taught to abhor the rape of a young girl along with condemning the implication of same-gender sex? Are our religious tenets again selective? Is the sin of the cities not more accurately one of inhospitality for the townsmen's failure to welcome Lot's visitors within their gates?[6]

The Bible was not always interpreted to view homosexuality negatively. During the early centuries of Christianity, the Church does not seem to have condemned homosexuality. Same-gender sexual behavior was apparently an accepted alternative in many circles, particularly in more urban centers. The beginning of its denigration seems to have coincided with intolerance toward Europe's Jews and witches during the Dark Ages preceding the Renaissance.[7]

MODERN TIMES

There are now religious organizations that open their doors to provide spiritual opportunities for gay and lesbian worshippers and their loved ones. Some, such as mainstream Catholicism, welcome us if we remain celibate or if we agree to be "cured." Some welcome us, even celebrate us, as we are. They recognize the divinity in all human life, and they offer inclusive interpretations of liturgy and ritual. *Dignity* is a grassroots movement from the gay community which seeks to work within the Catholic Church to gain acceptance of out gay men and lesbians as Catholics in good standing and as clergy. *Affirmation* is the gay and lesbian movement of the Methodist Church.

Churches and synagogues that specifically serve the gay and lesbian community are becoming widespread. Branch congregations of the Metropolitan Community Church (MCC) are in numerous cities across the country. Los Angeles is home to two synagogues that officially serve gays, lesbians, and their families and friends, and both are members of the Reform movement's Union of American Hebrew Congregations.[8] Many other gay-affirming and supporting Jewish congregations exist around the country. Local support groups, such as *Response* of Valley Beth Shalom, a Conservative Synagogue in Encino, California, and *Not Your Ordinary Christian Women's Support Group* in Northern California, are also becoming more common.

The Reform and Reconstructionist movements of the Jewish community, including their rabbis and lay leaders as well as grassroots community members, have officially endorsed the concept of legalizing civil marriage for same-gender couples. Reform rabbis are now formally supported in choosing to perform gay and lesbian "commitment" ceremonies. Clergy of many Christian denominations have officiated at "holy union" and "commitment" ceremonies for same-gender couples. Some have done so with the blessing of their parent organizations. Others have taken personal responsibility and risk of official censure in order to follow their personal conviction that lifelong commitment between loving individuals is important, regardless of their gender.

Despite these advances, there was a period of controversy in Los Angeles in 1996 because an openly gay rabbi had been approved to be the head rabbi at his mainstream Reform temple. The majority of congregants supported this selection, but there were detractors, and a heated debate about the ethics and efficacy of allowing gay and lesbian clergy to serve their Jewish congregants was carried out in the mainstream Jewish press.[9,10]

Rather than leaving our religious homes, perhaps it is time for gays and lesbians to come out and speak up in their houses of worship. Maybe hiding in our own churches, mosques, and synagogues is no longer effective or necessary. Could coming out to your fellow congregants be the vehicle by which you begin to heal the world of prejudice and ultimately to make your children safer? Chances are you are not alone. If we are "one in ten," there are other gays and lesbians, or their relatives and friends who worship where you do. Your courage will be much more likely to enlighten the ignorant about the benignness of homosexuality than to bring wrath upon you.

For many gays and lesbians, nontraditional paths provide a more appropriate way to express their spirituality. Whether we were raised in traditional Judeo-Christian homes or not, many of us feel more included in the messages of Wicca, of Native American traditions, or of New Age philosophies and rituals. We are a minority, and many of us are finding that inclusion comes more readily from other minorities than it does from the religious mainstream.

FAMILY VALUES

Many gay and lesbian parents and their children experience individual or familial crises of faith. They feel unwelcome in communities of worship and question both the existence of God and the usefulness of belonging to any movement that would deny the value of their lives and families. Yet gay and lesbian parents are like all parents in their desire to instill in their children a larger vision of the world than what is physically accessible. Like all parents, they wish to provide a code of ethics and morality that is bigger than "because I said so." They enjoy many of the rituals, the holiday celebrations, and the sense of community that they remember from their own youth.

There is a difference between feeling spiritual and following a religion. Spirituality emerges from an inner sense of the existence of something or someone greater than ourselves. Religion is the institutionalization of that recognition. The vast majority of people on Earth believe in some form of divine presence. Some call it God or Goddess, some refer to it as Spirit or simply as a higher power. There are emissaries of spiritual messages who have appeared in the persons of the Christ, the Buddha, Joseph Smith, Mohammed, and Abraham. There are great books and traditions through which the messages have been passed down through generations: the Bible, the Book of Mormon, the Koran, the Bhagavad Gita, the writings of Confucius and of Lao-tse, the rituals of the Wiccans, and the traditional ceremonies of the Native Americans. There are clearly many paths from which we each choose, even if that selection is made by the inertia of nonchoice.

Some of us are lucky to have been brought up along paths that do not conflict with our sense of self. Others do truly reach a point of such disharmony between their beliefs about themselves and their beliefs about the world that the only apparent reconciliation is to toss one aside. None of us throws away connections easily. When one path no longer suits our needs, we begin our search for another. Like the choice of gay men or lesbians to become parents, the choice of a spiritual path becomes very personal and individual. Simply following the path of one's parents does not necessarily work. As parents, gay men and lesbians give a great deal of thought to what they find appropriate to teach their children about the divine or spiritual nature of the world. They are careful about where they go to worship or to do service. Many choose to stay within the mainstream, but many others join the ranks of alternative worship. The alternative may take the form of a gay- or lesbian-focused synagogue or church of a mainstream denomination, or it may be found in a nontraditional faith.

Not all families place religious or spiritual concerns as a significant part of their lives. Most, however, have felt some sense of connection to a spiritual or religious path at some time in their lives, even if the association has now been severed.

The questions that face gay and lesbian parents are numerous and often difficult. Do we belong to a congregation? What denomination feels right? In what ways should we participate? Are we out to our congregation or to its leaders? Do we believe that we are sinning or not, and how do we explain that belief to our children? What does our life experience tell us about the existence or nature of God/Goddess/Spirit? How do we teach our children to respond to people who use their religion to deny our value? How do we inspire our children to live good lives in the face of spiritual controversy?

Family 1—Jeremy ▲▼▲ Gay Father—27—New York

"In speaking with a nun last week, I expressed to her how tired I am of hearing that gays should not be parents, that homosexuality is wrong, that we do not procreate and therefore do not deserve children for our own. 'My dear,' she said, 'Gays are God's form of population control. With so many children who need to be taken care of, I bet even Sally Struthers would agree that gays and lesbians make a perfect choice.'

I was raised Jewish, but through the years have become relaxed in my religious observance. I will try to instill in Micah to the best of my ability, a sense of the existence and love for God on a personal level"

Family 2—Alan ▲▼▲ Gay Father—46—Massachusetts

"We are Roman Catholic. I belong to a church community with activities in service and social aspects."

Margaret (straight mother . . . married to Alan—44—Massachusetts): "Most of our family's spiritual activities are centered around our Roman Catholic church community in both service and social activities."

Brett (Alan and Margaret's 15-year-old daughter—Massachusetts): "I'm Catholic. I don't really know what role it plays. I guess God or whoever is watching us helps me sometimes."

Family 3—Rob ▲▼▲ Gay Father—53—California

"My family is Conservative Jewish. I am Reform Jewish. My family attend services and has Shabbat dinners sometimes. My younger daughter attends a Conservative Jewish Day School. I joined a gay and lesbian temple, but the rest of my family belongs to a Conservative synagogue."

Family 4—Samantha ▲▼▲ Lesbian Mother—33—Vermont

"I was raised Catholic. Now I attend a Unitarian Church. Religion and spiritual beliefs play a minor role in our life."

Family 5—Linda and Donna ▲▼▲ Lesbian Mothers— 40 and 49—Utah

Linda: "Donna was a Mormon for over twenty years. I was Catholic. We have had Nicolas baptized into the Catholic Church to please my family, but we do not currently attend church or adhere to any kind of organized religion. We are very spiritual, although not religious. We try to live by altruistic ideals and values, and we teach the children to do so. We have some familiarity with Eastern philosophies like Taoism and Buddhism, and our principles are probably closer to them than anything else.

"We consider ourselves to be married. We had a holy union ceremony at the Unitarian Church 2 years ago."

Family 6—Leah and Ali ▲▼▲ Lesbian Mothers— 40 and 42—Texas

"We are both Jewish. Ethan was born of a non-Jewish mother and was converted through a *Mikvah* ceremony (ritual bath) at 6 months, followed by a naming ceremony. He was also circumcised at 16 days by a Jewish urologist. A *Brit Milah* ceremony (ritual of circumcision held on the eighth day of a boy's life) could not be held because of the time frame.

"We are raising Jacob in a Jewish home, learning to love and celebrate the Jewish heritage. He is currently attending a Jewish pre-school and next year will go to a different school which is a Jewish Day School through eighth grade."

Family 7—Lydia and Sari ▲▼▲ Lesbian Mothers— 43 and 42—California

"We have no formal religion, but we are very spiritual in the sense of truth, honor, and love of our higher selves. Our spiritual beliefs give us a code of ethics to live by and thus play a very important part in our daily lives."

Family 8—Carol and Rose ▲▼▲ Lesbian Mothers— 41 and 31—Kansas

"We're Methodist now. In the past, we attended MCC for several years. Religion and spiritual beliefs play very little of a role in our family life right now, but we expect it to play more as we attend church workshops in the summer, take church ski trips, and eventually go to church pre-school."

Family 9—Jenny and Ann ▲▼▲ Lesbian Mothers— 33 and 38—Illinois

Jenny: "We are members of a Christian church, and I have been a member there all of my life. Ann doesn't usually attend church with us. She feels that Christianity and homosexuality don't mix. She states that she is very spiritual, but not religious. I have never really figured out what that means.

I believe in God, and the rest of the family shares this belief. We give thanks before each meal and count our blessings every night before sleep. Jo and I used to be more active in our church, but when I became pregnant with Cait, there was a lot of gossip. The church frowned upon my being an unwed mother, and they just assumed I was promiscuous. I have since been in search of another church that may be more accepting of our family. I hope this will encourage Ann to participate in worship with us."

Jo (Jenny and Ann's 13-year-old daughter—Illinois): "I am Christian. I believe in God, and I believe God loves all individuals. We belong to a Christian church, and sometimes I go to a different church with my friend."

Family 10—Dee ▲▼▲ Lesbian Mother—31—California

"Sherry and I currently attend an Episcopal church. The boys (ages 17 and 15) generally do not attend with us. My spiritual beliefs on one hand strongly affect my beliefs and daily life. On the other hand, they are frequently in flux, because I feel constrained by church doctrine and duties. All of the things Sherry and I do at church mean we spend a lot of time there, which affects the boys in a way. We say grace at dinner. This is the one regular spiritual thing we share with the boys."

Sherry ▲▼▲ Lesbian Mother—46—California

"The boys attended church until about 3-1/2 to 4 years ago. My beliefs are an important part of my thoughts and how I approach people and situations. I also find spiritual strength in being more loving and accepting of my sons."

Family 11—Liz and Kathy ▲▼▲ Lesbian Mothers— both 32—Pennsylvania

"Originally from mixed backgrounds, we spent time together finding a church and congregation we both liked and felt comfortable with. After attending for about 9 months, we joined our church, not for the classification of religion, but for the supportive staff and congregation where there are many types of families, including some like ours. It is a place where we feel more than simply 'accepted.' We have been actively supported, included, and it is a place and people for our family to grow with.

"We go to church regularly and involve ourselves in helping our daughter as a part of our activities whether it's a crafts and pot-luck dinner or helping to make soup. We enjoy the company of the diverse congregation and are happy that our children will be fortunate enough to be able to experience all different types of families through their church experience."

Family 12—Joyce ▲▼▲ Lesbian Mother—52—Hawaii

"I was raised Catholic but have been Pagan since around my son's birth, so we've done seasonal rituals and earth blessings and goddess chants all along. My son is at this point very anti-religious. During the last 2 years of her life, my daughter became a Muktananda devotee, along with her dad!

"For myself, spirituality plays a strong role. Since my son was about fourteen or fifteen, he has chosen not to participate in rituals except candle lighting at Winter Solstice."

Family 13—Roz and Stacy ▲▼▲ Lesbian Mothers— 22 and 23—Arizona

"We are Wiccan. We are very earth-oriented, as well as believing in the existence of spirits, aliens, karmic fate, reincarnation, magic, the power of words, crystals, tarot cards, runes, etc.

"We are strong believers in Wicca, and as Skye grows, we will encourage our beliefs to her. But we will also teach her of other religions and beliefs so that when she feels it is time, she can decide for herself what faith to follow, if any. We do not attend a church or anything, but we study about our religion through books and research."

Family 14—Carole ▲▼▲ Lesbian Mother—47—California

"One parent in this family is Jewish with a fairly strong Reform Jewish background. The other parent is Catholic, but she is not connected to the Catholic Church.

"As a family, we discuss religion and God, and we celebrate holidays. We celebrate Jewish holidays with my family, and we generally host Christmas dinner for both families. We attend some Jewish services together."

Andrea ▲▼▲ Lesbian Mother—44—California

"I am Catholic but have not been involved with the Church since the development of this relationship. My partner is Jewish. Most of our religious activities are of the Jewish faith. We celebrate religious holidays, Jewish holidays with my partner's family."

Alix (Carole and Andrea's 13-1/2-year-old daughter—California): "I guess I'm Christian, but we don't go to church. It doesn't play a role really, except when we go to temple with Carole."

Family 15—Christine ▲▼▲ Lesbian Mother—60—California

"We were Roman Catholic, actively, as a family until about 1972. When that church no longer met my spirituality needs, I became aware of MCC. Once I was attending there, my children chose to attend with me. As the older girls were able to drive, they began attending other mainline Protestant churches that their friends attended.

"Religion and spirituality play a very large role in our lives. The children attended Catholic schools and services until about 1972. When I joined MCC, they began attending MCC Sunday School and services. Eventually, they chose to attend other churches with their friends. MCC remained vital to my spirituality. In time, I became a deacon, and then when I felt a call to the ministry, I completed studies through MCC to become a minister in 1986. By this time, the youngest two girls were twenty, still living at home with me."

Marybeth (Christine's 35-year-old daughter—California): "I was raised Roman Catholic until junior high. Then through my twenties, I don't know what I was. From my twenties to the present, I have been Roman Catholic.

"My husband and I are co-choir directors, and I am the choir director of the children's choir. I also am a Eucharistic Minister. I watch what happens in the youth group my daughter is in. I am on the Parish Council."

Jean (Christine's 29-year-old daughter, Tara's twin—California): "I grew up going to my mom's church (MCC). When I was 19 years old and got pregnant, it was the people at my mom's church who stood by my side, sometimes more than my family. When I gave up that baby for adoption, they stood by my side and supported me! I would have *never* been able to go through what I did without their help! They made a *very* big difference. I feel my mom's church has helped shape me into the person I am today.

"I believe that my God is with me all the time. I believe that she guides me with the help of my mom, we are very close."

Tara (Christine's 29-year-old daughter, Jean's twin—California): "I was Catholic, but my husband and I were baptized Southern Baptist. I don't go to church except at MCC.

"I believe in God. I pray every day. God is very important to me. I don't believe you need to go to church every week, as long as you believe in God. God helps me with my daily life. I also believe that if you ask God for forgiveness, you will go to heaven. Also, I don't believe that God is a judgmental person or a racist."

Barbara (Christine's 38-year-old daughter—California): "I went to church often until I became an adult. It's hard to explain the role that religion plays in my life. I know that God's here and will listen and help if I need him. For me, he's in the background but always there."

Family 16—Dale ▲▼▲ Lesbian Mother—38—Florida

"We don't practice a formal religion. I share with my children my beliefs in reincarnation. As with sex, I ask them not to discuss belief systems for the same reason as sex. Not everyone is tolerant of different views. It is tragic in a so-called democracy, we still have to walk on eggs.

"Kat and I feel all children ideally should be brought up in an organized religion that emphasizes an all-loving Higher Power. Unfortunately, we have not found that yet."

Family 17—Jim ▲▼▲ Gay Father—40—Massachusetts

"We are Unitarian-Universalist. It has a strong impact at chosen times."

Chelsea (Jim's 13-year-old daughter—Massachusetts): "I'm Unitarian-Universalist. I don't go to church."

Family 18—Becka ▲▼▲ Lesbian Mother—44—Washington State

"I am sixth generation Mormon. I survived, and now I practice no religion but have a deep and abiding spirituality.

Spirituality is all-encompassing in our lives. I also believe in education about the diversity of beliefs."

Family 19—Sandra and Kelly ▲▼▲ Lesbian Mothers—37 and 36—Ohio

"My kids grew up in a United Church of Christ (UCC) church. It was not a very liberal church, even though it's UCC. I've started looking for a more liberal UCC that might accept Kim and me and one where the children's father is not a member.

"The children have been in church a lot. We've pulled back some for several reasons specific to the congregation."

Miranda (Sandra and Kelly's 17-year-old daughter—Ohio): "I grew up in a UCC church. I've gone pretty regularly. I used to sing in the choir, and I've gone to three mission trips with my youth group. Now we're looking for a new church. I've been confirmed and baptized.

"I don't always agree with what religion says, but God has gotten me through a lot. I know he/she watches over me, loves me, and forgives me of my sins. When I am confused, frustrated or depressed, I try to talk to God. Sometimes, I get angry at him/her, and sometimes I question him/her, but I believe my pain and struggles have made me a stronger and more empathetic person. I know I can survive anything that doesn't kill me."

Family 20—Melissa and Trish ▲▼▲ Lesbian Mothers—37 and 39—New Jersey

"We are very spiritual, and we've recently joined our local Unitarian Church where we've been welcomed very warmly. Spirituality is very important to our family."

Dawn (Melissa and Trish's 14-year-old daughter—New Jersey): "My religion is whatever I believe in. It doesn't play a very big role in my life."

Family 21—Denise ▲▼▲ Lesbian Mother—33—New York

"I was raised Catholic but am not practicing. My partner was raised agnostic and remains so.

At this time, religion plays no role in our lives, although we wouldn't be opposed to belonging to a gay Catholic congregation."

Alisha ▲▼▲ Lesbian Mother—34—New York

"I have no religious or spiritual background. Though I'm tolerant of others' spirituality, it doesn't play a big part in my life. We may get involved with a church for the religious education and social activities, however it would have to be a gay-friendly parish, which could be a challenge."

Family 22—Werner ▲▼▲ Gay Father—31—Austria

"We are former Roman Catholics. Religion plays no role in our family life."

▲▼▲

We live in a country that guarantees religious freedom, including the freedom not to believe in or practice any religion or spiritual path. Because many gays and lesbians feel unwelcome in the congregations or faiths that embrace the majority of their neighbors, we frequently find ourselves closely examining our personal convictions rather than simply adopting the practices of our non-gay families. Yet many also have a need or desire to find a faith community in which we do feel welcome. When gay fathers, lesbian mothers, and our children make spiritual or religious choices, they seem to be made with a great deal of thought and conviction, and the search for the right community has led to a great deal of self-knowledge for many families.

How ironic and unfortunate that so many of us need to go outside of religious organizations that purport to teach love and inclusion in order to feel truly valued for our full humanity. On the other hand, let's give loud applause to the institutions and the individuals in their ranks that are making the changes that are welcoming gay and lesbian individuals and families into their fold.

Conclusion

7

"Up!," they cry "the day is
   come
On the smiling valleys;
We have beat the morning
   drum;
Playmate, join your allies!"

   Robert Louis Stevenson,
      "Night and Day," in *A
      Child's Garden of Verses*

Gay- and lesbian-headed families are establishing themselves
from a basis of love . . .

*F*rom a distance, I heard a deep, soulful moan that seemed nearly human, though clearly it was not. My entire body vibrated as the *basso* tones came in waves across the distance. I smelled salt and pitch in the air and felt the crowd's excitement as we neared the docks of New York Harbor. The ship's horn let out another blast, and I knew from its volume that we were almost at our destination. Soon my parents and I turned a corner, and I saw the huge black hull of the Queen Elizabeth II as she slowly and majestically maneuvered into her slip. She had just crossed an ocean carrying hundreds of stories that accompanied her many passengers who by now were hanging over the railings waving furiously at the throng of family and friends who waited excitedly for their arrival.

My grandmother was on the ship. Every summer, she visited "the old country" to do a little business and to indulge in a little relaxation at the baths. Her travels took her to a world that was completely foreign to me except in the moments when I could peek in through the window of her stories. Through those accounts, I came to know her better, to see beyond the life that she lived here in America, to understand the experiences that had made her who she was. The tales that she brought back with her, both the new ones and the newly remembered ones, became *my* journey into my grandmother's world.

Creating *Families of Value: Gay and Lesbian Parents and Their Children Speak Out* has taken me on such a journey. Although the terrain was not completely foreign to me, my venture into the lives of the families who so generously shared their experiences with me has indeed offered me a window to a better understanding of their worlds, and consequently a clearer view of my own.

My initial intent was to illuminate the fact that children of gay fathers and lesbian mothers have been and are growing up in healthy, nurturing homes, and my assumption that gay and lesbian families are healthy places for growing children was validated by "my" families. I am aware that the participants were self-selected, and perhaps poorly adjusted families were not interested in participating, but not all of the contributors to *Families of Value: Gay and Lesbian Parents and Their Children Speak Out* told completely rosy tales. I continue to believe, as a researcher, as an observer of human nature, as a psychotherapist, and as an essentially optimistic individual, that having bumps along one's road is in no way synonymous with living in an unhealthy situation.

I hope that the few problems that participants wrote about are being resolved. I did have the good fortune of hearing from one father, Rob, about developments in his relationship with his children. His teenage son is speaking with him again and seems to have accepted his dad's sexual orientation as just another aspect of Dad. Rob's younger daughter has attended events in the gay and lesbian community with her father and has become friendly with other children of gay and lesbian parents.

The developments in Rob's family are moving to me. They demonstrate the irrepressible capacity of the human heart and mind to grow. There may be setbacks for Rob or for other families like his, but for now at least he is once again enjoying the love, respect, and companionship of his children.

I am also touched by the sensitivity of so many of the children and teens who wrote to me. Their ability to see their parents as unique individuals and to focus on the strengths of their families certainly runs counter to the bad press that most young people are receiving these days. The children's contributions paint a picture of open-mindedness and understanding of human nature that seems to surpass their years. More than living in merely adequately healthy homes, these children are growing up in actively growth-promoting environments. They and their parents deserve a resounding ovation!

What did I find out about gay and lesbian families? For the most part, I saw a healthy variety of family life. Most of the information feels upbeat and encouraging to me. Gay- and lesbian-headed families are establishing themselves from a basis of love, making use of an incredibly wide range of methods for adding children to their lives and homes, including conception within straight relationships, alternative insemination, surrogate mothering, and various forms of adoption. They are living pretty average lives with little more than the normal amount of difficulty in raising their children.

Parents and children from the families who have participated in this study have clearly established mutually supportive relationships with each other. I am struck by the maturity of the children's understanding of their parents, and I am likewise impressed at the parents' sensitivity to their children's needs. There is an openness among the members of the families seen here that seems to come, at least in part, from their mutual respect for the struggles that each faces due to being different from the norm. Whether they are addressing issues of fashion or of sexuality, they generally offer each other support, understanding, and trust. There is a sense of commonality that all people face challenges and a willingness to help each other find personal satisfaction in life.

Parents are making decisions based on the best interests of the children. They are providing physical, emotional, and spiritual nourishment for their families. The children are developing a mantle of understanding and tolerance of individual differences in response to themselves so often being the targets of prejudice.

Most of the families felt that they are fairly comfortable being out in most if not all areas of their lives. Few expressed significant difficulty with extended family, although not all relatives were seen as helpful or even accepting. There are predictable hurdles to overcome in coping with schools, peers, neighbors, and religious communities, and gay and lesbian parents are often concerned that their children may not be safe in the world. They are very protective of their children's security outside of their homes, but this does not seem to infringe on their ability and even passion for encouraging their offspring to seek their own paths.

A number of both parents and children express concern that the children may be gay or lesbian. The parents wish for their children a life free of the pain that may accompany homosexuality, but they also reiterate their unconditional love and support of their sons and daughters. The children who are concerned about their own sexual orientation fear being seen by others as abnormal. The older teens and the adult children have generally come to believe that their own sexual orientation is not a product of their parents' homosexuality. The teens who are still unsure of their sexual orientation often express an openness to discovering over time what will be right and natural for them.

The chapter dealing with religion and spirituality, leaves me with a rather bittersweet feeling. That the area of our lives that most strives to elevate our existence should be the source of so much suffering for so many good people grieves me. I am saddened that so many people feel spiritually adrift and excluded by the religious communities by which they wish to feel included. Clearly, the more orthodox or fundamental a religion is, the more its followers castigate those who do not subscribe to their definitions of morality. For gay and lesbian families, comfort and accepting moral guidance is most likely to be found in the more liberal religious venues. My grief is tempered by the growing number of churches, synagogues, and other worship and service alternatives that are being created in the spirit of openness and true acceptance of all human beings.

Homosexual parenting has received a good deal of coverage in the political arena and in the media recently. On the positive side, *Newsweek*'s November 1, 1996, cover story shared upbeat, informative, and supportive information about several families, including that of singer Melissa Etheridge and partner Julie Cypher.[1,2] I have also seen numerous articles in my local paper that speak about gay fathering and lesbian mothering as simply another way to be a family.

In December 1996, Judge Kevin Chang of the First Circuit Court of Hawaii ruled that Hawaii State civil marriage law cannot discriminate against same-sex couples. In the case from which the ruling emanated, *Baehr v. Miike,* the State of Hawaii had attempted to demonstrate that marriage exists for the promotion of family and that children should not be raised by gay or lesbian parents. Judge Chang gave legal credence to the large body of research that endorses the capacity of gay men and lesbians to be good parents and indicated that the ability of same sex couples to enjoy the benefits of civil marriage would, in fact, protect their children.[3] In gay and lesbian communities across the nation, there is a sense of cautious optimism that perhaps we will see a day when our relationships and our families will be granted the same civil recognition, benefits, and protections that straight relationships and families now enjoy. While we wait, however, for the final Hawaii Supreme Court ruling on the appeal of this case, organizations such as the Lambda Legal Defense and Education Fund and the Freedom to Marry Coalition[4] are continuing to keep people informed about the need for such legal changes.

Not all the news has been so encouraging. As I worked on this book, gay and lesbian parents and their children continued to face discrimination. In Virginia, Sharon Bottoms lost her battle to expand her visitation with her son and even had visitation time cut. Custody of the boy had previously been awarded to his grandmother on the grounds that Ms. Bottoms' sexual orientation would create an unhealthy environment for him. In Florida, an 11-year-old girl was sent by the courts to live with her father, a convicted wife-murderer, because living with her lesbian mother, Mary Ward, was deemed to be too dangerous for the girl. On the eve of a presidential election, President Clinton signed into law the federal "Defense of Marriage Act," which defines marriage as being a union of one man and one woman and allows individual states to deny recognition of same-gender marriages that may be performed legally in other states. This flies in the face of constitutional law that guarantees recognition by all states of contracts deemed legal in any other state. As of September 1997, twenty-two states have passed or are considering legislation along the same lines.[5]

As a society, we have made large strides in acknowledging the gay and lesbian community and the parents and their children within it, but there are clearly many challenges yet ahead of us before we are truly living the credo that "all [men] are created equal." For all of us, gay or straight, there are crucial decisions to be made about our future. Debating whether or not gay and lesbian families should exist is irrelevant. They're here. Disputing the ability of gay fathers and lesbian mothers to provide nurturing environments for their children ignores the facts. For the most part, they, like *most* parents, *are* doing so. What, then, are the questions that we need to be asking in order to take the next step on this journey?

Do we even know where we want to go? Obviously there are as many answers to this question as there are respondents, and perhaps there are many valid destinations. I see as an essential goal, however, the creation of an environment in which all families, including gay and lesbian families, are welcomed into the mainstream of American life. In a country that espouses legal equality, no legitimate purpose can be served by excluding some players from the game.

What are the barriers that currently exist to full inclusion? One major hurdle for the gay and lesbian community to overcome is the sincere belief of a segment of society that homosexual people are less worthy than straight people. How do we dispute a belief system? What facts would constitute proof against an existing backdrop of faith? Is proof necessary, or should we simply agree to disagree without losing sight of our democratic principle of accepting dissenting views? Do we, as members of a free society, wish to maintain our right to hold personal beliefs, or do we want to teach a single proscribed ideology? Does accepting that others see and live life differently pose a danger to individuals or to society?

It is human nature to fear the unknown, and for many people within the straight community, homosexuality remains a great mystery. How do we educate the uninformed? What will "normalize" the differences between us? How do we demonstrate the commonalties that do truly outnumber those differences? What are the lessons to be learned from the struggles that have historically faced every minority group as it sought to become assimilated into the melting pot?

Despite the great wealth that surrounds us, we often tend to approach life from an assumption of limitation. We seem to fear that if someone else gets a goody, there will be fewer treats for us. What are the privileged afraid of losing? Are we talking about material goods such as housing and income? Are we talking about services such as health care and educational opportunities? Are we talking about abstract benefits such as social status and perceived morality? What is the likelihood that any real loss will occur, and is maintaining one's own advantage a legitimate argument for denying equal access to someone else?

These are some of the broad-stroke concerns that are apparent to me at this time. What, though, are the specific venues in which they are being played out? Same-gender marriage has been catapulted into the limelight as an umbrella issue for gay and lesbian rights. What are the fears that are associated with expanding the civil right of marriage to gays and lesbians? How will the legal union of same-sex couples affect morality, health care, child welfare, family structure, the economy, or the political system? Will there be dire consequences, or will the controversy prove to have been irrelevant?

Sex education is another major arena in which consensus eludes us. If children are to be taught about sex and sexuality at all, how much information about homosexuality is healthy and useful? At what point does information cease to be appropriate for the healthy development of individual students as well as for the larger community? Does sex education encourage children to act out behaviors in which they would not otherwise engage? Does it legitimize behavior that is dangerous? Does it destroy lives or save them?

Beyond sex education lies the realm of what used to be referred to as values clarification. Why clarifying our values has come to be perceived as detrimental is beyond me. As with sex education, the first question to ponder is whether or not we wish to teach children to examine their own thoughts and feelings. Within the context of such education, would information about sexual orientation be detrimental to young minds? Is learning about the variety of families that exists dangerous to children? How does knowing that some people have two mothers or two fathers, or any other nontraditional set of parents, affect children? How are children from alternative families affected by inclusion in or exclusion from school curricula, books, films, or TV shows? Does being aware of different ways of living promote disharmony or understanding? Do children make choices that are less healthy or less ethical if they know there are more options available to them?

Some of these questions are in the process of being answered, others still wait in the wings of our collective consciousness. The answers that we do find will themselves naturally lead to new inquiries. And so the trek continues.

Despite the difficulties that confront us, gay men and lesbians will continue to bear, to adopt, and to raise children. Some will blend quietly into their communities, facing challenges privately, and some will make themselves visible and become a vanguard for the future of American family life. I hope that we can travel the distance from arguing about who deserves to be a family to creating a universally nurturing environment in which to support the many and varied families of value who are living among us.

Notes

INTRODUCTION

1. *Both My Moms' Names Are Judy: Children of Lesbians and Gays Speak Out.* This ten-minute video of interviews with the children of homosexual parents is part of an in-service training for elementary school teachers and administrators. It is a production of the Lesbian and Gay Parent Association and the Gay and Lesbian Parenting Coalition International, 1994.
2. Chasnoff, Debra and Cohen, Helen, *It's Elementary, Talking About Gay Issues In School.* This film was reviewed in Gelnaw, Aimee, "Documentary Film Review . . . ," *Network* (Gay and Lesbian Parenting Coalition International, Montclair, New Jersey), Fall 1996.
3. Singer, Bennett L., and Deschamps, David, eds., *Gay and Lesbian STATS,* New Press, New York, 1994.
4. Martin, April, Ph.D., *The Lesbian and Gay Parenting Handbook: Creating and Raising Our Families,* HarperPerennial/Harper Collins, New York, 1993.

CHAPTER 1: WHAT IS A FAMILY?

1. *Webster's Ninth New Collegiate Dictionary,* Merriam-Webster, Springfield, Massachusetts, 1984.
2. Flexner, S. B., Editor-in-Chief, and Hauck, L. C., Managing Editor, *The Random House Dictionary of the English Language,* 2nd unabridged edition, Random House, New York, 1996.
3. Singer, Bennett L., and Deschamps, David, eds., *Gay and Lesbian STATS,* New Press, New York, 1994.
4. *Ibid.*
5. *Los Angeles Times,* August 18, 1996.

6. Singer, Bennett L., and Deschamps, David, eds., *Gay and Lesbian STATS*, New Press, New York, 1994.
7. *Avest Seventh Corp. v. R.*, 109 Misc., 2d, 248, 1981; *Yorkshire House Associates v. Lulkin*, 114 Misc, 2d, 40, 1982; *420 East 80th Co v. Chin*, 115 Misc., 2d, 195, 1982; *Evangelists Associations v. Bland*, 117 Misc., 2d, 558, 1983; *Hudson View Properties, v. Weiss*, 59, N.Y., 2d, 733, 1983; as well as court decisions in Denver and California; cited in Curry, Hayden, Clifford, Dennis, and Leonard, Robin, *A Legal Guide for Lesbian and Gay Couples*, 7th ed., Nolo Press, Berkeley, 1993.
8. *Ibid., Braschi v. Stahl Associates Co.*, 74 N.Y. 2d 201.
9. *Ibid.*
10. Kantrowitz, Barbara, "Gay Families Come Out," *Newsweek*, November 4, 1996.
11. Ocamb, Karen, "Lesbian Custody Case Shaking Up L.A.," *The Lesbian News*, Vol. 22, No. 4, November 1996.
12. Curry, Hayden, Clifford, Dennis, and Leonard, Robin, *A Legal Guide for Lesbian and Gay Couples*, 7th ed., Nolo Press, Berkeley, California, 1993.
13. Pacific Reproductive Services, 65 North Madison Avenue, Suite 505, Pasadena, California, 91101; 626 432-1680.
14. Curry, Hayden, Clifford, Dennis, and Leonard, Robin, *A Legal Guide for Lesbian and Gay Couples*, 7th ed., Nolo Press, Berkeley, California, 1993.
15. *Ibid.*

CHAPTER 2: IT'S ALL "RELATIVES"

1. Singer, Bennett L. and Deschamps, David, eds., *Gay and Lesbian STATS*, New Press, New York, 1994.
2. *Ibid.*
3. "Homosexual Parent: All in the Family," *Science News*, Vol. 147, No. 3, January 21, 1995.
4. Smith, Katherine, "Children Raised by Lesbian Mothers," Doctoral Dissertation, Department of Psychology, UCLA, 1981.
5. Goodman, B., "The Lesbian Mother," *American Journal of Orthopsychiatry*, Vol. 43, 1973.
6. "Homosexual Parent: All in the Family," *Science News*, Vol. 147, No. 3, January 21, 1995.
7. Green, R., "Sexual Identity of Thirty-Seven Children Raised by Homosexual or Transsexual Parents," *American Journal of Psychiatry*, Vol. 35, pp. 692–697, 1978.
8. Bowlby, J., *Child Care and the Growth of Love*, 2nd ed., abridged and edited by Margery Fry, with two new chapters by Mary D. Salter Ainsworth. Penguin Books, Baltimore, 1966.

9. Green, R., "Sexual Identity of Thirty-Seven Children Raised by Homosexual or Transsexual Parents," *American Journal of Psychiatry*, Vol. 35, pp. 692–697, 1978.
10. Mucklow, B. M., and Phelan, G. K., "Lesbian and Traditional Mothers' Responses to Adult Response to Child Behavior and Self-Concept," *Psychological Reports*, Vol. 44, pp. 880–882, 1979.
11. Harris, M. B., and Turner, P. H., "Gay and Lesbian Parents," *Journal of Homosexuality*, Vol. 12, No. 2, pp. 101–113, 1985/86.
12. Bozett, Frederick W., ed., *Gay and Lesbian Parents*, Praeger, New York, 1987.
13. Gottman, Julie Schwartz, "Children of Gay and Lesbian Parents," in Bozett, Frederick W., and Sussman, Marvin B., eds., *Homosexuality and Family Relations*, Haworth Press, New York, 1989.
14. Lewin, Ellen, *Lesbian Mothers: Accounts of Gender in American Culture*, Cornell University Press, Ithaca, New York, 1993.
15. Bozett, Frederick W., ed., *Gay and Lesbian Parents*, Praeger, New York, 1987.
16. Hanscombe, G. E., and Forster, J., *Rocking the Cradle: Lesbian Mothers, a Challenge in Family Living*, Alyson, Boston, 1982.
17. American Psychiatric Association, *Diagnostic and Statistical Manual of Mental Disorders III: DSM-III*, American Psychiatric Association, Washington, D.C., 1972.
18. Lewin, Ellen, *Lesbian Mothers: Accounts of Gender in American Culture*, Cornell University Press, Ithaca, New York, 1993.
19. Bozett, Frederick W., ed., *Gay and Lesbian Parents*, Praeger, New York, 1987.
20. Hanscombe, G. E., and Forster, J., *Rocking the Cradle: Lesbian Mothers, a Challenge in Family Living*, Alyson, Boston, 1982.
21. Miller, B., "Gay Fathers and Their Children," *The Family Coordinator*, Vol. 28, pp. 544–552, 1979.

CHAPTER 3: PARENTS AND CHILDREN TOGETHER

1. Falk, P. J., "Lesbian Mothers: Psychological Assumptions in Family Law," *American Psychologist*, Vol. 44, 1989.
2. Koss, Mary, *et al.*, *No Safe Haven: Male Violence Against Women at Home, at Work, and in the Community*, American Psychological Association, Washington, D.C., 1994.
3. Bozett, Frederick W., and Sussman, Marvin B., eds., *Homosexuality and Family Relations*, Haworth Press, New York, 1989.
4. Department of Children's Services, Los Angeles County, *Child Abuse Prevention Handbook*, Crime Prevention Center, Office of the Attorney General, California Department of Justice, Sacramento, California, 1993.

5. Chaidez, Lucy, ed., *The California Child Abuse and Neglect Reporting Law: Issues and Answers for Health Practitioners*, State Department of Social Services, Office of Child Abuse Prevention, Sacramento, California, 1991.

6. Patterson, Charlotte J., "Children of Lesbian and Gay Parents," *Child Development*, Vol. 63, 1992.

7. Harris, M. B., and Turner, P. H., "Gay and Lesbian Parents," *Journal of Homosexuality*, Vol. 12, No. 2, pp. 101–113, 1985/86.

8. Golombeck, S., Spencer, A., and Rutter, M., "Children in Lesbian and Single Parent Households: Psychosexual and Psychiatric Appraisal," *Journal of Child Psychology and Psychiatry*, Vol. 24, No. 4, pp. 551–572, 1985.

9. Green, R., "Sexual Identity of Thirty-Seven Children Raised by Homosexual or Transsexual Parents," *American Journal of Psychiatry*, Vol. 35, pp. 692–697, 1978.

10. Goodman, B., "The Lesbian Mother," *American Journal of Orthopsychiatry*, Vol. 43, 1973.

11. Gottman, Julie Schwartz, "Children of Gay and Lesbian Parents," in Bozett, Frederick W., and Sussman, Marvin B., eds., *Homosexuality and Family Relations*, Haworth Press, New York, 1989.

12. Smith, Katherine, "Children Raised by Lesbian Mothers," Doctoral Dissertation, Department of Psychology, UCLA, 1981.

13. Baron, Kathryn, "The Gaybie Boom," *Los Angeles Times*, Life and Style section, March 1, 1995.

14. Singer, Bennett L., and Deschamps, David, eds., *Gay and Lesbian STATS*, New Press, New York, 1994.

15. Bozett, Frederick W., and Sussman, Marvin B., eds., *Homosexuality and Family Relations*, Haworth Press, New York, 1989.

16. Johnson, Lee, "Words to Warm a Parent's Heart," *The Family Next Door* (Oakland, California), Vol. 1, No. 6, p. 32, 1994.

17. Bowlby, J., *Child Care and the Growth of Love*, 2nd ed., abridged and edited by Margery Fry, with two new chapters by Mary D. Salter Ainsworth, Penguin Books, Baltimore, 1966.

18. *Ibid.*

19. Bowlby, J., *Attachment and Loss*, 2nd ed., Basic Books, New York, 1982.

20. Mitchell, Valery, and Wilson, Diane, "Let's Talk About It," *The Family Next Door* (Oakland, California), Vol. 1, No. 6, pp. 22–24, 1994.

21. Kus, Robert J., *Keys to Caring: Assisting Your Gay and Lesbian Clients*, Alyson, Boston, 1991.

22. Rafkin, Louise, ed., *Different Mothers: Sons and Daughters of Lesbians Talk about their Lives*, Cleis Press, San Francisco, 1990.

23. Martin, April, Ph.D., *The Lesbian and Gay Parenting Handbook: Creating and Raising Our Families*, HarperPerennial/Harper Collins, New York, 1993.

24. Bozett, Frederick W., ed., *Gay and Lesbian Parents*, Praeger, New York, 1987.
25. Lewin, E., and Lyons, T., "Everything in Its Place: The Coexistence of Lesbianism and Motherhood," in Paul, W., Weinrich, J. D., Gonsiorek, J. C., and Hotvedt, M. E., eds., *Homosexuality: Social, Psychological, and Biological Issues*, Sage, Beverly Hills, California, 1982.
26. Goodman, B., "The Lesbian Mother," *American Journal of Orthopsychiatry*, Vol. 43, 1973.
27. Patterson, Charlotte J., "Children of Lesbian and Gay Parents," *Child Development*, Vol. 63, 1992.
28. McDonald, Helen, and Steinhorn, Audrey I., *Understanding Homosexuality: A Guide for Those Who Know, Love, or Counsel Gay and Lesbian Individuals*, Crossroads, New York, 1993.
29. Kus, Robert J., R.N., Ph.D., *Keys to Caring: Assisting Your Gay and Lesbian Clients*, Alyson, Boston, 1991.
30. Curry, Hayden, Clifford, Dennis, and Leonard, Robin, *A Legal Guide for Lesbian and Gay Couples*, 7th ed., Nolo Press, Berkeley, California, 1993.
31. Ginsburg, H., and Offer, S., *Piaget's Theory of Intellectual Development: An Introduction*, Prentice-Hall, Englewood Cliffs, New Jersey, 1969.
32. Furth, Hans G., *Piaget for Teachers*, Prentice-Hall, Englewood Cliffs, New Jersey, 1970.
33. Ocamb, Karen, "Lesbian Custody Case Shaking Up L.A.," *The Lesbian News*, Vol. 22, No. 4, November, 1996.
34. McDonald, Helen, and Steinhorn, Audrey I., *Understanding Homosexuality: A Guide for Those Who Know, Love, or Counsel Gay and Lesbian Individuals*, Crossroads, New York, 1993.
35. Frazier, Cynthia, "Keeping the Kids," *The Lesbian News*, Vol. 21, No. 9, April 1996.
36. Jullion, Jeanne, *Long Way Home: the Odyssey of a Lesbian Mother and Her Children*, Cleis Press, San Francisco, 1985.
37. Hanscombe, G. E., and Forster, J., *Rocking the Cradle: Lesbian Mothers, a Challenge in Family Living*, Alyson, Boston, 1982.
38. "Donahue," Transcript #4131, Multi-media Entertainment, Inc., November 29, 1994.
39. Martin, April, Ph.D., *The Lesbian and Gay Parenting Handbook: Creating and Raising Our Families*, HarperPerennial/Harper Collins, New York, 1993.
40. Kus, Robert J., R.N., Ph.D., *Keys to Caring: Assisting Your Gay and Lesbian Clients*, Alyson, Boston, 1991.
41. Pennington, S. B., "Children of Lesbian Mothers," and Bozett, Frederick W., "Children of Gay Fathers," in Bozett, Frederick W., ed., *Gay and Lesbian Parents*, Praeger, New York, 1987.

42. Bozett, Frederick W., ed., *Gay and Lesbian Parents,* Praeger, New York, 1987.

43. McDonald, Helen, and Steinhorn, Audrey I., *Understanding Homosexuality: A Guide for Those Who Know, Love, or Counsel Gay and Lesbian Individuals,* Crossroads, New York, 1993.

44. Corley, Rip, *The Final Closet: The Gay Parents' Guide for Coming Out to Their Children,* Editech Press, Miami, Florida, 1990.

45. Green, G. D., and Clunis, D. M., *Lesbian Couples,* Seal Press, Seattle, Washington, 1988.

46. Bozett, Frederick W., ed., *Gay and Lesbian Parents,* Praeger, New York, 1987.

CHAPTER 4: OUT AND ABOUT IN THE COMMUNITY

1. Harris, M. B., and Turner, P. H., "Gay and Lesbian Parents," *Journal of Homosexuality,* Vol. 12, No. 2, pp. 101–113, 1985/86.

2. Golombeck, S., Spencer, A., and Rutter, M., "Children in Lesbian and Single Parent Households: Psychosexual and Psychiatric Appraisal," *Journal of Child Psychology and Psychiatry,* Vol. 24, No. 4, pp. 551–572, 1985.

3. Smith, Katherine, "Children Raised by Lesbian Mothers," Doctoral Dissertation, Department of Psychology, UCLA, 1981.

4. Green, R., "Sexual Identity of Thirty-Seven Children Raised by Homosexual or Transsexual Parents," *American Journal of Psychiatry,* Vol. 35, pp. 692–697, 1978.

5. Goodman, B., "The Lesbian Mother," *American Journal of Orthopsychiatry,* Vol. 43, 1973.

6. Kantrowitz, Barbara, "Gay Families Come Out," *Newsweek,* November 4, 1996.

7. Lewin, Ellen, *Lesbian Mothers: Accounts of Gender in American Culture,* Cornell University Press, Ithaca, New York, 1993.

8. Rafkin, Louise, ed., *Different Mothers: Sons and Daughters of Lesbians Talk about Their Lives,* Cleis Press, San Francisco, 1990.

9. Jullion, Jeanne, *Long Way Home:The Odyssey of a Lesbian Mother and Her Children,* Cleis Press, San Francisco, 1985.

10. Smith, Katherine, "Children Raised by Lesbian Mothers," Doctoral Dissertation, Department of Psychology, UCLA, 1981.

11. Kantrowitz, Barbara, "Gay Families Come Out," *Newsweek,* November 4, 1996.

12. Chasnoff, Debra, Producer-Director, and Cohen, Helen, Co-producer, *It's Elementary, Talking About Gay Issues In School* [film], 1996.

13. Lesbian and Gay Parents Association, *Both My Moms' Names Are Judy: Children of Lesbians and Gays Speak Out* [video], 1994.

14. Lambda Legal Defense and Education Fund, 6030 Wilshire Boulevard, Suite 200, Los Angeles, California 90016; 666 Broadway, 12th Floor, New York, New York 10012.
15. Kantrowitz, Barbara, "Gay Families Come Out," *Newsweek*, November 4, 1996.
16. Singer, Bennett L., and Deschamps, David, eds., *Gay and Lesbian STATS*, New Press, New York, 1994.

CHAPTER 5: TO BE OR NOT TO BE

1. *Highlights for Children*, 803 Church Street, Honesdale, Pennsylvania, 18431.
2. Kus, Robert J., R.N., Ph.D., *Keys to Caring: Assisting Your Gay and Lesbian Clients*, Alyson, Boston, 1991.
3. Blommer, Stephen J., "Answers to Your Questions About Sexual Orientation and Homosexuality," American Psychological Association, Office of Public Affairs, Washington, D.C., 1994.
4. Bell, Alan P., Weinberg, Martin S., and Hammersmith, Sue K., *Sexual Preference, Its Development in Men and Women*, Indiana University Press, Bloomington, Indiana, 1981.
5. Haldeman, D. C., "The Practice and Ethics of Sexual Orientation Conversion Therapy," *Journal of Consulting and Clinical Psychology*, Vol. 62, pp. 221–227, 1994.
6. Singer, Bennett L., and Deschamps, David, eds., *Gay and Lesbian STATS*, New Press, New York, 1994.
7. *Ibid.*
8. American Psychiatric Association, *Diagnostic and Statistical Manual of Mental Disorders III: DSM-III*, American Psychiatric Association, Washington, D.C., 1972.
9. Blommer, Stephen J., "Answers to Your Questions About Sexual Orientation and Homosexuality," American Psychological Association, Office of Public Affairs, Washington, D.C., 1994.
10. American Psychiatric Association, *Diagnostic and Statistical Manual of Mental Disorders III-R: DSM-III-R*, American Psychiatric Association, Washington, D.C., 1989.
11. American Psychiatric Association, *Diagnostic and Statistical Manual of Mental Disorders IV: DSM-IV*, American Psychiatric Association, Washington, D.C., 1994.
12. Hamer, Dean, *et al.*, *Nature Genetics*, November 1993.
13. *Ibid.*
14. "Homosexual Parent: All in the Family," *Science News*, Vol. 147, No. 3, January 21, 1995.

15. Goodman, B., "The Lesbian Mother," *American Journal of Orthopsychiatry*, Vol. 43, 1973.
16. Bandura A., and Walters, R., *Social Learning and Personality Development*, Rinehart and Winston, New York, 1963.
17. Hoeffer, Beverly, R.N., D.N.Sc., "Children's Acquisition of Sex-Role Behavior in Lesbian Mother Families," *American Journal of Orthopsychiatry*, Vol. 51, No. 3, pp. 536–543, July 1981.
18. Kirkpatrick, Martha, M.D., Smith, Catherine, and Roy, Roy, M.D., "Lesbian Mothers and Their Children: A Comparative Survey," *American Journal of Orthopsychiatry*, Vol. 51, No. 3, pp. 545–551, July 1981.
19. Hoeffer, Beverly, R.N., D.N.Sc., "Children's Acquisition of Sex-Role Behavior in Lesbian Mother Families," *American Journal of Orthopsychiatry*, Vol. 51, No. 3, pp. 536–543, July 1981.
20. McDonald, Helen, and Steinhorn, Audrey I., *Understanding Homosexuality: A Guide for Those Who Know, Love, or Counsel Gay and Lesbian Individuals*, Crossroads, New York, 1993.
21. Rafkin, Louise, ed., *Different Mothers: Sons and Daughters of Lesbians Talk aboutTheir Lives*, Cleis Press, San Francisco, 1990.
22. Fisher, Tim, "Everything Possible," *Network* (Gay and Lesbian Parenting Coalition International, Montclair, New Jersey), Winter/Spring 1996.
23. Martin, April, *The Lesbian and Gay Parenting Handbook: Creating and Raising Our Families*, Harper Perennial/Harper Collins, New York, 1993.
24. Troiden, R. R., "The Formation of Homosexual Identities," *Journal of Homosexuality*, Vol. 17, No. pp. 43–73, 1989.
25. Martin, April, Ph.D., *The Lesbian and Gay Parenting Handbook: Creating and Raising Our Families*, HarperPerennial/Harper Collins, New York, 1993.
26. Miller, Deborah A., Ph.D., *Coping When a Parent Is Gay*, Rosen, New York, 1993.
27. Cass, Vivienne C., "Homosexual Identity Formation: A Theoretical Model," *Journal of Homosexuality*, Spring 1979.

CHAPTER 6: GOD AND GODDESS

1. Kushner, Harold S., *When Bad Things Happen to Good People*, Avon, New York, 1981.
2. Barrett, Martha Barron, *Invisible Lives*, Morrow, New York, 1989.
3. *Ibid.*
4. Baetz, Ruth, *Lesbian Crossroads: Personal Stories of Lesbian Struggles and Triumphs*, Morrow, New York, 1980.
5. Boswell, John, *Christianity, Social Tolerance and Homosexuality: Gay People in Western Europe from the Beginning of the Christian Era to the 14th Century*, University of Chicago Press, Chicago, 1980.

6. *Ibid.*
7. *Ibid.*
8. Beth Chayim Chadashim (BCC) was admitted to the Union of Reform Hebrew Congregations in 1972. Congregation Kol Ami was admitted in 1995. Other lesbigay-friendly Jewish congregations are in existence throughout the United States and the world.
9. "Prager Pro and Con" [Letters to the Editor], Dannenbaum, Lisa; Silverman, Daniel, Ph.D.; Pearlston, Carl; Comess-Daniels, Rabbi Neil; Simon, Joseph; and Kleinerman, Margy, *Jewish Journal*, Vol. 11, No. 42, December 13–19, 1996.
10. Prager, Dennis, "Homosexuality, Judaism and Rabbis," *Jewish Journal*, Vol. 11, No. 39, November 22–28, 1996.

CHAPTER 7: CONCLUSION

1. Kantrowitz, Barbara, "Gay Families Come Out," *Newsweek*, November 4, 1996.
2. McGuire, Megan, "Growing Up With Two Moms," *Newsweek*, November 4, 1996.
3. Lambda Legal Defense and Education Fund 6030 Wilshire Boulevard, Suite 200, Los Angeles, California 90016; 666 Broadway, 12th Floor, New York, New York 10012.
4. Freedom to Marry Coalition, 1625 North Schrader Boulevard, Los Angeles, California 90028; www.ftm.org.
5. "News for Our Families; Custody and Visitation," *Network* (Gay and Lesbian Parenting Coalition International, Montclair, New Jersey), 1996.

Appendix A ▲▼▲ Groups, Services, and Information in the United States and Abroad

SUPPORT AND INFORMATION SERVICES

GLPCi (Gay and Lesbian Parents Coalition International)   ▲▼▲
P.O. Box 50360
Washington, DC 20091
Tel: (202) 583-8029
FAX: (202) 783-6204
e-mail: GLPCINat@ix.netcom.com
Website: http://www.qrd.org/QRD/www/orgs/glpci/HOME.HTM.

GLPCi is a grassroots international organization in its third decade of providing advocacy, education, and support for gays and lesbians in child-nurturing roles and their families worldwide. The GLPCi newsletter, *Network*, is published four times a year. GLPCi offers an affordable annual international family conference with workshops for parents and children and has chapters across the United States as well as in Europe, Africa, Canada, and Oceania.

Selected local GLPCi Chapters:

International

Gay Fathers of London   ▲▼▲
649 Colborne Street
London, Ontario, N6A 3Z2
Canada
Tel: (519) 432-1061, ext. 1

▲▼▲　*Johannesburg Gay and Lesbian Parents Group*
47 Silwood Road
Bramby 2090
Johannesburg
South Africa
Tel: (27-11) 786-7794

▲▼▲　*Lesbian Parenting and Reproductive Law Project, Rights of Women*
52–54 Featherstone Street
London GC14 8RT
England
Tel: (44-0171) 251-6575

United States

▲▼▲　*Connecticut Moms Support Group/Our Kids*
77 North Main Street
West Hartford, CT 06107-1923
Tel: (860) 561-5329

▲▼▲　*Gamofites* (Gay Mormon Fathers)
6401 East Nohl Ranch Road, #28
Anaheim Hills, CA 92807
Tel: (714) 998-2052

▲▼▲　*Gay Fathers of Greater Boston*
Box 1373
Boston, MA 01105
Tel: (617) 742-7897

▲▼▲　*Houston Gay and Lesbian Parents*
P.O. Box 35709-262
Houston, TX 77235-5709
Tel: (713) 980-7995

▲▼▲　*Lambda Family Circle*
101 South Pine Avenue
Albany, NY 12208
Tel: (518) 482-3268

Lesbian and Gay Families of Central Virginia ▲▼▲
Box 767
Charlottesville, VA 22902

Lesbian and Gay Parents of Northwest Ohio ▲▼▲
3521 Rushland Avenue
Toledo, OH 43606
Tel: (419) 473-9289

Love Makes a Family, Inc. ▲▼▲
P.O. Box 11694
Portland, OR 97211
Tel: (503) 228-3892

Minnesota Families ▲▼▲
Box 11970
St. Paul, MN 55111

Parents and Wanna Be's ▲▼▲
9035 Greenway Lane
Lenexa, KS 66215

Philadelphia Family Pride ▲▼▲
P.O. Box 4995
Philadelphia, PA 19119
Tel: (215) 843-1596

Lesbian Mothers and Our Children ▲▼▲
(310) 397-5646

A grassroots support and networking group for lesbian mothers, coparents, children, and lesbians considering parenthood, Lesbian Mothers and Our Children offers monthly rap meetings, family outings, social events, and an informative newsletter.

Momazons ▲▼▲
P.O Box 82069
Columbus, OH 43202
Tel: (614) 267-0193

A national organization and referral network by and for lesbians choosing children.

▲▼▲   *Gay Fathers Coalition of Washington, DC*
P.O. Box 19891
Washington, DC 20036
Tel: (202) 583-8029

▲▼▲   *Gay Fathers of Long Beach*
2017 East Fourth Street
Long Beach, CA 90504
Tel:(310) 434-4455

▲▼▲   *PFLAG* (Parents and Friends of Lesbians and Gays)
1101 14th Street, NW, Suite 1030
Washington, DC 20005
Tel: (202) 638-4200/(800) 4-FAMILY
FAX: (202) 638-0243
e-mail: PFLAGNTL @aol.com

PFLAG began in 1973 and was founded nationally in 1981 by parents, families, and friends as a grassroots organization to build local, regional, national, and international coalitions to counter threats to their gay and lesbian relatives and friends. PFLAG offers active chapter affiliates in about 350 cities in the United States and abroad. Regular rap and discussion meetings, and support, assistance, and educational materials are available through local chapters. Contact the national headquarters (above) for information on local affiliates.

Selected local PFLAG chapters:

Akron, OH (216) 923-1883
Palm Springs, CA (619) 346-3228
Denver, CO (303) 333-0286
Roanoke, S.W., VA (703) 890-3957
Ephrata/Grant, WA (509) 754-4776
Santa Cruz, CA (408) 662-4780
Las Vegas, NV (702) 438-7838
Spokane, WA (509) 489-2666
Lubbock, TX (806) 799-5466
St. Louis, MO (618) 344-7765
New York, NY (212) 463-0629
Tulsa, OK (918) 749-4901
Pittsburgh, PA (412) 372-4059
West Palm Beach, FL (407) 272-1634

EDUCATION RESOURCES

GLSEN (Gay, Lesbian, and Straight Education Network) ▲▼▲
2124 Broadway, #160
New York, NY 10023
Tel: (212) 387-2098
e-mail: GLSTN@aol.com

Southern Poverty Law Center ▲▼▲
400 Washington Avenue
Montgomery AL 36104

Supports diversity and tolerance education for all communities, publishes
quarterly magazine *Teaching Tolerance*, provides information on educational
and other tolerance-related materials and resources.

GAY AND LESBIAN CENTERS

Gay, Lesbian and Bisexual Community Services Center of Colorado ▲▼▲
P.O. Drawer 18E
Denver, CO 80 218-0140
Tel: (303) 831-6268

Gay and Lesbian Community Center of Baltimore ▲▼▲
241 West Chase Street
Baltimore, MD 21201
Tel: (410) 837-5445

The Gay and Lesbian Community Center of Tampa ▲▼▲
1222 South Dale Marby, #350
Tampa, FL 33629
Tel: (813) 273-8919

Gay and Lesbian Helpline of Wake County ▲▼▲
P.O. Box 36307
Raleigh, NC 27606-6207
Tel: (919) 821-0055

Lambda Community Center ▲▼▲
1931 L Street
Sacramento, CA 95814
Tel: (916) 442-0185

▲▼▲ *The Lesbian and Gay Community Services Center*
208 West 13th Street
New York, NY 10011
Tel: (212) 620-7310

▲▼▲ *Los Angeles Gay and Lesbian Community Services Center*
1625 North Schrader Boulevard
Los Angeles, CA 90028
Tel: (213) 993-7600

▲▼▲ *Panhandle Gay and Lesbian Support Services*
P.O. Box 1046
Scottsbluff, NE 63963-1046
Tel: (308) 635-8488

▲▼▲ *Wingspan*
422 North Forth Avenue
Tucson, AZ 85708
Tel: (602) 624-1779

RELIGIOUS AND SPIRITUAL RESOURCES

▲▼▲ *Affirmation* (United Methodists for Gay, Lesbian, and Bi Concerns)
P.O. Box 691283
West Hollywood, CA 90069
Tel: (213) 969-4664

▲▼▲ *A Common Bond* (gay and lesbian ex-Jehovah's Witnesses)
203 Main Street, Box 2A
Lyndora, PA 16045
Tel: (412) 285-7334

▲▼▲ *Dignity L.A.* (Roman Catholic)
P.O. Box 3886
South Pasadena, California 91031
Tel: (213) 344-8064

▲▼▲ *Mormons Gay and Lesbian Affirmation*
P.O. Box 8922
Fountain Valley, CA 92728
Tel: (714) 502-8844

Universal Fellowship of Metropolitan Community Churches (MCC) ▲▼▲
5300 Santa Monica Boulevard, #304
Los Angeles, CA 90029
Tel: (213) 464-5100

World Congress of Gay and Lesbian Jewish Organizations ▲▼▲
P.O. Box 23379
Washington, DC 20026-3379
c/o B.M. World Congress
London WC1 N3XX, U.K.
Website: http://www.wcgljo.org/wcgljo/
Tel: (44-0181) 809-0877

LEGAL AND RELATED SERVICES

Bayside Legal Advocates ▲▼▲
3163 Mission Street, Suite 300
San Francisco, CA
Tel: (415) 282-9300

A lesbian law collective providing legal services for lesbian and gay families including adoptions, coparenting, and donor insemination agreements, wills, trusts, powers of attorney, and property and relationship contracts.

CALM. Inc. (Custody Action for Lesbian Mothers) ▲▼▲
P.O. Box 281
Narberth, PA 19072
Tel: (215) 667-7508

CALM. Inc. has provided custody litigation support for lesbian mothers since 1974

Human Rights Campaign Fund ▲▼▲
1012 14th Street, NW, Suite 607
Washington, DC 20005
Tel: (202) 628-4160

Hawaii Gay Marriage Bureau or GLEA Foundation ▲▼▲
P.O. Box 37093
Honolulu, HI 96837
Tel: (808) 532-9000

▲▼▲   *Lambda Legal Defense and Education Fund*
6030 Wilshire Boulevard, Suite 200
Los Angeles, CA 90016
Tel: (213) 937-2728

666 Broadway,12th Floor
New York, NY 10012
Tel: (212) 809-8585

Lambda Legal Defense and Education Fund also has regional offices in Chicago and will soon be opening an office in Atlanta. The Fund uses the legal system to defend the rights of gays and lesbians in the area of equality, family rights, access to health care, and free speech.

▲▼▲   *National Freedom to Marry Coalition*
c/o Los Angeles Gay and Lesbian Community Services Center
1625 North Schrader Boulevard
Los Angeles, CA 90028-6213
Tel: (213) 860-7350
Website: www.ftm.org

▲▼▲   *National Gay and Lesbian Task Force*
1734 14th Street, NW
Washington, DC 20009
Tel: (202) 332-6483

▲▼▲   *Texas Human Rights Foundation*
1519 Maryland
Houston, TX 77006
Tel: (713) 526-9139

ADOPTION AND FERTILITY RESOURCES

▲▼▲   *Fenway Community Health Center Lesbian and Gay Family and Parenting Services*
7 Haviland Street
Boston, MA 02115
Tel: (617) 267-0900, ext. 282

Insemination, newsletter, education, support, and advocacy for gay and lesbian families.

▲▼▲   *GLASS* (Gay and Lesbian Adolescent Social Services)
650 North Robertson Boulevard

West Hollywood, CA 90069
Tel: (310) 358-8727

GLASS provides help with regard to group homes, foster parenting, and adoption of gay and lesbian youth.

Growing Generations ▲▼▲
6310 San Vicente Boulevard, Suite 410
Los Angeles, CA 90048
Tel: (310) 475-4770
FAX: (310) 470-7196
e-mail: growinggen@earthlink.net

Growing Generations is a new surrogate-parenting facilitation organization that provides multiple services, including matching fathers to surrogate mothers, adoption referrals, support group referrals, coparent referrals, outreach, and psychological support.

Infertility Center of America ▲▼▲
2601 Fortune Circle East, Suite 102B
Indianapolis, IN 46241
Tel: (317) 243-8793

Founded by Noel Keane, J.D. Also has offices in New York City and the San Francisco area. Provides matching of surrogate mothers with donor fathers.

International Concerns Committee for Children ▲▼▲
911 Cypress Drive
Boulder, CO 80303
Tel: (303) 494-8333

Report on Foreign Adoption: annual listing of domestic (U.S) agencies faciltating in international adoptions.

Lyon-Martin Women's Health Services ▲▼▲
1748 Market Street, Suite 201
San Francisco, CA 94102-5806
Tel: (415) 565-7674

National Adoption Information Clearinghouse ▲▼▲
1400 I Street NW, Suite 600
Washington, DC 20005
Tel: (202) 842-1919

Supplies adoption information and referrals and publishes an annual directory of agencies and support services for adoptive parents.

▲▼▲ *Pacific Reproductive Services*
65 North Madison Avenue, #505
Pasadena, CA 91101
Tel: 888-469-5800

444 DeHaro, Suite 222
San Francisco, CA 94107
e-mail: PacifRepro@aol.com

Pacific Reproductive Services is a sperm bank and insemination clinic for alternative families, first established in San Francisco in 1984. Services include fertility services, donor insemination ("yes" and anonymous donors), shared ovum insemination, private donor screening, co-parenting connections, surrogate mothers, and information on legal and community support.

▲▼▲ *Pact, An Adoption Alliance*
3315 Sacramento Street, Suite 239
San Francisco, CA 94118
Tel: (415) 221-6957
FAX: (415) 457-4432

▲▼▲ *Reproductive Technologies, Inc.*
2115 Milvia Street, 2nd Floor
Berkeley, CA 94704
Tel: (510) 841-1858
FAX: (510) 841-0332

▲▼▲ Resolve, Inc.
5 Water Street
Arlington, MA 02174
Tel: (617) 643-2424

Provides infertility support and education as well as information about adoption.

▲▼▲ *The Sperm Bank of California*
3007 Telegraph Avenue, Suite 2
Oakland CA, 94609
Tel: (510) 444-2014

Provides "yes" donors.

▲▼▲ *Vista del Mar*
3200 Motor Avenue
Los Angeles, CA
Tel: (310) 836-1223

Adoptions.

SUMMER CAMPS

Camp It Up!   ▲▼▲
4000 Waterhouse Road
Oakland, CA 94602
Tel: (510) 530-0107

Mountain Meadow Summer Camp   ▲▼▲
35 West Mt. Airy Avenue
Philadelphia, PA 19119
Tel: (215) 242-3037

Camp Westwind   ▲▼▲
YMCA of Greater Portland
1111 SW 10th Avenue
Portland, OR 97205
Tel: (503) 294-7472

YOUTH SERVICES

COLAGE (Children of Lesbians and Gays Everywhere, GLPCi)   ▲▼▲
2300 Market Street, #165
San Francisco, CA 94114
Tel: (415) 861-KIDS
FAX: (415) 255-8345
e-mail: KidsOfGays@aol.com

This offshoot group of GLPCi offers newsletters, pen pals, support groups, a writers' program, leadership opportunities, media advocacy, and programs at the GLPCi annual family conference for the children of gay fathers and lesbian mothers.

Lyric (Lavender Youth Recreation and Information Center)   ▲▼▲
San Francisco, CA
Tel: (415) 703-6150
Peer-staffed Talkline: (800) 246-7743

Gay and lesbian youth.

Young Adult Support Group   ▲▼▲
Atlanta, GA
Tel: (414) 876-5372

Gay and lesbian youth.

▲▼▲   *Horizons Youth Service*
Chicago, IL
Horizons Helpline: (312) 472-6469

Gay and lesbian youth.

▲▼▲   *Lambert House Gay, Lesbian, and Bisexual Youth Center*
Seattle, WA
Tel: (206) 322-2735

▲▼▲   *Second Generation*
57–59 Second Avenue
New York, NY 10003
Tel: (212) 673-2926

Gay or lesbian children of gay or lesbian parents.

Appendix B ▲▼▲ Media Resources

BOOKS FOR CHILDREN

Abramchik, Lois, *Is Your Family Like Mine?*; Tel: (718) 788-5146; ages: 4 to 9.

Greenberg, Keith Elliot, *Zack's Story: Growing Up With Same-Sex Parents* (photographs by Carol Halebian), Lerner Publications, Minneapolis, Minnesota; ages: 5 to 13.

Heron, Ann, ed., *Two Teenagers in Twenty: Writings by Gay and Lesbian Youth*, 1994, Alyson Publications, 40 Plympton Street, Boston, Massachusetts 02118.

Skutch, Robert, *Who's In a Family?* (illustrations by Laura Nienhaus), Tricycle Press, Berkeley, California, 1995; available through GLPCi, Box 43206, Monclair, New Jersey 07043; ages: 3 to 7.

BOOKS FOR PARENTS

Corley, Rip, *The Final Closet: A Gay Parents' Guide for Coming Out to Their Children*, Editech Press, Miami, Florida, 1990.

Curry, Hayden, Clifford, Denis, and Leonard, Robin, *A Legal Guide for Lesbian and Gay Couples*, Nolo Press, Berkeley, California, revised periodically.

Martin, April, Ph.D., *The Lesbian and Gay Parenting Handbook: Creating and Raising Our Families*, HarperPerennial, New York, Harper Collins, 1993.

BOOKS FOR EXTENDED FAMILY

Buxton, Amity Pierce, *The Other Side of the Closet: The Coming Out Crisis for Straight Spouses and Families*, Wiley, New York, 1991.

Cohen, Susan, and Cohen, Daniel, *When Someone You Know is Gay, A Book for Everyone,* M. Evans, New York, 1989; available from PFLAG, 1101 14th Street NW, #1030, Washington, D.C. 20005; Tel: (202) 638-4200, FAX: (202) 638-0243, e-mail: PFLAGNTL@aol.com.

Fairchild, Betty, and Hayward, Nancy, *Now That You Know: What Every Parent Should Know About Homosexuality,* 2nd updated edition, Harcourt Brace Jovanovich, San Diego, 1989; available from PFLAG, 1101 14th Street NW, #1030, Washington, D.C. 20005; Tel: (202) 638-4200, FAX: (202) 638-0243, e-mail: PFLAGNTL@aol.com.

Griffin, Carolyn W., Wirth, Marian J., and Wirth, Arthur G., *Beyond Acceptance: Parents of Lesbians and Gays Talk about Their Experiences,* revised and updated edition, St. Martin's Press, New York, 1966; available from PFLAG, 1101 14th Street NW, #1030, Washington, D.C. 20005; Tel: (202) 638-4200, FAX: (202) 638-0243, e-mail: PFLAGNTL@aol.com.

PERIODICALS

In the Family, P.O. Box 5387, Takoma Park, Maryland 20913; Tel: (301) 270-4771.

The Family Next Door ["for lesbian and gay parents and their friends"], Next Door Publishing, P.O. Box 21580, Oakland, California 94620.

VIDEO AND FILM

Both of My Moms' Names Are Judy: Children of Lesbians and Gays Speak Out, a project of the Lesbian and Gay Parents Association, 1994; available with workshop materials from GLPCi, Box 43206, Monclair, New Jersey 07043; ages: 7 to 11.

Other Mothers, CBS Schoolbreak Special.

It's Elementary: Talking About Gay Issues in School, Debra Chasnoff and Helen Cohen, JPD Communications; Tel: (510) 843-8048, e-mail: Jilldavey@aol.com.

Bibliography

Abcarian, Robin, "The Bonds of Family Hold Fast Against the Tide," *Los Angeles Times*, Life and Style section, February 14, 1996.

American Psychiatric Association, *Diagnostic and Statistical Manual of Mental Disorders III: DSM-III*, American Psychiatric Association, Washington, D.C., 1972.

American Psychiatric Association, *Diagnostic and Statistical Manual of Mental Disorders III-R: DSM-III-R*, American Psychiatric Association, Washington, D.C., 1989.

American Psychiatric Association, *Diagnostic and Statistical Manual of Mental Disorders IV: DSM-IV*, American Psychiatric Association, Washington, D.C., 1994.

Associated Press, "Study Links Homosexuality and Heredity," *Los Angeles Times*, October, 31, 1995, p. A18.

Baetz, Ruth, *Lesbian Crossroads: Personal Stories of Lesbian Struggles and Triumphs*, Morrow, New York, 1980.

Bandura, A., and Walters, R., *Social Learning and Personality Development*, Rinehart and Winston, New York, 1963.

Baron, Kathryn, "The Gaybie Boom," *Los Angeles Times*, Life and Style section, March 1, 1995.

Barrett, Martha Barron, *Invisible Lives*, Morrow, New York, 1989.

Bell, Alan P., Weinberg, Martin S., and Hammersmith, Sue K., *Sexual Preference, Its Development in Men and Women*, Indiana University Press, Bloomington, Indiana, 1981.

Benkov, Laura, *Reinventing the Family: The Emerging Story of Lesbian and Gay Parents*, Crown, New York, 1994.

Blau, Melinda, "Gay Parents: Another Kind of Family," *Child*, June/July 1996.

Blommer, Stephen J., "Answers to Your Questions About Sexual Orientation and Homosexuality," American Psychological Association, Office of Public Affairs, Washington, D.C., 1994.

Boswell, John, *Christianity, Social Tolerance and Homosexuality: Gay People in Western Europe from the Beginning of the Christian Era to the 14th Century*, University of Chicago Press, Chicago, 1980.

Bowlby, J., *Child Care and the Growth of Love*, 2nd ed., abridged and edited by Margery Fry, with two new chapters by Mary D. Salter Ainsworth, Penguin Books, Baltimore, 1966.

Bowlby, J., *Attachment and Loss*, 2nd ed., Basic Books, New York, 1982.

Boxall, Bettina, "Hawaii Justices Open Door to Legalizing Gay Marriages," *Los Angeles Times*, March 26, 1995, pp. A1, A22.

Bozett, Frederick W., "Gay Fathers: Evolution of the Gay-Father Identity," *American Journal of Orthopsychiatry*, Vol. 51, No. 3, July 1981.

Bozett, Frederick W., ed., *Gay and Lesbian Parents*, Praeger, New York, 1987.

Bozett, Frederick W., "Children of Gay Fathers," in Bozzett, Frederick W., ed., *Gay and Lesbian Parents*, Praeger, New York, 1987.

Bozett, Frederick W., and Sussman, Marvin B., eds., *Homosexuality and Family Relations*, Haworth Press, New York, 1989.

Buxton, Amity Pierce, *The Other Side of the Closet: The Coming Out Crisis for Straight Spouses*, Wiley, New York, 1991.

Cameron, Anne, "Looking for a Mommy," *The Lesbian News*, October 1994.

Cass, Vivienne C., "Homosexual Identity Formation: A Theoretical Model," *Journal of Homosexuality*, Spring 1979.

Chaidez, Lucy, ed., *The California Child Abuse and Neglect Reporting Law: Issues and Answers for Health Practitioners*, State Department of Social Services, Office of Child Abuse Prevention, Sacramento, California, 1991.

Chasnoff, Debra, Producer-Director, and Cohen, Helen, Co-producer, *It's Elementary, Talking About Gay Issues In School* [film], 1996.

Clunis, D. Merilee, and Green, G. Dorsey, *Lesbian Couples*, Seal Press, Seattle, Washington, 1988.

Coleman, Daniel, "Studies Find No Disadvantage in Growing Up in a Gay Home," *New York Times*, December 2, 1992.

Corley, Rip, *The Final Closet: The Gay Parents' Guide for Coming Out to Their Children*, Editech Press, Miami, Florida, 1990.

Curry, Hayden, Clifford, Dennis, and Leonard, Robin, *A Legal Guide for Lesbian and Gay Couples*, 7th ed., Nolo Press, Berkeley, California, 1993.

Davidson, Jerome K., "On Welcoming Jewish Gays," *The Jewish Week*, October 20, 1995.

D'Emilio, John, "Family Matters," *Network* (Gay and Lesbian Parenting Coalition International, Montclair, New Jersey), Winter/Spring 1996.

Department of Children's Services, Los Angeles County, *Child Abuse Prevention Handbook*, Crime Prevention Center, Office of the Attorney General, California Department of Justice, Sacramento, California, 1993.

"Donahue," Transcript #4131, Multi-media Entertainment, Inc., November 29, 1994.

Dulaney, D. D., and Kelly, J., "Improving Services to Gay and Lesbian Clients," *Social Work*, Vol. 27, 1982.

Essoyan, Susan, and Boxall, Bettina, "Hawaii Ruling Lifts Ban on Marriage of Same-Sex Couples," *Los Angeles Times*, December 4, 1996.

Falk, P. J., "Lesbian Mothers: Psychological Assumptions in Family Law," *American Psychologist*, Vol. 44, 1989.

Fisher, Tim, "Everything Possible," *Network* (Gay and Lesbian Parenting Coalition International, Montclair, New Jersey), Winter/Spring 1996.

Flexner, S. B., Editor-in-Chief, and Hauck, L. C., Managing Editor, *The Random House Dictionary of the English Language*, unabridged 2nd edition, Random House, New York, 1996.

Frazier, Cynthia, "Keeping the Kids," *The Lesbian News*, Vol. 21, No. 9, April 1996.

Furth, Hans G., *Piaget for Teachers*, Prentice-Hall, Englewood Cliffs, New Jersey, 1970.

Gelnaw, Aimee, "Documentary Film Review: *It's Elementary, Talking About Gay Issues In School*, a film by Debra Chasnoff and Helen Cohen," *Network* (Gay and Lesbian Parenting Coalition International, Montclair, New Jersey), Fall 1996.

Ginsburg, H., and Offer, S., *Piaget's Theory of Intellectual Development: An Introduction*, Prentice-Hall, Englewood Cliffs, New Jersey, 1969.

Golombeck, S., Spencer, A., and Rutter, M., "Children in Lesbian and Single Parent Households: Psychosexual and Psychiatric Appraisal," *Journal of Child Psychology and Psychiatry*, Vol. 24, No. 4, pp. 551–572, 1985.

Goodman, B., "The Lesbian Mother," *American Journal of Orthopsychiatry*, Vol. 43, 1973.

Goodman, B., and Bandura, A. "Social Learning Theory: Identificatory Processes," in Goslin, David A., ed., *Handbook of Socialization Theory and Research*, Rand McNally, Chicago, 1969.

Goodman, B., and Bandura, A., *Social Learning Theory*, Prentice-Hall, Englewood Cliffs, New Jersey, 1977.

Gottman, Julie Schwartz, "Children of Gay and Lesbian Parents," in Bozett, Frederick W., and Sussman, Marvin B., eds., *Homosexuality and Family Relations*, Haworth Press, New York, 1989.

Green, G. D., and Clunis, D. M., *Lesbian Couples*, Seal Press, Seattle, Washington, 1988.

Green, R., "Sexual Identity of Thirty-Seven Children Raised by Homosexual or Transsexual Parents," *American Journal of Psychiatry*, Vol. 35, pp. 692–697, 1978.

Haldeman, D. C., "The Practice and Ethics of Sexual Orientation Conversion Therapy," *Journal of Consulting and Clinical Psychology*, Vol. 62, pp. 221–227, 1994.

Hamer, Dean, *et al.*, *Nature Genetics*, November 1993.

Hanscombe, G. E., and Forster, J., *Rocking the Cradle: Lesbian Mothers, a Challenge in Family Living*, Alyson, Boston, 1982.

Harris, M. B., and Turner, P. H., "Gay and Lesbian Parents," *Journal of Homosexuality*, Vol. 12, No. 2, pp. 101–113, 1985/86.

"Hawaii Court: Lesbian and Gay Couples Should Be Allowed to Marry," Lambda Legal Defense and Education Fund, News Release, December 3, 1996.

Hoeffer, Beverly, "Children's Acquisition of Sex-Role Behavior in Lesbian Mother Families," *American Journal of Orthopsychiatry*, Vol. 51, No. 3, pp. 536–543, July 1981.

"Homosexual Parent: All in the Family," *Science News*, Vol. 147, No. 3, January 21, 1995.

Hotvedt, M. E, and Mandel, J. B., "Children of Lesbian Mothers," in Paul, W., Weinrich, J. D., Gonsiorek, J. C., and Hotvedt, M. E., eds., *Homosexuality: Social, Psychological, and Biological Issues*, Sage, Beverly Hills, California, 1982.

Howlett, Debbie, "Supreme Court Reaffirms Gay Parents' Rights," *USA Today*, November 14, 1995.

Johnson, Lee, ""Words to Warm a Parent's Heart," *The Family Next Door* (Oakland, California), Vol. 1, No. 6, p. 32, 1994.

Jullion, Jeanne, *Long Way Home: The Odyssey of a Lesbian Mother and Her Children*, Cleis Press, San Francisco, 1985.

Kantrowitz, Barbara, "Gay Families Come Out," *Newsweek*, November 4, 1996.

Kirkpatrick, Martha, Smith, Catherine, and Roy, Roy, "Lesbian Mothers and Their Children: A Comparative Survey," *American Journal of Orthopsychiatry*, Vol. 51, No. 3, pp. 545–551, July 1981.

Koss, Mary *et al.*, *No Safe Haven: Male Violence Against Women at Home, at Work, and in the Community*, American Psychological Association, Washington, D.C., 1994.

Kus, Robert J., *Keys to Caring: Assisting Your Gay and Lesbian Clients*, Alyson, Boston, 1991.

Kushner, Harold S., *When Bad Things Happen to Good People*, Avon, New York, 1981.

Lesbian and Gay Parents Association, *Both My Moms' Names Are Judy: Children of Lesbians and Gays Speak Out* [video], 1994.

Lewin, Ellen, *Lesbian Mothers: Accounts of Gender in American Culture*, Cornell University Press, Ithaca, New York, 1993.

Lewin, E., and Lyons, T., "Everything in Its Place: The Coexistence of Lesbianism and Motherhood," in Paul, W., Weinrich, J. D., Gonsiorek, J. C., and Hotvedt, M. E., eds., *Homosexuality: Social, Psychological, and Biological Issues*, Sage, Beverly Hills, California, 1982.

Maddox, Brenda, *Married and Gay: An Intimate Look at a Different Relationship*, Harcourt Brace Jovanovich, New York, 1982.

Martin, April, Ph.D., *The Lesbian and Gay Parenting Handbook: Creating and Raising Our Families,* Harper Perennial/Harper Collins, New York, 1993.

Martin, April, "Same-Sex Marriage and Parenting," *Network* (Gay and Lesbian Parenting Coalition International, Montclair, New Jersey), Fall 1996.

McDonald, Helen B., and Steinhorn, Audrey I., *Understanding Homosexuality: A Guide for Those Who Know, Love, or Counsel Gay and Lesbian Individuals,* Crossroads, New York, 1993.

McGuire, Megan, "Growing Up with Two Moms," *Newsweek,* November 4, 1996.

Metz, Holly, "Support for Kids of Gay Parents," *Commentary,* Vol. 60, No. 1, January 1996.

Miller, B., "Adult Sexual Resocialization: Adjustments Toward a Stigmatized Identity," *Alternative Lifestyles,* Vol. 1, 1978.

Miller, B., "Gay Fathers and Their Children," *The Family Coordinator,* Vol. 28, pp. 544–552, 1979.

Miller, B., "Unpromised Paternity: The Lifestyles of Gay Fathers," in Levine, M. P., ed., *Gay Men,* Harper and Row, New York, 1979.

Miller, Deborah A., Ph.D., *Coping When a Parent Is Gay,* Rosen, New York, 1993.

Mitchell, Valery, and Wilson, Diane, "Let's Talk About It," *The Family Next Door* (Oakland, California), Vol. 1, No. 6, pp. 22–24, 1994.

Morgen, Kenneth B., *Getting Simon: Two Gay Doctors' Journey to Fatherhood,* Bramble Books, New York, 1995.

Mucklow, B. M., and Phelan, G. K., "Lesbian and Traditional Mothers' Responses to Adult Response to Child Behavior and Self-Concept," *Psychological Reports,* Vol. 44, pp. 880–882, 1979.

Nemeth, Mary, "American Dreamers," *Maclean's,* Vol. 105, No. 41, October 12, 1992.

"News for Our Families; Custody and Visitation," *Network* (Gay and Lesbian Parenting Coalition International, Montclair, New Jersey), 1996.

Ocamb, Karen, "Lesbian Custody Case Shaking Up L.A.," *The Lesbian News,* Vol. 22, No. 4, November 1996.

Pagelow, M., "Heterosexual and Lesbian Single Mothers: A Comparison of Problems, Coping, and Solutions," *Journal of Homosexuality,* Vol. 5, 1980.

Patterson, Charlotte J., "Children of Lesbian and Gay Parents," *Child Development,* Vol. 63, 1992.

Pennington, S. B., "Children of Lesbian Mothers," in Bozett, Frederick W., ed., *Gay and Lesbian Parents,* Praeger, New York, 1987.

Peterson, N., "Coming to Terms With Gay Parents," *USA Today,* April 30, 1984.

Pollack, Jill S., *Lesbian and Gay Families: Redefining Parenting in America,* Franklin Watts, New York, 1995.

Prager, Dennis, "Homosexuality, Judaism and Rabbis," *The Jewish Journal*, Vol. 11, No. 39, November 22–28, 1996.

"Prager Pro and Con" [Letters to the Editor], Dannenbaum, Lisa; Silverman, Daniel; Pearlston, Carl; Comess-Daniels, Rabbi Neil; Simon, Joseph; and Kleinerman, Margy, *The Jewish Journal*, Vol. 11, No. 42, December 13–19, 1996.

Preston, John, *The Big Gay Book*, Penguin Books, Balitmore, Maryland, 1991.

Quintanilla, Michael, and Koenenn, Connie, "Legalities Aside, Gays Still Stand on Ceremony," *Los Angeles Times*, Life and Style section, December 6, 1996.

Rafkin, Louise, ed., *Different Mothers: Sons and Daughters of Lesbians Talk about Their Lives*, Cleis Press, San Francisco, 1990.

Rath, Kate, "A Daughter's Inheritance," *Teaching Tolerance*, pp. 62, 63, Spring 1995.

Rees, R. A., "A Comparison of Children of Lesbian and Single Heterosexual Mothers on Three Measures of Socialization," Doctoral Dissertation, California School of Professional Psychology, Berkeley; *Dissertation Abstracts International*, Vol. 40, pp. 3418–3419B, 1979.

Reske, Henry J., "Lesbianism at Center of Custody Dispute," *ABA Journal*, Vol. 81, July 1995.

Schulenberg, J., *Gay Parenting*, Doubleday, New York, 1985.

Singer, Bennett L., and Deschamps, David, eds., *Gay and Lesbian STATS*, New Press, New York, 1994.

Skutch, Robert, *Who's In a Family*, Tricycle Press, Berkeley, California, 1995.

Smith, Katherine, "Children Raised by Lesbian Mothers," Doctoral Dissertation, Department of Psychology, UCLA, 1981.

Smith, Lynn, "Do We Have Any Idea What We're Agreeing On?" *Los Angeles Times*, Life and Style section, June 23, 1996.

Tate, Julia J., *Artificial Insemination and Legal Reality*, American Bar Association, Chicago, 1992.

Tepper, "Once, Interracial Marriage Was Banned, Too," Community Essay, *Los Angeles Times*, December 7, 1996.

Troiden, R. R., "The Formation of Homosexual Identities," *Journal of Homosexuality*, Vol. 17, pp. 43–73, 1989.

Tucker, Rabbi Gordon and Freundel, Rabbi Barry, "Two Views: Homosexuality and Halachic Judaism," *Moment*, June 1993.

Van Gelder, Lindsay, "Mothers of Convention," *Lifestyles*, Vol. 3, No. 1, July 1992.

Wallerstein, J., and Kelley, J., *Surviving the Breakup: How Children and Parents Cope With Divorce*, Basic Books, New York, 1980.

Webster's Seventh New Collegiate Dictionary, Merriam-Webster, Springfield, Massachusetts, 1967.

Webster's Ninth New Collegiate Dictionary, Merriam-Webster, Springfield, Massachusetts, 1984.

Weeks, B., Derdeyn, A. P., and Langman, M. "Two Cases of Children of Homosexuals," *Child Psychiatry and Human Development*, Vol. 6, 1975.

Weiss, Andrea, and Schiller, Greta, *Before Stonewall: The Making of a Gay and Lesbian Community*, Naiad Press, Tallahassee, Florida, 1988.

Weston, Kath, *Families We Choose: Lesbians, Gays, Kinship*, Columbia University Press, New York, 1991.

Woodman, Natalie Jane, ed., *Lesbian and Gay Lifestyles: A Guide for Counseling and Education*, Irvington Publishers, New York, 1992.

Index